THE REPUBLIC
OF VENICE

De magistratibus et republica Venetorum

THE LORENZO DA PONTE ITALIAN LIBRARY

THE REPUBLIC OF VENICE

De magistratibus et republica Venetorum

GASPARO CONTARINI

Edited and introduced by Filippo Sabetti

Translated by Giuseppe Pezzini with Amanda Murphy

UNIVERSITY OF TORONTO PRESS
Toronto Buffalo London

ISBN 978-1-4875-0584-4

Printed on acid-free, 100% post-consumer recycled paper
with vegetable-based inks.

The Lorenzo Da Ponte Italian Library

Library and Archives Canada Cataloguing in Publication

Title: The republic of Venice : De magistratibus et republica Venetorum /
Gasparo Contarini ; edited and introduced by Filippo Sabetti ;
translated by Giuseppe Pezzini with Amanda Murphy.
Other titles: De magistratibus et republica Venetorum. English.
Names: Contarini, Gasparo, 1483–1542, author. | Sabetti, Filippo,
1940–, editor. | Pezzini, Giuseppe, 1984–, translator. |
Murphy, Amanda C. (Amanda Clare), translator.
Description: Series statement: The Lorenzo Da Ponte Italian
library | Translation of: De magistratibus et republica Venetorum. |
Includes bibliographical references and index.
Identifiers: Canadiana 20190151358 | ISBN 9781487505844 (hardcover)
Subjects: LCSH: Venice (Italy) – Politics and government. |
LCSH: Venice (Italy) – History.
Classification: LCC JN5269 .C613 2020 | DDC 320.0945/311 – dc23

This volume is published under the aegis and the financial assistance of
Agincourt Press Ltd. and Casa Italiana Zerilli Marimó of New York University.

Casa Italiana Zerilli - Marimò
New York University

University of Toronto Press acknowledges the financial assistance to its
publishing program of the Canada Council for the Arts and the Ontario Arts
Council, an agency of the Government of Ontario.

**Canada Council
for the Arts**

**Conseil des Arts
du Canada**

ONTARIO ARTS COUNCIL
CONSEIL DES ARTS DE L'ONTARIO

an Ontario government agency
un organisme du gouvernement de l'Ontario

Funded by the
Government
of Canada

Financé par le
gouvernement
du Canada

Canadä

MIX
Paper from
responsible sources
FSC® C016245

Contents

Illustrations

Figure

Maps

Acknowledgments

/

I wish to thank Professors Luigi Ballerini and Massimo Ciavolella for including this volume in the series Lorenzo Da Ponte Italian Library. This is the third volume I have contributed to this exciting and important project, and I am grateful to the series editors for their hospitality, collaboration, and support stretching over many years. I also thank the two anonymous readers for the thoroughness of their responses to my project; even where I disagreed, their comments stimulated me to further reflection, and this book is the better for it. Translation from Ciceronian Latin is a difficult art, and I greatly appreciate the good and patient work to this effect by Giuseppe Pezzini with Amanda Murphy, as well as the readers' scrutiny of the translation. It has been a pleasure and an enriching experience for me to learn from, and exchange views with, Beppe and Mandy on how best to convey Contarini's ideas; the result, again, is a better work of scholarship.

I wish to acknowledge the support of the Social Science and Humanities Research Council of Canada (SSHRC 410-2011-0698) and the generous sabbatical leave from McGill University that allowed me to work on this project over the past ten years. The benefit I derived from reading the authors listed in the bibliography is self-evident. There are others whom I can acknowledge more directly, and I hope I may be pardoned if I fail to remember some.

Moving from the study of modern comparative politics to the study of Renaissance Venice was challenging, but the trespass was relatively easy to make for two reasons. I took the study of Contarini's Republic of Venice as a case study of how different communities of people across time and space face and address issues of collective action and governance, a life-long interest. The trespassing was made easier by the warm assistance of historians and Venetianists alike. First of all, I am most grateful to Edward Muir for valuable discussions and directions over the years since my first chance encounter with him at Renaissance Society of America meetings in Montreal in 2011. I remain deeply touched by his support, generosity, and help. I also greatly thank Paul Dragos Aligica, Salvatore Ciriacono, Paula C.Clarke and Edoardo Giuffre, Daniel H. Cole, William J. Connell, Elisabeth Crouzet-Pavan, Eric Dursteler, Robert Finlay, Maria Stella Florio, Elisabeth Gleason, Wai-Fung Lam, Peter Mentzel, Claudio Negrato, Dennis Romano, Karol Soltan, and Mark Sproule-Jones. I have learned a great deal from subjecting my work to critical interdisciplinary scrutiny. The comments, critiques, and suggestions I received strengthened my understanding of the history of the Republic of Venice and Contarini's account, and where I disagreed with critics, I felt compelled to amplify and thus fortify my argument to meet their objections, again to the betterment of this work. I also wish to acknowledge the assistance of the IstitutoVeneto di Scienze Lettere ed Arti and Professor Francesco Vallerani of the Università di Venezia Ca' Foscari in facilitating my participation in the international conference on waterscapes and canals as cultural heritage held in Venice in May 2015. Francesco D'Amaro, Rosella Mamoli Zorzi, Maria Stella Florio, and Lonnie Weatherby generously responded to my calls for help. Finally, Suzanne Rancourt and Janice Evans, in different capacities at the University of Toronto Press, oversaw the transformation of the manuscript into the book with skill and care. Terry Teskey did splendid work with the copyediting. Judy Dunlop prepared the index, help which I also wish to acknowledge. I dedicate the book to H. Scott Gordon and to the memory of the late John A. Marino.

FS
Alta Valle del Fortore
Summer 2019

Gasparo Contarini, 1483–1542.
The History Collection / Alamy Stock Photo.

Introduction: Gasparo Contarini and Enduring Institutions

FILIPPO SABETTI

Gasparo Contarini was a Venetian gentleman born in 1483 who died a prince of the church in Bologna in 1542. He belonged to an old Venetian family and had a distinguished career, first as a patrician and then as a prelate. Since the 1950s, a succession of specialized monographs on Renaissance history and the discovery of archival material have added much knowledge about Contarini's social, intellectual, and spiritual journey as a young man and his emergence and presence on the stage of public and ecclesiastical life. The various phases of Contarini's life were brought together in the early 1990s in a biography (Gleason 1993). Since then, additional research – largely undertaken at the Ca' Foscari University of Venice – has amplified our knowledge of Contarini as a diplomat and writer (e.g., Florio 2009; Negrato 2012). Yet he is best remembered for his reflections on the government of the Republic of Venice that he penned, and circulated among his friends, between 1522 and 1525 and then again between 1533 and 1534 (e.g., Bowd 1998, 174–5). These reflections were posthumously published as *De magistratibus et republica Venetorum* in Paris in 1543. This book presents the first modern English-language edition of Contarini's work to be translated from the original Latin.

Contarini was the eldest of seven sons and two daughters of Alvise Contarini and Polissena Malpiero. His life has been generally broken down into four periods: his education up to 1509; his years as a scholar and member of the Great Council between 1508 and 1518; his service to the Venetian republic, 1518–35; and his career as a churchman, 1535–42 (e.g., Bowd 1998; Donnelly 2002, 9; Fragnito 1988; Gilbert 1967, 1968, 1969; Jedin 1958; Matheson 1972; Ross 1970, 1972). As a young man, Contarini took seriously the challenge of deciding which path to follow: the contemplative life, like some of his close friends who entered the cloister, or the active life of a patrician gentleman. The decision came, as he recounted, by chance and from an unexpected source: a monk, hearing his confession on Holy Thursday in 1511, made him realize that it was possible to live in the presence of Christ in the secular world, and to achieve human happiness and salvation in the midst of the city (Bowd 1998, 52–63; Fragnito 1969, 101–4; Gleason 1993, 14–15).

Contarini accepted a strong union of faith and reason and drew on St Thomas to assert the capacity of human beings to understand the world around them through the use of their faculties, properly exercised. He acknowledged that original sin and nature set limits to human knowledge without, however, denying the human striving to use reason as much as possible (Gleason 1993, 84–5). At the same time, he recognized that not all questions about the meaning of human life and destiny could be answered by philosophical enquiry. Revelation, tradition, and faith provided satisfactory answers where and when philosophy could not. Thus Contarini combined, to put matters in modern terms (Savorana 2017, 998), the pessimism that Christians associate with the nature of man and the optimism about human affairs that they derive from the incarnation of Christ. Human action is fallible but capable of instruction and certainly is not predetermined by original sin. Against this backdrop, it comes as no surprise that Contarini, while in public life and before becoming a priest and cardinal, initially wrote about theological and religious matters (Fragnito 1969; Gleason 1993, 83).

As a member of one of Venice's most distinguished families, Contarini had the necessary pedigree for an active role in the governance of the Republic.[1] In 1508 he entered the Great Council, the sovereign assembly of the Republic consisting of all patricians over twenty-five years of age. He served initially in various junior capacities, including as state attorney and surveyor of reclaimed land. Between 1520 and 1525, he was the Venetian ambassador to the court of the Holy Roman Emperor Charles V, and was present at the signing of the Peace of Bologna in 1530. In over four hundred dispatches[2] he reported, with the aid of two secretaries, on

---

1   Elisabeth Gleason (1993, 2) recalls that the Contarini clan gave the Republic eight doges, the first of whom helped to start the construction of St Mark's Basilica in the eleventh century. By the time of Gasparo's birth, three of his ancestors had been elected doge (and another five would hold that post after his death). The *Dizionario biografico degli Italiani* has entries on more than seventy Venetian Contarini, and that on Gasparo by Gigliola Fragnito (1983) is the longest, covering twenty pages. See Appendix C listing the principal events of Contarini's life.

2   For useful guides on how to read Contarini's diplomatic dispatches, see de Vivo 2011, Halikowski Smith 2017, and Negrato 2012. Halikowski Smith also maps Contarini's travels throughout Europe, Britain included, while serving as Venetian envoy to Charles V (see fig. 3, p. 196).

the international events he observed while travelling, mostly on horse-back, through the German lands, the Low Countries, England, Spain, and France (e.g., Contarini 1525). Contarini was a first-hand witness to Venice's shifting position in continental affairs, from independent strength to relative powerlessness among European states. He was later the Venetian ambassador to the Holy See. Beyond diplomatic postings, he served the Republic – among other capacities – as one of the heads of the Council of Ten, where he dealt with myriad issues, including wheat provision, murder, censorship, and carrying concealed weapons. He became a member of the most prestigious and powerful steering committee of the Senate, the Collegio, where he served as a *savio grande* responsible for general governmental affairs.[3] Made cardinal in 1535, he advocated various proposals for internal reform of the church. He also gave his support to the emerging Jesuit order. Perhaps the highest point of his ecclesiastical career came in 1541, when he attended a conference of Catholic and Protestant theologians at Regensburg to see if their theological differences could be bridged. Contarini helped to draft a document on justification of salvation that both sides accepted, but the discussion reached an impasse when it came to sacraments, church structure, and the papacy.[4] On his return to Italy, the pope named him the legate/governor of Bologna. He died there the following year. Contarini was eventually interred in the family tomb in the Santa Maria dell'Orto church in Venice.

By all accounts, Contarini showed "a remarkable continuity" in public life as a devoted servant, first of Venice and then of the church (Gleason 1993, 90). A shrewd observer of diverse ways of life, he held firm to the ethos of his patrician class as well as to the faith of his church, moving with ease in the secular and ecclesiastical worlds. He accepted hierarchy and inequality but without failing to notice their shortcomings in Rome as in Venice. He gained, as Elisabeth Gleason notes, a reputation for being a fair-minded and skilled diplomat with a clear sense of when to take a stand and when to compromise. "His experience, self-confidence, and knowledge of psychology" (Gleason 1993, 44) were mirrored in the diplomatic reports he wrote while serving both Venice and Rome. Even when he was not consistent in his position – for example, his description of how a public official or bishop ought to behave did not always accord with his own behaviour when faced with the exigencies of office – few doubted his good will, sincerity, moderation, and strong sense of civic

---

3 For a glossary of governmental terms, see Appendix B.

4 He was tainted with Protestantism in the later years of his life, but his ecclesiastical work has received a less controversial and more positive re-evaluation since his death. See, more recently, the unsigned commentary on his life in *L'Osservatore Romano* (2017).

duty. He succeeded in combining his various commitments "in an harmonious way" (Gleason 1993, 44, 67–71, 80–92; see also Contarini 1571; Gilbert 1969, 265; Negrato 2012).

In drafting *De magistratibus et republica Venetorum*, Contarini drew on both the history of Venice and his own experience to provide a host of normative, historic, and contemporary details that would educate Venetians and foreigners alike about the machinery of Venice's government. The volume was not concerned with the political behaviour of Venetians, but with the formal institutions by which political aims were realized. The reflections are thus as much a description of the institutions of governance as they are a prescription for how those institutions ought to work to meet expectations. In this way, *De magistratibus* contributed to a particular view in the sixteenth century that has come to be known by modern historians as "the myth of Venice,"[5] celebrating the Republic's well-being and accomplishments, and presenting its aspirations and self-image as reality.

What continues to lend support to Contarini's portrait is that, by his time, Venice had managed to preserve its liberty inviolate (unlike most other Italian states), had avoided long-lasting factional violence, and had experienced the benefits of established institutional forms of elite interaction and organizational ways of processing and addressing problems: what some modern social scientists studying the requirements for human development identify as "perpetually lived organizations" (North, Wallis, and Weingast 2013, 158). The Republic withstood and survived the 1509 attack on its liberty by an alliance of great powers known as the League of Cambrai. It has been suggested that Contarini's treatise was written in response to the Venetian defeat at Agnadello in 1509, to combat the sense of insecurity that had been mounting since 1500 and to restore confidence in the image of Venice as a serene and long-lasting republic (e.g., Bowd 1998, xv, and 196–7, 235, and supporting sources cited therein). By 1600, support for the myth of Venice came from outside Venice as the political vicissitudes of the other Italian republics exposed them to absolutist rule and both Milan and Naples became part of the sprawling empire of Spain. The fate of the Italian peninsula was increasingly determined by large European territorial states (Bowd 2000a, 408–9). Against this backdrop, Brian Pullan found that now the political atmosphere in Italy favoured the myth of Venice, "for only Venice kept its old character and its republicanism and independence" (1964, 95). For "Venice endured as a republic while its neighbors did not, thus achieving for itself an

---

5 For an elaboration of this point, see Appendix A, "The Myth and Anti-myth of Venice."

international reputation as a state in which the interests and passions of the citizens were almost mystically bound to the system of government ... Until its capture by Napoleon in 1797, Venice had been an independent community for nearly a millennium" (Muir 1981, 13).

Contarini may not have anticipated the success and influence of his work, which became a primary source of knowledge about Venice. Not only does his text capture the characteristics that make Venice unique, but the popularity of the text itself added to Venice's reputation and myth of greatness. The treatise was in circulation as a manuscript in France and Germany before its publication in 1543 in Paris (Bowd 2000b), and went through several reprints in the sixteenth century and beyond. Since the 1543 Latin edition published in Paris, other Latin editions followed: first at Basel in 1544 and 1547, and then at Venice in 1589 and 1592. The Elzevirs brought out new Latin editions in 1626, 1628, and 1722. A French translation by Jean Charrier first appeared at Paris in 1544 and later at Lyon in 1557. The first Italian translation, edited by E. Anditimi and offering a modified version of the Latin original, seems to have been published at Venice in 1544; others followed in 1548, 1551, 1564, 1591, and 1650 (Florio 2010; Fink 1945, 39n50; see also sixteenth-century sources discussing Contarini in Cozzi 1963–4, 282–3).[6] These reprints can be taken as proxy measures of the work's success in reaching readers throughout Europe. A more direct indication that Contarini was read in the sixteenth century is suggested by the research of Stephen Bowd (2000b). He found that "most sixteenth-century readers were full of praise for the work, which according to the first French translator, allowed the reader to understand how by a combination of prudence and good laws, Venice had resisted natural decline." Bowd quotes the French translator who in 1544 noted to his readers that "if you read this marvellous book (as I advise you to do) you may easily see Venice from [the comfort of] your home" (83n2).

De magistratibus captures both the characteristics that rendered the Republic of Venice unique among Italian city states and the significance of Venice "as a fermenting element" (Lane 1966a, 415) "in the political education of Europe" (Bouwsma 1973), by modelling a different way of organizing public affairs at a time when monarchical and absolute rulers dominated Europe and dictated political practices (see also Koenigsberger 1997; Pullan 1974; Venturi 1971, 1979). Contarini's *De magistratibus* sharply differs from Domenico Morosini's design of a well-managed republic in his work *De bene instituta re publica*, begun in 1497 but still unfinished at

---

6 Several Italian editions continue to be available (e.g., Conti, *La Republica e i magistrati di Vinegia*, 2003).

the time of his death in 1509 (Finzi 1969). Like Contarini, Morosini was deeply attached to Venice and was concerned with the threat of domestic dissidence and faction among patricians. But unlike Contarini's, Morosini's treatise is "rambling and inconsistent" (Chambers and Pullan 2004, 66) and is unrealistic in its expectations of how a well-managed republic might be constituted. It was unrealistic for example to expect, as Morosini does, that factions can be eliminated and the whole of patrician citizens be of one mind both in accumulating wealth and in sharing a single conception of the common good (e.g., Cozzi 1970; King 2014, 140–50). Against this backdrop, it comes as no surprise that successive generations of scholars have recognized Contarini's treatise as "the most celebrated work ever composed on the Venetian government" (Libby 1973, 17; see also Gilbert 1967, 183; Muir 1981, 31; Romano 2007, xix), "with a traceable impact in many countries" (Pocock 1975, 320). In fact, it "became the great source that fed republican thought in monarchical centuries" (Gilbert 1967, 184; see also Pullan 1974; Voltaire, cited in Venturi 1979). In its long history as an organized political community, Venice had suffered no revolutionary change, and almost every institution of its government maintained deep and lived roots in the past. Venice had not styled itself as "the most serene and eternal Republic" for nothing.

The present volume, titled *The Republic of Venice*, is the first modern translation of the original Latin text available in Contarini's collected works, his *Opera*, which was published in Paris in 1571 under the supervision of his nephew, Alvise Contarini, then living in Paris as the Venetian ambassador. While some of his *Opera*'s passages on theology were revised to allay the fear of inquisitors (Fragnito 1985, 31–43), this does not appear to be the case with *De magistratibus*, which is thought to be unexpurgated. Moreover, the *Opera* edition used for translating *The Republic of Venice* is the text that modern historians of Venice have often used in quoting Contarini from the Latin (e.g., Bouwsma 1968; Gleason 1993; Pocock 1975; Skinner 2002, 128). While remaining faithful to Contarini's Latin, the present translation is easily accessible to modern readers who wish to gain a first-hand appreciation of what it was that Contarini actually wrote that earned his treatise on Venice its status across the centuries. In this way, the present volume recovers for modern readers a classic work in the history of Venice and Renaissance Italy.

This is not the first time that *De magistratibus* has been published in English. That distinction was gained in 1599, when Lewes Lewkenor published the work in London under the title *The Commonwealth and Government of Venice*. But Lewkenor's edition was not a translation from the original and definitive Latin edition of 1571. As he himself admitted, he used the Italian version of 1544, and as philological research by Maria

Stella Florio (2009) found, his translation was occasionally faulty. In addition, Lewkenor mistranslated, amplified, or deviated from the Italian text in several places in order to make the treatise more acceptable to the English. He interpolated an argument in favour of English civil liberties, and he also elected to use "commonwealth" rather than "republic," since the latter term was at the time rife with controversial assumptions (Florio 2009, 103–15). Lewkenor added eighty pages to the book, by including excerpts from five other books[7] on Venice and by adding a list of the doges in chronological order. Imperfect as it is, Lewkenor's edition with its unmistakable Elizabethan prose has acquired historical value in its own right and remains a rich source for philologists studying English-Italian translations (e.g., Florio 2009, 2010; see also McPherson 1988). In 1969 the work was reprinted in a facsimile edition by Da Capo Press and the Theatrum Orbis Terrarum (Amsterdam and New York), but this reprint is no longer available. The 1599 English translation is now easily accessible through EEBO and Google Books, making it possible to compare and contrast this Elizabethan edition with our modern English translation, which is another project in itself. By going back and directly translating the original Latin, the present edition makes Contarini's actual text immediately accessible to modern readers.

In the remainder of this introduction I present Contarini's portrait of Venice, with both its strengths and its weaknesses, and then examine the extent to which his analysis illuminates the factors that account for Venice's status as "a stable oasis" (Dursteler 2013, 5) in the peninsula and a source of envy throughout much of Europe (sources cited in, e.g., Pullan 1974, 453; see also Wills 2001).

Reality and Myths

Contarini divided his treatise into five "books" or chapters of various lengths. The first deals with the location and origins of the city of Venice and the form of its governmental system, focusing on the basic political institution, the Great Council (Maggior Consiglio). The second book

---

7 Of these, perhaps the most noteworthy excerpts are taken from Donato Giannotti's *Libro della Repubblica de' Veneziani* ([1540] 1840). Giannotti, who wrote his book during a sojourn in Venice and Padua in 1525–6, read widely and discussed his topic with various Venetian gentlemen, possibly including Contarini himself. He reinforces the work of Contarini on many points. As William J. Bouwsma notes, Giannotti differs from Contarini in that the former's book "is less lofty and academic, and less concerned to inspire feelings of awe, more concrete, more interested in practical details. Above all, Giannotti adds to Contarini's vision of static perfection a realistic awareness of historical development" (1973, 154).

discusses the office, election, and prerogatives of the doge as the head of state and chief magistrate. The third and fourth books discuss the Senate, the Council of Ten, and the main judicial tribunals and various magistracies. The final book concludes with a discussion of the government of the Venetian *terraferma* and various community organizations. In sum, *The Republic of Venice* clearly lays out the complex structure of the machinery of government and puts the Venetian experience in a philosophical context, inviting comparative historical and contemporary analysis.

Contarini began his treatment in book 1 by recalling that he had often noticed that foreigners visiting the city for the first time were admiring of and astonished by the magnificence of Venice. One such foreigner was a Sicilian nobleman, the prince of Bisignano, who described it as "a truly excellent city," a description duly recorded by Marin Sanudo in his diary of 23 June 1521 (cited in Labalme and White 2008 and used on their book cover). Contarini then drew attention to geography's importance in creating an advantageous and secure location for the city. Very few cities, in fact, had been founded on sites as opportune as that of Venice. He described in some detail how Venice's location attracted people seeking refuge from calamities elsewhere in Italy. "Fortified by a marvelous expedient of nature," Venice thus was safe from attack from land and sea (book 1:8). This location made Venice equally well positioned for trading with others and amassing an abundance of commodities for its citizens. But these factors were not enough. Echoing Aristotle, whose work he was said to know by memory, Contarini observed that "a city is more than just walls and houses" (book 1:10). Thus, more important than geography per se was the use of environmental resources to create organized existence that revealed human creativity, or what Jacob Grygiel (2006, 22) recently characterized as "the human factor within geography." "Centuries of creative energy" (Crouzet-Pavan 2002, 10; see also McNeill 1974, chap. 2) went into what Contarini referred to as the "system and form of government by which men attain a happy life" (book 1:10). The rest of *The Republic Venice* is devoted to a description of the imaginative ways Venetians organized their system and form of government.

Venice was not, Contarini noted, "the work of immortal gods but rather of men" (book 1:3). For he noted (in book 1:11) that Venetians were not like "famous philosophers, who created forms of government according to the desires of the mind." Venetians were the co-creators of the institutional world in which successive generations of people lived. Despite his piety, Contarini dismissed the view that the Venetian Republic rested on divine will or miraculous origin,[8] which was an ancient myth of Venice

---

8 See also the accompanying note on translation by Giuseppe Pezzini in which he shows that Contarini pruned his Latin vocabulary of Christian and vernacular borrowings.

(see Fasoli 1958; Gaeta 1961, 59; Muir 1981, chap. 1; Rose 1974, 479). Contarini did not call up Saint Mark or the Virgin Mary to explain why Venice became a great republic, though there is little doubt that "the cult of Saint Mark strengthened [the] feeling of sovereign independence" (Lane 1973, 88) and was "the nucleus of Venetian civic consciousness, a nexus of popular piety and patriotism" (Muir 1981, 78–92, 299). Similarly, in spite of being a patrician from an old Venetian family, Contarini did not claim that Venetians succeeded where other Italians had failed because of the faith or virtues of the former. He invoked Aristotle and Plato from time to time and demonstrates familiarity with medieval political ideas, but it is generally agreed that political writers of the twelve and thirteenth centuries seemed to have little or no influence in Venice during the formulation of its constitutional arrangements – although there was considerable *ex post facto* praise of the sort of balanced constitution that Venice was supposed to have created (Lane 1966b, 306).

Contarini attributed the organizational arrangements of the Venetian republic to "wise and prudent ancestors" and mundane political acumen that brought together ideas and practices over time. He may have made too much of the "wise and prudent ancestors" in his narrative. But, as has been noted, "'the wise ancestors' to whom Contarini attributed the merits of Venetian government were not writers on political theory or architects of utopian states; they were practical men of·quotidian politics who build the constitution piecemeal, responding to immediate problems as they perceived them" (Gordon 1999, 137). John G.A. Pocock echoed the same idea when he observed that "Venetian history proceeds through pragmatic reflection on past experience, and far from hitting upon some miraculous recombination of elements, displays in 1170 a political sagacity exceeding that of the Roman patricians after the expulsion of the kings" (1975, 281).[9] In fact, Contarini points to a long tradition of equating experience with age, for "the slow-moving Venetian *cursus honorum* tended to weed out men who were brash, favoring instead those who were given to compromise and deliberation" (Romano 2007, 330; see also Finlay 1980, 134–7). Contarini also reached into the past to advance a moralizing and educational agenda: the enhancement of the Republic's independence and stability that had become all the more important following the War of the League of Cambrai, when its position in European affairs was being

---

9 It is not entirely clear what event in 1170 Pocock has in mind. Most likely it was the creation of the Grand Council (Pocock 1975, 279). At about the same time, in 1172, the dogeship changed into a magistracy, and 1178 saw the creation of ducal councillors coming from each of the *sestieri* into which the city was divided (Lane 1973, 92, 96). In Venetian constitutional history the 1170s were indeed "a critical moment" (Pocock 1975, 279).

challenged and eclipsed by the growth of national monarchies (see also Gilbert 1969). Appeals to wise and prudent ancestors was thus a way to reiterate the view of history promoted by Cicero and widely accepted until the Enlightenment: that history is both a life of memory and a mistress of life (*historia magistra vitae est*) (see also Sabetti 2010, 66).

Equally important, Contarini stressed that Venice was not created by a "hero legislator" (Pocock 1975, 280) or absolute ruler, but by many individuals across generations. Recent research supports the view that the development of both the patriciate and the various institutions of governance was an ongoing process (e.g., Chojnacki 2000; Rösch 2000). Contarini admitted that "more than a few [cities] in the past centuries have surpassed the city of Venice in the extent of their dominion, the number of people, and the abundance and magnificence of material things" (book 1:1). But, as noted earlier, a city is more than "just walls and houses"; "the city is specifically the system and form of government by which men attain a happy life." And it is this "outstanding" and "marvelous quality" that "makes Venice especially shine, seeming to surpass antiquity," for "none can compare with this city of ours in institutions and laws suitable for living well and happily." No other city has "ever endured for such a long time" (book 1:10; see also 2:33 and 4:76).

Contarini here hints at (but does not develop) something that the modern literature on city origins and economic development has, arguably, established: that prosperous cities came first, and rural development followed later. Contarini did not, and could not be expected to, cover Venice as a commercial republic. But because of its lagoon foundation the Venetian commercial republic developed in the reverse of the traditional economic model,[10] which starts from agriculture and progresses to manufacturing, service, and a knowledge economy. Venice began with a transportation service economy, trading salt and fish for grain to become what has been aptly described as a "forest on the sea" (Appuhn 2009; see also Griffith 2004; Lane 1973, 1). Already by the thirteenth century Venice's knowledge industry was at the forefront of developments affecting changing social relations and the circulation of ideas and architectural designs in western Europe (e.g., Febvre and Martin 2010). Focusing on the architectural imagination, Sophia Psarra recalls that by the

---

10 A point that Machiavelli also noted but did not quite seem to appreciate when in *The Discourses* (1, 55) he observed that "gentlemen in this republic [i.e., Venice] are so in name rather in point of fact: for they do not derive any considerable income from estates; their great wealth is based on merchandise and movable goods. Moreover, none of them have castles nor have they any [feudal] jurisdiction over men" (2003, 247–8). Cf. the impression of Venetian gentlemen in Thomas Koryat's account [1611] 1905, vol. 1. See also Jacobs 1970, 18–19; Sabetti 2010, chaps. 5 and 7.

sixteenth century "Venice and the Veneto were home to more than 450 printers, publishers and booksellers, who fueled with books, woodcuts and engravings the interest in the ancient world shown by architects and scholars" (2018: 7). The nobility of Venice was for the most part made up of merchants, traders, printers, and writers.[11]

Contarini advances a temporal and secular view of republican government with particular twists. First, unlike other parts of Italy, Venice had never been conquered or occupied, and alternations in rule were achieved not through assassination but via the ballot box. Second, Venetian republicanism reinforces the view that there is not a single scale on which a republican discourse can be weighted and classified.[12] Until the fourteenth century, the term *republica* retained the old meaning of any legitimate form of government, thus applying to a wide variety of regimes (see, e.g., Leonardo Bruni cited in Hankins 2010, 464). In the course of the fifteenth century the term and the accompanying "republican idea" came to refer almost exclusively to non-monarchical regimes, even if at times it included different forms of oligarchies, like those of Florence, Lucca, and Venice (Hankins 2010, 465). As William J. Connell notes in his discussion of the republican idea in the Renaissance, "it bears keeping in mind that oligarchies are still republics, and there is still something distinctly different about the rule of a self-governing, self-legitimating oligarchy as compared with the rule of a monarch or a tyrant" (Connell 2000, 25).

A distinctive feature of Venetian republicanism repeatedly noted by Contarini was that the political imaginary and repertoire shared by patricians – what in modern social science is called shared understanding, cognitive rules, and epistemic knowledge (V. Ostrom 1997, chap. 4; see also Greif and Mokyr 2017; Sabetti 2010, chap. 6) – possessed no single centre of authority with the final say over public affairs (e.g., Contarini,

---

11 Some Asian diplomats, inspired by the work of Frederick C. Lane, have suggested Singapore as the new Venice of the twenty-first century (e.g.,Koh 1998). Economists Daron Acemoglu and James A. Robinson (2012, 152–8) argue the opposite, that Venice "became a museum" by the fourteenth century. Unfortunately, their exploration of the Republic of Venice is conducted at such a high level of generality that the discussion misleads and undermines what they sought to do, to understand the origins of power, prosperity, and poverty in the modern world. More recently, Chrystia Freeland (2012), by uncritically building her argument on their analysis, makes the same error.

12 A point made more generally by several contributors to van Gelderen and Skinner's (2002) two-volume study of republicanism as a shared European heritage. One contributor, Donald Winch, suggests that even when confined to Scottish thinkers alone, the term "republican" is "a sophisticated term of political and interpretative art" to challenge how best to make sense of particular conceptualizations: "civic or moral humanism," "Commonweathmen," "Country" forms of opposition, "neo-Harringtonian or ne-Roman ideology," or more simply, "classical republicanism" (294).

book 4:73). The shared understanding among patricians and the very practice of governance excluded the notion of an undivided, monocentric conception of political rule. What Venice had was corporate rule. As Dennis Romano recalls, "especially between the fourteenth and seventeenth centuries, as the European state system took shape and matured under the tutelage of kings seeking to fulfil their dynastic ambitions, Venice served as the model for an alternative pathway to political development, one based upon republican rather than monarchical principles, and in so doing garnered great admiration for the stability and constancy of its regime" (2007, xix). What Romano describes adds to the significance of Venice in history (Pullan 1974), and it helps to explain why, for observers like James Harrington in the seventeenth century and Voltaire in the eighteenth, Venice remained a model of liberty to be admired, esteemed, and if possible emulated (Harrington [1656] 1992, 34; Venturi 1979, 209). For this reason, Contarini's book may have prominence in early modern political thought: it shows how it was possible to have lived institutional arrangements that could serve as constitutional and political alternatives to national monarchies and monocentric states and, and at the same time, hold violence in check. Contarini's account demonstrated that violence could be reined in by non-centralized systems of rule (see also Pocock 1975, chap. 11; Wilson 2016; cf. North et al. 2013).

At the same time, Contarini saw patrician rule as unproblematic. He held the then-widespread view, both in and beyond Venice, that not everyone who lived in the city was, and should be regarded as, a citizen. The population of Venice was divided into three social orders (see Pullan 1999). First, the status of citizen was confined to those of noble birth and, in some cases, those who acted meritoriously towards the Republic (book 1:17–18). Citizens were free men, whereas those who worked for a wage were under some form of servitude (book 1:17). Contarini refers to the hereditary patriciate as the "citizens" in Latin, but there were others immediately below the patriciates known as *cittadini originari*. These were the second level of elites who held bureaucratic posts as secretaries and state notaries but did not have political rights. These original citizens were also a hereditary class enrolled in the silver book, just as the nobility were enrolled in the golden book (Edward Muir, personal communication, 14 March 2017; Pullan 1971, 103–5). Brian Pullan notes that to some extent, noblemen and citizens did intermarry, though it caused some concern in the seventeenth century as patricians seeking to alleviate financial difficulties took wealth from below by marriage (1971, 106). Only the third layer of residents, the common people below both the patriciate and the *cittadini originari*, were excluded from participation in the governance of the city.

Contarini's defence of the patricians' natural position to govern with the aid of *cittadini originari*, his support for the exclusion of the common people from a share in the conduct of the Venetian government, and, more generally, his acceptance of the unequal social and political conditions among Venetians – all of these were unexceptional at the time. He offered the standard justification, used as far back as the ancient Greek city states and as late as the end of nineteenth-century Europe, to confine political participation to a select few and exclude the great majority of people: namely, the assumption that humans possessed varying and unequal qualities, abilities, and endowments, and hence only some were fit to rule (e.g., Bagehot [1867] 1968, 272; Wilson 2016, 240; cf. Brennan 2017). For Contarini, as for Aristotle and Plato and medieval writers and more recent analysts like Walter Bagehot, the unequal distribution of human qualities, abilities, and endowments resembled that found in the human body and the physical, natural world. Contarini applied this analogical way of reasoning to politics and religion. In book 1, he observed: "consider that a living creature has been shaped by nature in the same way that a city is organized by men. In a living creature, there are many parts which are not alive, and yet the creature needs them in order to survive" (1:17; 5:97–8; see also Bowd 1998, 203–10).

What was particularly Venetian in Contarini's defence of the city's hierarchic arrangement and social inequality was his depiction of the ancestors from whom his generation had received such a flourishing republic. As Contarini described them, these were people "without exception of the same mind in their desire to strengthen and advance the country, almost without regard for their own private benefit and personal honour." They "were never ambitious when it came to themselves, and were infinitely more devoted to the well-being of the country" (book 1:10). Research by Brian Pullan on caring for the poor draws attention to the complex interplay of religious and secular reasons that gave expression to Contarini's assertion: a highly developed sense of the state as "an entity binding rulers and rules, a corporate political enterprise demanding service and self-sacrifice," for the public offices were not "intended to be primarily a source of gain or a means of rewarding private persons" 1960, 20, 32). But no matter how sage, selfless, and devoted to the public good any particular individuals might have been, the view that the entire Venetian patriciate was wholly and consistently patriotic, self-sacrificing, devoted to civic-minded service, decorous, and wise is difficult to accept.

What allowed Contarini to convey the image of a timeless and serene Republic with a selfless patriciate was his tendency to fuse time, brushing aside tumultuous events in the history of Venice that challenged such a portrayal. Edward Muir notes that "the early political history of Venice was certainly violent enough." He adds that "if the chronicles can be trusted, between 697 and 1172, five doges ... were forced to abdicate, nine exiled or deposed, five blinded and five murdered. The early doges and their

families were famous for their involvement in conspiracies and vendettas"
(1999, 384). Other turbulent events, elided by Contarini, include the conspiracy to overthrow the constitution involving Doge Marin Falier in 1355;
the decades of doubt brought about by the wars against Genoa in the fourteenth century; the repeated challenges to Venice posed by the Ottoman
Empire in the fifteenth and sixteenth centuries; and the future stagnation,
decay, and despair among rich and poor patricians revealed by the constitutional crisis of 1628–9 (see, e.g., Rose 1974; see also Romano 2007).

Modern research has seriously challenged the image of a Venetian patriciate endowed with unparalleled self-possession and selfless devotion
to public service that Contarini sketched and that many foreign observers believed. Research by Donald E. Queller documents – with what a
reviewer called "cascades of evidence" (Chojnacki 1988, 601) – that "Venetian nobles were deterred by no spirit of sacrifice in their zeal for the public welfare" (1986, 147). Queller produces many instances that call into
question Contarini's depiction of patricians over the centuries as extraordinarily patriotic and altruistic, and seeks to replace that depiction with a
view of the patricians as essentially self- and rent-seeking. Robert Finlay's
research notes that many patricians in the sixteenth century campaigned
relentlessly for public positions, electioneering, cheating, conspiring, and
bribing to gain desirable offices and avoid undesirable ones; and the leadership of the Republic tended to be kept in the hands of some factions –
prominent patricians in the Senate, the so-called *primi di la terra* – and
not in the hands of the "common" patricians in the Great Council (1980,
chap. 1 and 200–286; Queller 1986, 118, 189). Contarini took justifiable
pride in drawing attention to an "ancient" aspect of the Venetian judicial system (book 3:65–6) that allowed poor defendants the right to state-
funded counsel, but he did not reveal what we now know from scholarly
sources: he failed to notice that there were less meritorious, class-based
features of the justice system that put most ordinary Venetians at a disad-
vantage (e.g., Ruggiero 1980; Shaw 2006). But there is more.

The Venetian legislation, as Queller (1986, chaps. 3–7) suggests, can
equally be taken to demonstrate that the Venetian governing class sought
to *curb* the evasion of public responsibilities and opportunistic tendencies
among its members. The legislation conveys "the remarkable degree to
which Venetians sought to find some solution to the human frailties that
made them as imperfect as others" (Muir 1988, 290). At the same time,
the electioneering and canvassing for votes highlighted by Finlay must not
have appeared as a defect to many young patricians: those activities helped
them to lessen the cost of securing information about and to increase the
value of their vote. Dorit Raines's (1991, 140–5, 161–2; 2003) research
on those Venetian practices recalls what is familiar to modern students

of electoral and legislative politics in and beyond the American Congress –
for voters and legislators alike, to be well informed is not cost free, but
requires a considerable outlay of time and effort; the modern folk theory
of democracy glosses over the dark realities of democratic politics (Achen
and Bartels 2017; Brennan 2017). In the words of one reviewer, Finlay
"does not seem to have made up his mind … whether to treat electoral
corruption as a positive or a negative factor, as an essential part of the
system or a threat to it. He does not seem to have decided whether to
argue that the Venetian political system was essentially stable, capable of
absorbing conflict and of being altered in matters of detail to avoid structural changes, or whether the crisis of the early 16th century led to a real
change of system" (Burke 1980, 22). Still, Contarini himself was aware of,
and drew attention to, the potential for human fallibility, political corruption, and institutional weaknesses and failures throughout his treatise.

In book 1, Contarini noted that "men endowed with both prudence
and integrity are extremely rare, and men generally err in judging because the force of the mind's passions tends to powerfully divert from
the right judgment … [for] man's nature is mortal and frail … and easily succumbs to his frail disposition" (1:14–15). He recognized that procedures and rules for admission to the Great Council needed to avoid
fraud and prevent "some ignoble person from stealthily creeping in their
congregation of gentlemen" (1:20). He also acknowledged the challenge
of maintaining honest elections, without voting irregularities. Elections
in the Great Council were suspended after sunset precisely to prevent
patricians from committing "any illicit acts under the cover of darkness"
(1:28, 29, 30). A principal reason that public power was vested in and
alternated between so many hands was precisely to minimize the potential that those who were excluded would "plot something" against the
Republic (1:29). He allowed that even the doge could be bribed (2:29,
36, 38). In book 3, Contarini recognized different motives, interests, and
knowledge among senators (3:55), and in book 4, concerning the magistracies of the Republic, he saw the possibility of patricians being convicted for embezzling public money and converting it into private wealth
(4:78–9, 80, 94). In book 5, he noted the prospect of arrogance and mis-
chievousness among patricians if they were allowed to command a large
number of attendants, since "it is human nature to incline to the worse"
(5:94). Recalling Aristotle, he conceded what Montesquieu and Madison
and Hamilton in *The Federalist* would later place in sharp relief: "such
is our human disposition that those who are in power do not conduct
themselves well unless they are checked by another authority" (5:98).
In the same book, he noted that "many young men, corrupted by ambition or luxury since the expansion of the empire, have neglected" their

duties (5:96). Finally, Contarini recognized that no matter how perfectly things may have been originally constituted, after some time everything experiences "the crumbling deterioration of nature and stands in need of repair" (5:96), for "nature has disposed things in such a way that nothing can be permanent among men" (5:96).

In brief, Contarini's book may have promoted a certain idealized view of Venice that some historians call "the myth of Venice," but its author also gave reasons to question it. His work did not just convey the image of a perennially harmonious republic. He was aware of the contrast between expectations and practice in the face of exigencies of security, though he "did not fear that the Council of Ten might become tyrannical" (Gleason 1993, 66). The emphasis on the complex system of chance and choice in elections can be viewed as indications of efforts to discourage arbitrary behaviour (Jones 1997, 93) and to make personal virtue the automatic or routinized consequence of the elections and institutional balances – what John Pocock calls "mechanized virtue" (1975, 284; see also Conti 2002; de Vivo 2007, 27). One also suspects that Contarini was not troubled by the discrepancy between the ideal and the reality of Venetian institutions for other reasons. One reason might be that corruption actually facilitated stability because it gave some, often poor, nobles a vested interest in the election process from which they might profit. Elections might be another kind of patronage/clientage system (see Burke 1980; Muir 2017). Another reason, for Contarini, was that the very reality of Venice was itself a mental creation that served to shape action; and, like officials in the Holy Roman Empire of his time (Wilson 2016, 45), he tended to consider that discrepancy between reality and appearance to be an expression of the imperfection of the human condition itself. At the same time, Queller's preoccupation with discrediting the "myth" distracted him from "confronting the structural issue at the heart of the myth, which is the tension between the patriciate as a regime and the patriciate as collection of flawed individuals – between patrician ideology and patricians' behavior" (Chojnacki 1988, 601). Similarly, from the perspective of those who study modern institutions for collective action, the tensions highlighted by both Queller and Finlay are unsurprising for several reasons (e.g., Fotos 2017; E. Ostrom 1990, 2005, 2014; Sabetti 2000). All human interests are rooted in the self, and a function of the political process is the extent to which it is possible to bias individual decision making towards taking into account a wider community of people and longer time horizon. Moreover, bureaucratic politics and corruption can be viewed as permanent features of government organizations. For these reasons students of institutions for collective action would expect Venetian governance to experience weakness and failure, and to find some patricians shirking responsibility, pursuing ambition, and engaging in corrupt practices. They would also expect that the substantial social and economic disparities among social orders would show in the way that members of those orders experienced the application of different standards in criminal law.

Beyond Myths

The contrasts between the norms and practices of Venetian governance, between how the order of patricians were supposed to behave and how they individually sometimes actually behaved, highlight *ex adverso* Contarini's message of institutional resilience and political stability – for, in the words of Margaret L. King, "it would be foolish ... to deny that Venice ... was a uniquely successful city" (2014, xix). So the question about long-enduring institutions becomes: How was it that Venetian institutions "proved strong enough to absorb many shocks without violent revolution" (Lane 1973, 186)? This question can itself be refined further to ask: How did the Republic of Venice largely manage to avoid the bloody factional violence and battles characteristic of other parts of Italy, and maintain a semblance of liberty not found elsewhere in most of Europe (Muir 1999; Terpstra 2006, 5)? And in the words of modern social science advanced by, among others, the Bloomington school of political economy (e.g., E. Ostrom 1990; Sabetti and Aligica 2014; see also Voigt 2013), how is it possible for fallible human beings to construct and operate an enduring system of governance? It would be too much to expect Contarini to provide a response that would meet twenty-first-century standards of scholarship. His work does not match those standards, and it may be anachronistic to hold him to them.

For Contarini the key to the strength and success of the Republic lay in its combination of Aristotle's and, later, Polybius's three forms of ideal rule: the doge offering the monarchical element, the Senate the aristocratic, and the Great Council the democratic. This is the idea of mixed government (e.g., Casini 2002; Gaille 2005). This conception permeates Contarini's treatise and is used to account for the success of the Republic but, I argue (see also Pullan 1974), this is not the whole story about why the government of Venice endured. In fact, it can be argued that Contarini's analysis itself points to additional factors as determinants of stability and institutional longevity, and that these factors have been addressed at some length in the later social science literature on what makes institutions work and endure (e.g., E. Ostrom 1990; Rodrik 2002; Tocqueville [1835] 1969, 1, chap. 9).

This literature identifies three factors as the "deep determinants" that account for the durability of political regimes: geography; institutions; and trust, or the habits of the heart and mind that animate institutions. Each set of factors has different functions, and they all supplement each other in complex fashion. The literature, starting with Tocqueville, argues that institutions are more important than geography, while habits of heart and mind are more important than geography and institutions for making institutions work well and endure. This social science conclusion seems echoed by historian Edward Muir when he observed that "a well-ordered system of magistracies ... was insufficient to maintain political stability without an auxiliary ethic of political service" (1981, 21). While there are differences between the modern self-governing institutions noted by institutionalists like Douglass C. North, John Wallis, and Barry Weingast, Vincent and Elinor Ostrom, and Tocqueville, and the institutions discussed by Contarini, it is nonetheless apparent that Contarini's approach to understanding political and institutional stability, as we shall see when we turn to the text, shares or seems to be informed by, *mutatis mutandis*, similar characteristics.

We saw earlier that Contarini focused, as a point of departure, on the importance of geography for understanding the advantages and disadvantages posed by a country's location (see Crouzet-Pavan 2002; see also 2000, 2013). Contarini devoted a large portion of his work to describing, in effect, the importance of institutions in shaping the habits of the heart and mind in order for Venice to remain "secure not only from the domination of foreign men, but also from significant civil sedition" (book 5:104). He continued in book 5, "this has not been achieved by force, armed garrison, or a well-fortified citadel but rather by a just and balanced system of government such that the people obey the nobility of their own accord and do not wish for any revolution, while retaining a strong affection toward the nobility" (5:104). The compound system of rule is conveyed in Figure 1.

The Pien Collegio was the executive body and consisted of the Consulta and the Signoria. The Consulta involved six *savi grandi*, five *savi di terraferma*, and five *savii agli ordini*. The *savi grandi* were the highest-ranking members of the Collegio; the *savi di terraferma* were responsible for military affairs on the mainland; and the *savi agli ordini* were responsible for maritime affairs and by the sixteenth century were the lowest-ranking members of the Collegio. All the *savi* (literally, wise men) were individually elected by the Senate for a six-month term.

The diagrammatic depictions of the relations among those bodies help us to appreciate the complex organization of the Venetian system of government, but, in the words of one economic historian, they

mislead more than they inform because their membership composition covers the whole range of possible relations – in the language of set theory, they display, in various cases, independence, identity, inclusiveness, and intersection. Unless it were complex to the point of incomprehensibility,

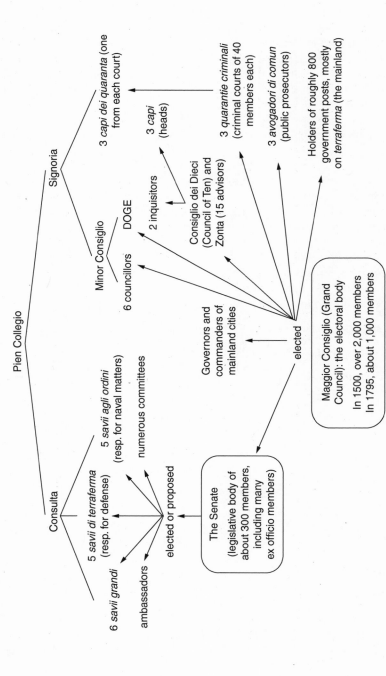

Figure 1. Structures of the Venetian Government. From Gleason (1993), appendix 2.

a diagram would also fail to capture other essential features of the Venetian system, such as short, staggered, terms of office of most officials, the complex method of election, the frequent practice of electing a person to office in a different body upon the conclusion of his service in another one, the restrictions that did not permit more than one member of a family to hold simultaneous office in the smaller councils and so forth. (Gordon 1999, 138–9)

The basic point is that Venice had a complex system of plural centres of powers.

Contarini described at some length the intricate mechanisms of elections that governed public affairs and goes into great detail about the selection and voting procedures, and how members drew balls from particular urns. Electoral mechanisms can best be understood as part of a larger system of multiple centres of decision and authority. Book 2, in particular, describes the system of electing a doge as simultaneously an effective technique to prevent elections from being rigged and a means of ensuring broad support for the person ultimately chosen. Lane (1973, 111) represents this procedure for the election of the doge as follows:

From the Great Council there were chosen by lot 30;

The 30 were reduced by lot to 9;

    The 9 named 40;

        The 40 were reduced by lot to 12;

            The 12 named 25;

                The 25 were reduced by lot to 9;

                    The 9 named 45;

                        The 45 were reduced by lot to 11;

                            The 11 named 41;

                                The 41 nominated the doge,

                                    For approval by the Assembly.[13]

---

13 Scott Gordon presents a simplified schematic description of the procedure as follows:

$30L \rightarrow 9L \rightarrow 40E \rightarrow 12L \rightarrow 25E \rightarrow 9L \rightarrow 45E \rightarrow 11L \rightarrow 41E \rightarrow D$

L refers to selection by lot, E to selection by election.

Contarini suggests that the electoral system succeeded in preventing rigging by generating considerable discussion of the leading candidates for office. As Dennis Romano notes, appropriately in my view, "the procedure for electing the doge was not a perverse joke or a mere flight of fancy: it was carefully designed to reduce the danger of factional interference in elections by incorporating a generous element of chance. The several rounds of lottery made it difficult for anyone to guarantee that he or his allies would have a place in the nominating committees. Chance served to underscore the essential equality of all members of the Great Council" (2007, 37). Even when the doge was elected, he could still not conduct state business on his own initiative. He wielded power with others while retaining all the pomp of a revered and dignified leader. The doge's wealth was audited after his death to insure that he did not profit from his office. There is another aspect of the decision-making process that merits recognition: the importance of delay and consultation in slowing down the process of deliberation to defuse passion or, in other words, the importance of time in gaining reflection. In a fine study of James Madison's thought, Greg Weiner characterizes the natural power of time in deliberation as "temporal republicanism" (2012, ix), and it seems that this form of temporal republicanism was also at work in the Republic of Venice and can be read into Contarini's treatise.

The electoral process, rotation in office for magistracies below the doge, and multiplicity of individual magistracies remained practically unchanged from the thirteenth century onward in Venetian history. More than simply a system of "mixed" government, as Contarini suggests, these institutional arrangements as well as temporal delay contributed to the system of checks and balances. Of course, the system was not free of bureaucratic conflict, organizational rivalry, and time-consuming negotiations. But together, Contarini hinted, the electoral system and the checks and balances inherent in the system of government sought to do three things: secure a high degree of reflection and support among patricians, minimize the danger of factional politics and violence, and make the authority of governing accountable. The basic point is that Venice had achieved and perfected an equilibrium of plural centres of powers, and that sovereignty understood in Hobbesian terms or as monocratic rule is a concept inapplicable to the governance of Venice.

Contarini draws attention to the dynamic aspects of system performance, but he does not – and could not have been expected to – deal with possible trade-offs between different aspects of system performance in the temporal republicanism of Venice. Contarini's biographer, Elisabeth Gleason, suggests that his stands show he sometimes prized efficiency and order in the day-to-day workings of the government and did not fear that the Council of Ten might become tyrannical (1993, 66). Two types of trade-offs are in fact particularly important to Contarini's analysis of the workings of the Venetian machinery of governance. The first is concerned with a trade-off between efficiency and stability or durability. To attain maximum performance with regard to a particular set of criteria – say, rapid rotation in office, lengthy voting procedures – the rules and norms of a system would have to be aligned to those criteria to the point that the entire system of government could become vulnerable to fluctuations and disturbance in other areas. A second issue not discussed by Contarini is the possibility of trade-offs between criteria. Durability is always construed with reference to a particular set of criteria. In other words, the Venetian Republic could not be strong or robust in the face of all types of disturbances at all times. The procedure for electing the doge bet more on stability than efficiency. Thus, building stability with regard to a particular set of criteria – how to avoid factional politics and domination by one particular group – can and did make the system vulnerable to other criteria.

Historians have generated many case studies pointing to these issues and problems in the long history of the Republic. Over time, Venetians themselves came to realize that what applied to elections and office rotation did not and could not apply, for example, to questions of defence. When drawing up an order of battle in naval defence, or setting up land fortifications through the *provveditori alle fortezze*, one found that elaborate group discussions did not work well (see Hale 1971; Mallett 1973). Finlay highlights these challenges employing concepts more familiar to historians:

> Venice's flaws were indissolubly linked to its virtues ... rapid rotation in office, diverse responsibilities within individual magistracies, dedication to collective decision making, a multitude of temporary commissions, overlapping competencies of councils, complex and lengthy voting procedures, and a consistent weakness of executive authority at almost all levels of government. Inefficiency, confusion and bureaucratic conflict were prices that Venetian patricians were apparently willing to pay for maintaining their republican order. (1980, 38)

Though Contarini does not tell us so, we can surmise, judging by the long-term sustainability of the Republic, that the Venetians had somehow addressed and resolved the trade-offs between multiple criteria of institutional performance (see also Appuhn 2009 on environmental issues).

At the same time, Contarini was aware that the strength of the government of Venice did not derive just from a secure geographical location and the excellence of its institutions and laws. In fact, he suggested that its strength derived more from the set of attitudes, beliefs, sentiments, and rituals that gave order and meaning to the political architecture and process and provided the underlying assumptions and rules that governed them and instilled and nurtured support. As he noted, "it is something hard to believe, indeed scarcely credible, that for so many years the multitude, though deprived of a place in government, has never yet refused or been unwilling to support the government of the patricians" (book 5:98). And then he immediately suggested that the loyalty of the common people also rested in letting them share in "the offices and charges that could be entrusted to them without detriment to the common good" (5:99).

Contarini discussed a chief reason for the strength of the social and political order in books 4 and 5. Research has abundantly demonstrated over the last four decades that the Venetian social order was characterized by the existence of a thick web of religious, charitable, and occupational institutions within and beyond the parish level. These institutions served as an essential foundation for the cultivation of the arts and of the practice of crafting institutions and neighbourhood associations of all sorts (see also map 3 on public buildings and facilities and map 4 on the Venetian administrative divisions). This polycentric and shared system of governance was "the foundation stone of Venice's social stability" (Lane 1973, 12; see also Fortini Brown 1987; Humphrey and Mackenney 1986; Martin and Romano 2000, 24; Pullan 1971; Psarra 2018, 52–65). The presence of these neighbourhood associations helps to understand why there was no sedition among the lower classes (Pullan 1971, 106–8).

The first *scuole*, which Contarini refers to as societies or companies (book 5:103), were founded in the thirteenth century as clubs in which members could worship together, providing charity for the poor and mutual aid for each another. By the sixteenth century, there were six big companies (the *scuole grandi*) and many smaller ones. The *scuole grandi* were reserved for the *cittadini originari*. Begun as pious flagellant companies for the well-to-do, these associations were principally charitable institutions that supplied processioners for public rituals, housed the poor, and engaged in other kinds of charitable activities. While nobles could be (and often were) members of the *scuole grandi*, only non-nobles could hold office in these associations. Members of the *scuole grandi* presented the greatest revolutionary danger to the nobility. Artisans per se were usually not members; they were generally members of the *scuole piccolo*, which were linked to guilds and specific trades (Lane 1973, 105–6; Muir 2017; Pullan 1971, 55). On the other hand, the internal organization of each *scuola* was modelled on the constitution of the Venetian republic – even in some cases copying the outfits and regalia of the government's officers. Similarly, just as the Republic was represented symbolically by the relic of St Mark, each of the *scuole grandi* had its own prized relics. In this way, "each [*scuola*] became a kind of mini-Venice" (Wills 2001, 125). It has been suggested that "an important reason why [ordinary] Venetians quietly accepted patrician rule was that the government itself offered them a measure of political involvement along with a form of social security" (Finlay 1980, 47). This helps to account for the loyalty the peasantry showed to Venice during the War of the League of Cambrai and for Contarini's warm portrait of *terraferma* loyalty in book 5.

While institutions like the *scuole* helped integrate different elements of the city's population by imitating the Republic's central institutions, something similar was observable in the Venetian territories on the mainland. Going beyond what Contarini presented, Edward Muir (2000) offers a fascinating account of how the institutional and legal framework of the Republic reached the farthest parts of the Venetian *terraferma* and fostered the political education of local communities in resisting outside and often arbitrary rule, maintaining the liberty of their own little *res publicae*, and institutionalizing conflict into litigation through legal channels. Muir is quick to point out that "these [local] practices were not so much exported from Venice as licensed by Venice" (2000, 159). Villagers learned to successfully resist arbitrary local rule by invoking the protection of the written word from Venice. This suggests how shared were the mental images of the working of instrumentalities of governance, the strategic opportunities provided by those instrumentalities, and the common knowledge required to pursue contrasting community interests (see also Muir 1981; cf. cases of collective action among peasants and villagers in the Holy Roman Empire, Wilson 2016, 581–2; and compare also villagers from Spanish Lombardy appreciating the liberty in nearby Bergamo provided by the Republic of Venice in Manzoni's classic novel *The Betrothed*, [1827] 1909, chaps. 16 and 17).

Conclusion

In a sweeping tour of how the coercive power of the state has been historically controlled through a pluralistic distribution of political power, Scott Gordon suggests that Contarini's *The Republic of Venice* may be just as instructive as Machiavelli's *The Prince* to students of politics, if not far more so (1999, 161–2). For Gordon, Machiavelli's chief contribution to the modern study of politics is twofold: a secular view of the state and construing humankind as self-interested creatures. That, in Gordon's compelling view, is the extent of Machiavelli's contribution to the study of politics, for Machiavelli "does not examine the organization of government as a means for making collective decisions, and despite his republicanism, he does not consider how the liberty of the citizen may be preserved, or how the self-interest of the governors may be directed to the service of the general welfare" (162). Contarini, he continues, is as secular as Machiavelli and as realistic in his view of human nature, but he goes much further, "examining in detail the machinery of Venetian government and analyzing its dynamics" (162). This leads Gordon to suggest that Contarini "did for political science what Adam Smith's model of the marketplace later did for economics: it showed how a stable social order can be achieved without a hierarchical structure of authority" (162).

Suggesting that Contarini be placed alongside Machiavelli and favourably comparing Contarini with Adam Smith may be fitting for a political economist like Gordon who specializes in the history of theoretical and institutional economics; but I suspect that those who have invested much of their professional lives in the study of Renaissance political thought may not be persuaded as I am by Gordon's assessment. They may find it easier to accept the view offered by historian Frederic Lane when he noted that "compared to all other political organizations prior to the American and French revolutions, the government of ... communes [like Venice] was the one which offered [in the words of Robert Lopez] to the 'greatest number a chance to make [the] voice [of the people] heard in the conduct of public business'" (1966b, 523; see also Fink 1945, 31–4). Better still, they may accept, or not object to, the assessment of S.E. Finer, who in a multivolume study of government from the earliest times advances the view that the government of Venice

> *was* the best in the world and it would remain so till perhaps the eighteenth century ... Although the city was ruled by an aristocracy of perhaps only one fortieth of the total population, that proportion of active citizens was a far wider band of participants than was to be met with in the late feudal monarchies and principalities. (1997, 1016–17, italics in the original)

Finer continues:

> Admittedly Venice's structure was better designed than most [of the city republics] ... But if the active citizenry who manned the councils and rotated through the ever-more numerous boards and commissions had been even a fraction as contentious and violent as those in cities like Florence, the Venetian constitution would hardly have worked any better. It worked so splendidly because, in the last resort, the aristocracy that worked it – and for that matter the quasi aristocracy of *cittadini originari* with their names in

their own "Silver Book" – were imbued with a sense of responsibility for the
Republic that transcended their rivalries ... The rules of debate, especially
in the Senate, which forbid insult and slander, reprove emotionalism and
demagoguery and seek ... to keep discussion low-key, practical, and con-
sensual, are another manifestation of their attitudes. In their great crises
this Venetian aristocracy behaved like Roman senators and magistrates in
their golden days, during the Hannibalic wars. They exhibited a respect
for the *mos maiorum*, the laws of the Republic, and then exhibited what one
can only call, really, a sense of state. (1018; see also conclusion in Norwich
1989)

Against this backdrop, the significance of Contarini's *Republic of Venice*
resides in this: it shows that it is possible for fallible human beings to
create and operate a complex system of accountable and productive governance over a long period of time. It equally shows that it is possible, on
a smaller scale and in a more efficacious way than the Holy Roman Empire, for a polycentric system of governance in premodern times to hold
violence in check, to endure as an alternative to national monarchies
and unitary rule, and to represent another pathway to economic and
political development. Contarini's account of the Republic of Venice
broadens and enriches our understanding of the "generative capacity"
(Psarra 2018) of people to devise systems of governance for themselves
to the point of inspiring the search for other such experiments in world
history and in our own time.

Appendix A

The Myth and Anti-myth of Venice

The word "myth" generally is loaded with pejorative or unverifiable con-
notations, but this understanding is not always found among historians
of Venice for a complex set of reasons. Like most other Italian cities in
the Renaissance, Venice had an official historian charged with promoting the memory of the city's past and its good name (Cozzi 1963–4).
Gina Fasoli, the historian who fashioned the expression "the myth of
Venice," notes that "no other modern state possessed like Venice a sense
of the practical value of history in the educational and civic formation
of citizens and in the shaping of public opinion abroad" (1958, 450; see
also Gaeta 1961, 1981). Modern historians have followed Fasoli in using
the expression to draw attention to the historical reputation enjoyed by
the Republic of Venice over the centuries. The myth of Venice as a good
republic encompasses multiple positive dimensions: Venice's distinctive
origins, its place in geography and history, the longevity of its republican government and institutions, its cultural activities, the spiritual and
moral association of the republic with St Mark the Evangelist, and the
symbols, rituals, and ceremonies that characterized public life and instilled the civic patriotism that reached down to the common people
and that described what patricians were expected to wear and how to
behave in public and in transacting government business. The myth of
Venice thus derives from multiple sources, but its various dimensions
sought to create, maintain, and regenerate solidarity and trust among
the population, while offering lessons and images of city life that awed
visiting foreign observers. Several modern historians of Venice have built
on, and extended, observations gleaned from travelogues, local chronicles, and official city histories to show that people create their own realities and often act on those realities. This ritualization of society and
the resulting civic patriotism were important elements in accounting for
Venice's long-term stability (e.g., Burke 1994; Muir 1981; Robey and Law

1975; cf. Trexler 1980). The myth thus had a fixed text. But, as Patricia Fortini Brown notes, "its strength lay in its mutability. Within the main lines of the myth, succeeding generations of Venetians could respond to the vicissitudes of political necessity" (1991, 527; cf. on myth Darnton 1990, 3, 329–31).

The myth of Venice is comparable to what social scientists refer to as "folk theory of democracy, a set of accessible appealing ideas assuring people that they live under an ethically defensible form of government that has their interests at heart" (Achen and Bartels 2017). Just as in the case of the myth of Venice, the credibility of the folk theory of democracy has been severely undercut by a growing body of evidence presenting a considerably darker view of democratic politics by examining what actually happens in democratic politics. What researchers have found is that the practice of politics sharply differs from founding "myths" or justifications. Voters are poorly informed, and even those who claim they are well informed often choose parties and candidates on the basis of social identities and partisan loyalties. Voters tend not to choose on the basis of policies, there is little or no internal party democracy (as Gaetano Mosca [1896] 1939 noted of parliamentary government more than a century ago), elections do not produce responsive government, and bureaucratic administration is not accountable. Even when growing economic inequalities are acknowledged, taxing the rich remains a challenge. There is a huge gap between the practice and the doctrine ("the foundational myth"?) of democratic governance. The list of reported dissatisfactions with democratic politics is long and for the most part convincing. This state of affairs has led some analysts, particularly in the American case, to build up a case against democracy in favour of epistocracy, the rule of the knowledgeable (e.g., Brennan 2017).

Just as comparativists have been revising the accepted view of democracy, so have historians of Venice. Several decades of modern historiography have made clear that the myth of Venice as a good republic has lost the power it once had, and that that very myth helped to generate a counter- or anti-myth of Venice (Grubb 1986; see also Martin and Romano 2000, 2; Romano 2007, 339–43). The origins of the counter- or anti-myth of Venice can be traced back as far as the fifteenth century, when Venice was expanding its hold over the mainland, the *terraferma*. Venice was now being portrayed as governed by a secretive oligarchy, utterly controlled by a group of wealthy families who established a police state using torture and a network of informers to maintain power, plagued from time to time with eruptions of the social tension that existed between the highly stratified classes, and regarded by most of its neighbours as a dangerous and arrogant bully, with much of its wealth guaranteed by vigorously enforced monopolies over trade and, of course, by simple plunder. Not surprising, the anti-myth became prominent in France, where Venetian ideas of government countered the dominant absolutist tendencies of late sixteenth- and seventeenth-century political thought and practices (Muir 1981, 50). Jean Bodin gave theoretical coherence to the anti-myth in his work on sovereignty (see, e.g., Gianturco 1938; Gordon 1999, 21–4). By the eighteenth century, the republicanism of Venice appeared to people like Rousseau, who had spent time there as secretary to the French ambassador, a "simulacrum" or an anachronism in an age characterized by large unitary states. The democratic aspirations generated by the French Revolution and Napoleon Bonaparte's threat to take the city by force in 1797 "snuffed out" the Republic (Romano 2007, 343).[14] By the end of the twentieth century the anti-myth of Venice had gained considerable credibility and power among historians (Grubb 1986; Martin and Romano 2000, 3). Not surprisingly, in modern scholarship Venice "is no longer represented as the Exemplary Republic" (Martin and Romano 2000, 8).

Yet, just like the folk theory of modern democracy, the reality of Venice as a good republic is built on more than a myth or a grain of truth. Its undeniable social and economic inequalities were commonplace in the pre-modern world. When matters are put in comparative historical perspective, the Venetian inequalities and oligarchic tendencies did not appear as such to many Renaissance writers (Fink 1945, 32–3; see also Fink 1940; Gilmore 1973). Even Bodin, no admirer of Venice, admitted that the city attracted "those who aspired to live in the greatest freedom and tranquility; people who wished to engage in trade or industry, or to pursue studies worthy of free men" (quoted in Gordon 1999, 135). While other communes degenerated into unstable *signorie* (e.g., Jones 1997), "Venice avoided the dominance of any single family and perfected a system of checks and balances within its ruling class" (Lane 1966a, 412). For most of its history, Venice avoided the internecine warfare, political assassinations, and religious chaos that bedevilled most of its neighbours in Italy and the Balkans. The aspects of Venice that most intrigued foreign observers were, in fact, its relatively high degree of social and political tranquility and its economic wealth and cultural creativity. Often against overwhelming odds, Venice retained, across time and space, its independence, political resilience, and constitutional robustness to be the admiration or envy of many thinkers, included the Florentines Machiavelli and Guicciardini (see also Muir 1981, 45–50). One political

---

14 Perhaps the best expression of the anti-myth of Venice in the second half of the nineteenth century may be found in chapter 22 of Mark Twain's *Innocents Abroad* (Gordon 1999, 134n3).

economist summed things up this way: "What historians have come to call 'the myth of Venice' refers to the conception of Venice as an *ideal republic* that in itself influenced Western political theory and constitutional development" (Gordon 1999, 156). For as historian Robert Darnton (1990, 3) notes in another context, "myths can move mountains. They can acquire a rocklike reality as solid as the Eiffel Tower, which the French built to celebrate the one hundredth anniversary of the Revolution in 1889." It is truly hard for any society, organized political community, or "perpetually lived organizations" (North, Wallis, and Weingast 2013) to exist without myth, good and bad.

Appendix B

Glossary of Terms[15]

Auditori nuovi. Supervisory magistrates for newly acquired Venetian lands on the *terraferma*.

Auditori vecchi. Auditors served both as courts of first instance in Venice and its lagoon and appellate tribunals.

Avogaria / Avogadori di común. Attorneys general or chief law officers of Venice. Three state attorneys (*avogadori*), elected to sixteen-month terms by the Great Council, served as state prosecutors in the three supreme appeal courts known as the Quarantie, with one attorney required to be present in all councils to guard against violations of the law.

Ballottini. Generally non-patrician youths entrusted with circulating the urns during voting (*ballottar*) in the Great Council.

Bucintoro. The doge's private barge used for ceremonial occasions. The peculiar name is thought to be based on an archaic word for boat (*bucio*) and the word "gold" (*d'oro*). The first such boat was constructed in 1277; the last one, built in 1728, was destroyed by Napoleon's soldiers, who chopped it to pieces in order to salvage the gold leaves.

Collegio. The steering committee of the Senate charged with setting the agenda and making proposals to the body. It comprised the doge, the ducal councillors, the heads of the Quarantie, and the three sets of *savi* or sages: the *savi grandi, savi di terraferma,* and *savi agli ordini.*

Council of Ten. Council responsible for public order. Originally created after the Tiepolo-Querini conspiracy of 1310, it had become a permanent feature by the fifteenth century. It consisted of the elected ten, the doge, and the six ducal councillors. In time, the concern for protecting the security of the state diminished the authority of the Senate and increased that of the Council of Ten. The diarist Marin Sanudo, a contemporary of Contarini,

---

15 Adapted from Chambers and Pullan 2004; Labalme and White 2008; and Crouzet-Pavan 2002.

recognized this dynamic situation in his lifetime when he described the
Council of Ten as "a severe magistracy of the top nobles [*primi*] of the city"
(in Cozzi 1973, 303, and in Chambers and Pullan 2004: 54–6). But this
exacting magistracy sometimes raised fears of overreaching and sought
to appease apprehension by broadening the number of people making
decisions, through the creation of an additional group in the deliberation.
See **Zonta** below.

Council of the Forty. The supreme appeals court for criminal cases, composed of
forty judges who had served on the other two Quarantie during the previous
six months. The Council was part of the Senate.

Doge. The titular and ceremonial head of the Venetian republic, also called
principe or *serenissimo.*

Ducal councillors. The six ducal councillors, each representing a *sestiere* or
district of the city, and part of the Signoria.

Giudici del forestier. Judges with jurisdiction over disputes involving foreigners.

Giudici di mobile. Judges with jurisdiction over property disputes on mainland
territory.

Giudici di petizion. These judged questions of debt and related matters.

Giudici di piovego. Judges with jurisdiction to maintain, and prevent
encroaching of, public streets, waterways, and common property.

Giudici di proprio. One of the oldest courts in Venice; the judges originally had
wide jurisdiction, which was narrowed as other courts were established. It
retained jurisdiction over such matters as dowry, intestate succession, division
between brothers, and some property disputes.

Governatori delle Entrate. Office in charge of collecting taxes on merchandise
and from office holders, among others.

Great Council. Made up of all patricians over the age of twenty-five, it was the
sovereign organ of the government and the keystone of the system.

Magistrate alla sanità. The Health Office, responsible for overseeing public
sanitation, fighting plagues, and enforcing quarantines.

Podestà. Title usually reserved for some provincial governors.

Primi di la terra. The most important and influential patrician politicians. What
diarist Marin Sanudo referred to as "*primi di la terra*" (prominent patricians,
literally "first of the land") while the Great Council remained the "*Signor de la
terra*" (Cruzet Pavan 2002, 209; see also Finlay 1980).

Procurators of San Marco. The procurators of Saint Mark were nine men
originally elected for life by the Great Council. The procurators acted as
treasurers for the government and as fiduciaries for private individuals. The
doge was generally chosen from among this number.

Provveditore (pl. provveditori). Commissioner or patrician appointed to serve as
official in charge or superintend particular spheres of administrative responsibility,
like military or defence (*provveditori alle fortezze*) or commercial activities.

Provveditori alle biave. From 1365, the generally three *provveditori alle biave* controlled the import and distribution of grain inside the Republic of Venice, fixed prices, and had judicial powers.

Provveditori sopra ori e argenti. Controller of finances.

Quarantia civile nuova. Court of appeals for cases originating outside the city of Venice.

Quarantia civile vecchia. Court of appeals for civil cases originating in the city of Venice. After eight months on this court, its judges went on to serve on the Quarantia criminal and to sit as voting members of the Senate.

Quarantia criminal. Supreme appeals court for criminal cases; could also initiate legislation. Its judges received a salary and had previously served on the Quarantia civile nuova and Quarantia civile vecchia. They were included as voting members of the Senate. The three heads of the Quarantia criminal were members of the Signoria, along with the doge and the six ducal councillors.

Savi. Sages or what Contarini calls preconsultors, the sixteen members of the Collegio organized in three "orders" or ranks. First came the *savi del consiglio*, five patricians usually from the most prestigious (*primi*) families. Second in importance were the five *savi di terraferma*, with responsibilities for military affairs on the mainland. The third order, six *savi agli ordini*, were charged with maritime affairs. The sixteen sages and the Signoria formed the Collegio, also known as the Pien Collegio, whose twenty-six members included some of the most prominent representatives of the Venetian patriciate.

Scuola. Confraternity.

Senate. Known until the fourteenth century as the Consilio dei Pregadi or dei Rogati, it was the Venetian assembly that became the principal organ of the Republic. The Senate was composed of four groups: sixty ordinary senators, sixty extraordinary senators (the *Zonta*), the Court of the Forty (Quarantia criminal), and about 140 magistrates who entered by virtue of their offices.

Sestiere (pl. sestieri). One of the six administrative and geographical districts of Venice, each represented by a ducal councillor.

Signori di notte. "Lords of the night" or judicial magistracy charged with keeping public order especially at night, with jurisdiction over each district, assigned by the heads of the *sestieri*, over cases of petty crimes.

Signoria. The Signoria was constituted by the doge, the six ducal councillors (one from each *sestiere*), and the three heads of the Quarantia, and was responsible for the collegial direction of the Venetian state. Generally viewed as superior to all the councils, it set the agenda of the Great Council, among other responsibilities.

Stato da mar. The overseas territories of the Republic.

Terraferma. Venetian lands and possessions on the mainland.

Zonta (pl. Zonte). Groups of patricians elected to serve as adjuncts to particular councils (such as the Senate or the Council of Ten) with the aim of expanding the circle of deliberation, often among the *primi di la terra*.

Principal Events in Gasparo Contarini's Life[16]

1483	Contarini is born in Venice
1501–9	Lives and studies in Padua; between 1502 and 1505, he prepares for the practice of law
1508–9	Interrupts his cultural activities in Padua, returns to Venice and enters the Grand Council
1512	Competes unsuccessfully for several public offices
1517	Writes booklet on the office of bishop, *De officio episcopi*
1518–20	Wins first public appointment, in the loans office of the republic, and then surveys and measures reclaimed land in the Po valley
1520–5	Ambassador to Charles V, emperor of the Holy Roman Empire; sojourns in several cities of the empire and visits England
1522	Begins draft of his *De magistratibus et republica Venetorum*
1526–7	Assumes the office of *savio di terraferma*, one of the five officials overseeing the affairs of the mainland areas, especially with regard to war and defence
1527	Elected as one of the advisors to the Senate, to the advisory board *Zonta dei pregadi*; dispatched as an envoy to the duke of Ferrara
1528–9	Served briefly as Venetian ambassador to Pope Clement VII and the Holy See
1530–5	During this period, he reaches highest levels in the governance of the Republic, beginning on 1 April 1530 with

---

16 This chronology relies in part on the chronology of Contarini's life prepared by Claudio Negrato (2012).

assumption of the prestigious office of *savio grande* or *del consiglio*. During this period, he also serves as member and head of the Council of Ten. Takes part in the meetings surrounding the Peace of Bologna in 1530, from which he emerged as a chief architect of a new image of Venice as a city and as a people of peace governing a relatively small Italian state

1536–9 Named cardinal by Pope Paul III in 1535, he celebrated his first mass in 1537

1540–1 As representative of the Catholic Church, takes part in meetings with Protestant counterparts in Germany aimed, without success, at resolving differences

1542 Named papal legate for Bologna, the most important legateship of the Holy See, where he died in August 1542

1543 First posthumous edition of *De magistratibus* appears

Notes on the Translation: The Latin
of *De magistratibus et republica Venetorum*

GIUSEPPE PEZZINI[17]

The Text

This translation is based on the Latin text as printed in Contarini's collected works (*Opera*, Paris 1571), edited and revised by Alvise Contarini and his assistants, and reprinted in Venice with small variations in 1578. This is the edition generally used by modern scholars who quote Contarini from Latin. We have intentionally overlooked earlier editions – the first Latin edition (1543) and its various reprints, the Italian translation by an anonymous hand (1544) – and Lewkenor's English translation (1599), which draws on multiple sources (including the Italian translation of 1544, deriving from the 1543 Latin edition), collated with the Latin text from the 1571/8 edition (as recently discussed by Florio 2010). We have thus avoided the tendency to group versions of the text before the 1571 edition as a single entity. There are significant divergences between the different versions of *De magistratibus* circulating before 1571, which include substantial interpolations, mistranslations, amplifications, stylistic simplifications, and at times (intentional) meaning alterations.

The most common type of alterations have a stylistic nature, and are motivated by a classicizing intent on the part of Alvise Contarini, aiming to make the language adhere more closely to the standards of Ciceronian Latin[18] as regards lexicon and phraseology, syntax and word order, emphasis and *ornatus* (cf. Florio 2010, 90–101).

---

17 I am very grateful to Amanda Murphy for valuable comments and suggestions on several drafts of these notes.

18 On humanistic Ciceronianism see below. Cf. also Jensen 1996, investigating the origin of the "Ciceronian ban" advocated by "Ciceronianist" humanists and intended to "banish medieval neologisms and replace them with classical equivalents" (689). This ban is already traceable in the first edition of Contarini's treatise, but becomes

For instance, in the very opening of the treatise (1.1) the 1543 edition has:

> [...] *inde evenit, ut complures civitates conditæ sint, aut in montium salebris, aspero difficilique accessu, aut locis palustribus.*
>
> "For this reason, many cities were founded either **on mountain passes**, with rough and uneasy access, or **in marshy areas**."

In contrast, this is the text found in the final edition of 1571 (262):

> [...] *inde evenit, ut complures civitates conditæ sint, aut in editioribus et præruptis, aspero difficilique accessu, aut palustribus demissisque locis.*
>
> "For this reason, many cities were founded either **in elevated and steep places**, with rough and uneasy access, or **in marshy and remote areas**."[19]

Other changes are not (only) stylistic but significantly alter the original meaning of the text. For instance, at 1.9 the 1543 edition has:

> [the law-makers] *neque odio tunc aut amicitia aliave animi perturbation a veritate deduci queunt.*
>
> "[The law-makers] cannot be diverted from truth by animosity, friend-ship, or any other passion of the mind."

In contrast, the 1571 edition (265) has *a virtute deduci queunt*: if the alteration *queunt > possunt* is purely stylistic (the archaic form *queunt* is never attested in Cicero) the change *veritate > virtute* produces a different sense (cf. Florio 2010, 94–6). In this particular case the rationale for the change (perhaps a mere typographic correction) is not clear. There are, however, changes that betray a precise intention to modify the original sense. For instance, at 2.33 the 1543 edition has:

> *Huius* [i.e., the doge] *nulla privata est functio, nulla etiam est in universa Republica cuius expers esse debeat.*
>
> "He does not have any private function, and yet there is nothing in which he must not take part."

In contrast, the 1571 edition has:

> *Huius nulla certa functio tamen est in universa Republica, cuius expers esse debeat.*

---

a systematic criterion in the final revision of 1571. Ciceronianism originated in papal Rome, but became less fashionable in the context of the Counter-Reformation, and by the end of the sixteenth century was associated with Protestantism.

19 Cf. also ed. 1543 *praediti publica authoritate* (2.34) vs. ed. 1571 *publica auctoritate ornati* (280–1); ed. 1543 *ut opes adipiscantur* (1.14) vs. ed. 1571 *ut opes accumulent* (1.268), ed. 1543 *tum etiam ad molliorem quendam vitæ luxum* (1.2) vs. ed. 1571 *tum ad molliorem atque elegantiorem vitae cultum* (261–2); etc.

"He does not have any specific function, and yet there is nothing in which he must not take part."

The change *privata* > *certa* aims to clarify the ambiguity of the original text, in which the adjective *privatus* could be construed as evoking the (potentially unpleasant) notion "that the doge's duty of supervision extended to anyone's 'private' sphere" (Florio 2010, 99). Lewkenor collates the two versions and produces yet another sense:

"This Duke of ours hath not any certaine private//office alotted him, yet nevertheles ther is not in the whole commonwealth any thing done." (2.40–1)

This is not the place for a systematic overview of the variations between the 1543 and 1571 editions and their cultural, political, and theological implications (see Florio's [2010] analysis). Here I only stress that our translation, unlike Lewkenor's, is not based on an arbitrary collation of the different versions of the text but on the 1571 edition generally viewed as definitive. In this way we aim to connect modern readers directly to the final codified version of Contarini's work and the one that most widely circulated in later ages.

Contarini and the Classical Tradition

Gasparo Contarini's treatise is anchored to the "classical tradition," that is, the idealized cultural world created and nourished by the reception of Greco-Roman antiquity, which served as the canonical backbone of European education from late antiquity to the (early) twentieth century. This tradition received an important (and distinctive) boost in Contarini's times, thanks to the work of humanistic writers, who constitute the ideal readership of *De magistratibus et republica Venetorum* and with whom Contarini aspired to be associated (see also Florio 2010, 19–21, 35–6).[20]

Classical antiquity and its tradition not only provide the linguistic paragon for the elegant classical Latin of *De magistratibus* but represent an important cultural archetype for its narrative and political discourse. This is shown, for instance, by the many classical anecdotes Contarini cites as historical *exempla* for his Venetian narrative,[21] and even more by his constant reference to ancient political systems, as handed down in classical

---

20 On Venetian humanism see King 2014 and Branca 1998.
21 Cf. book 1:15, "The same thing happened to the Romans for almost the same reason, and the foremost Roman senators were conscious that this was going to happen," and 3:51–2, 3:58, 3:59, 5:94.

historiographies. Indeed, for Contarini the political parallels to which Venice's institutions are compared are not found among contemporary sixteenth-century (Christian) states, but rather among the ancient Greek and Roman "illustrious republics" (cf., e.g., book 3:57). Moreover, in Contarini's narrative the "wisest" founders of Venice are said to have modelled the political structure of their government on ancient polities (especially Sparta, Athens, and Rome) or to have adhered to ancient political theories (book 1:17; 3:51–2, 60, 64, 68; 4:6; and 5:99).

Not only did the founding fathers of Venice imitate ancient laws and customs, but they often *improved* them. One illustration suffices: "This was an ancient custom of the Spartans and Cretans, whose republics were illustrious, which our ancestors adopted in a *less ostentatious* form [*moderatum*]" (book 2:38; see also 3:65–6). In doing so they either fulfilled the ideal aspirations of ancient philosophers (1:15, 17) or, in some cases, even surpassed them (e.g., 1:11).

Venice's government is described according to classical models (historical, political, or moral), which, in truth, belong more to an idealized classicized world than to the historical realities of ancient Greece and Rome. The ancient exempla are literary rather than historical: Contarini brings in the classical tradition in order to anchor Venice's enduring institutions to an idealized cultural tradition, with a noble ancestry and a shared European identity. The primary interlocutors of *De magistratibus* are thus the Renaissance humanists,[22] Venetian, Italian, or European, keen readers of Greek and above all Roman writers, who were the first creators of that cultural tradition.

This intellectual, humanistic approach is also shown, for instance, by Contarini's references to the *auctoritas* of ancient theorists: the authorities cited by Contarini in support of his statements are the great classical writers, above all the *princeps philosophorum* Aristotle (book 1:14, 24; 2:37; 3:52; 5:98–9, 101; see also Gleason 1993, 8–9, and Florio 2010, 17–19) and also Plato and Xenophon (1:24; 3:52, 66; 5:93). In sum, for Contarini the classical world does not (just) provide the historical exemplum for Venice's government; rather, it represents the ideal cultural framework through which that government is described and assessed. This effort of anchorage within an idealized classical framework contributes to the creation and promotion of a certain view of Venice, the myth of Venice, which is traceable at all levels of his work, including above all language.

---

22 Alluded to, for instance, at book 1:11: "[...] seeing that none of the many learned men of these times, who excel in intellect, knowledge of things, and eloquence, have undertaken this task in writing."

Contarini's Classical Latin

In Contarini's times "Latin" was not a monolithic notion, and could refer to a multiplicity of linguistic entities. This includes, first of all, medieval Latin, that is, the lingua franca of European culture in a broad sense from the fifth to the sixteenth century AD. This variety had remained "alive" for centuries, being used both as a language of literature, science, and theology and as a documentary language for records, chronicles, and the like; across the centuries it had been enriched (or spoiled) by a vast number of borrowings from vernacular or other languages, and often featured a number of grammatical and syntactical "irregularities" (according to classical standards) (see Waquet 2001, 41–79).

Second, under the umbrella of "Latin" was also the Latin of the Catholic Church, used and, especially after the Council of Trent (1545–64), imposed as the common language of the liturgy, against the promotion of vernacular advocated by the Protestants:[23] this variety of Latin was modelled on the *Vulgata* and characterized by Christian lexicon and biblical style.

Third, Latin also came in the standardized variety of classical writers (Cicero, Livy, Virgil, etc.), imitated by poets and scholars: although this variety of Latin was also constantly used throughout the Middle Ages, it had recently been championed by many humanist writers, in polemic contrast with the "barbarities" of medieval Latin. It featured a standardized grammar and syntax (similar to the one still learnt by students in Latin primers) as well as a degree of lexical filter (on this variety and Latin in the age of humanism, see Leonhardt 2013, 198–244).

Finally, as an extreme version of the preceding, the idealized Ciceronian Latin was strictly modelled on the rhetorical and philosophical writings of Cicero, "purified" of all vernacular or Christian borrowings, and characterized by elaborate syntax and style: this puristic variety was advocated by the so-called Ciceronians, originally members of the papal curia (see Jensen 1996), for whom Erasmus himself had severe words of reproach in his *Ciceronianus* (1528). In this work, Erasmus argued that Cicero himself would have incorporated lexical borrowings if he had lived in a different age.

There are traces of all of the above varieties in Contarini's work,[24] but it is clearly the last two varieties, classical Latin and the idealized Latin

---

23 On this cf. Waquet 2001, 41–79.
24 Cf. book 3:64: "Therefore, it would not be unreasonable to call them [the magistrates of the Avogaria] the tribunes of the laws [*legum tribuni*]. However, to avoid ambiguities (which is a great concern of ours), we will not depart from the common and accustomed terms."

of Cicero in particular, in which *De magistratibus* was written, especially in its final "Cicerionanist" revision by Alvise Contarini. This is first of all revealed by the abundance of Roman terminology, even when it denotes anachronistic notions and institutions. Dates, for instance, are provided according to the Roman calendar (cf. 282G[25] [= book 2:40] *duodecimo Calendas Iulias die* [15 June]; 291A [= book 3:52] *ad tertium Calendas Octobris* [29 September]) rather than the modern system (cf. the exceptional 269D [= book 1:19] *diem quartam mensis Decembris* [4 December]). More significantly, Venice's magistracies are indicated by their Roman (anachronistic) counterparts, to which they are analogically assimilated. For instance, the *pioveghi* (urban officers) are referred to as *aediles* (310E [= book 4:82–3]), the *podestà, capitan(i)o,* and chamberlain as *praetor, praefectus, quaestor* (316F–G [= book 5:91]), the grand chancellor as *scriba magnus* (274F [= book 1:22]), and so on.

These linguistic choices, some but not all ascribable to Alvise Contarini's revision, were not the only ones available in sixteenth-century Latin, which could in fact dispose of a plethora of Latinized vernacular forms (e.g., *chancellarius, capitanus, camerlengus*). An emblematic example is *cives*, which Contarini uses to refer to the patrician members of Venice's Great Council, and which could have been easily (and more lucidly) substituted by *patricii* or *nobiles* (also classical Latin): however, *cives* programmatically assimilates Venetian nobility to the citizens of the Roman republic, thereby putting forward a republican construction of Venice's government, which is a primary goal of *De magistratibus*. These linguistic choices are not stylistic or antiquarian pedantries, but betray the effort to anchor Venice, its history and institutions, to the idealized world of the classical tradition as conceived by Renaissance humanists, often in polemic contrast with the "corruptions" of the (Christian) Middle Ages.[26]

At times, Contarini explicitly comments on his linguistic program, defending the preference for "ancient neologisms," that is, unusual words yet ones anchored to classical authorities. For example, in book 5:98 one reads: "Our ancestors, however, added to them, like a crown or a top, magistrates we usually call syndics [*sindici*], a vernacular word derived from a Greek noun. We refer to them as 'recognitors' [*recognitores*], a name that is perhaps new, but appropriate to clarify the function of that office" (cf. also book 3:55–6 on his use of the term *preconsultores* for *savi*). Here the contrast is not between Latin and vernacular – both *syndici* and *recognitores* are Latin(ized) words) – but rather between different

25 All references to the Latin original are from the 1571 Parisian edition (see above).
26 On humanistic Latin see Jensen 1996.

varieties of Latin: the "corrupt" post-classical Latin versus the idealized classical Latin of Cicero.

Indeed, the Latin vocabulary of *De magistratibus* is blatantly pruned of Christian and vernacular borrowings, which even Erasmus might have used: all words used in *De magistratibus* are recorded in the Oxford Latin Dictionary, only covering Latin lexicon attested in sources up to the second century AD. I have found fewer than ten exceptions, of late, Christian, or medieval words (e.g., *temporaneus, charitas, sanctitas, schedula, quadragintaviralis, iurisconsultor*); to these one might add some classical terms used in non-classical senses (e.g., *syngraphus* as "signed note," *cancellatus* as "gated," *praerogativus* as "pre-emptive," *emolumentum* as "emolument," *auditor* and *gubernator* in a legal sense). In some cases the classical Latin form has been introduced in the revision of the work (see above). For instance, in the first edition of *De magistratibus* (1543) the term "city" is normally rendered as *civitas*, a standard sense of the word in medieval Latin but rarely attested in classical Latin (where it instead means "citizenship"); in contrast in the final edition of 1571/8, *civitas* has normally been substituted by the standard classic term *urbs*, perhaps also to evoke Rome, the *Urbs par excellence*.[27]

The rendition of Christian terminology is also indicative: saints are referred as *dei* (*immortales*) or *divi* (evoking analogically the deified *divus Iulius, divus Augustus*) rather than *sancti* (their standard epithet in ecclesiastical Latin);[28] *Deus* is often qualified as *optimus maximus* (just like the Roman Jupiter);[29] a church is a *templum* or *aedes*, never an *ecclesia*,[30] years are never identified with the *anno Domini* formula, but always with a relative reference (cf., e.g., 297C [= book 3:62] *anno ab hinc decimo supra ducentesimum*; 309B [= book 4:79] *anno ab hinc XV accidit*). Again, this is not a linguistic pedantry but a deliberate choice, with interesting theological implications.

The adherence to classical standards is also shown by the explicit declarations of (Latin) literary inadequacy, themselves modelled on classical (and humanistic) precedents. In book 1:11, the writer notes: "And although I know for certain that the weakness of my style cannot add any radiance, the topic is so splendid that it will bestow more than enough brightness and dignity on itself and my style alike."[31] And again in the same book, "I am aware that it is extremely difficult to explain these

---

27 Cf. Florio 2010, 91–2.

28 Cf., e.g., 264E (= book 1:11) *iuxta templum Divo Stephano dicatum* (and passim); 282E (= book 2:39) *in aedem divi Marci*; 298G (= book 3:63) *in deos immortales*.

29 Cf. e.g. 286G (= book 2:46), 287C (= book 2:47).

30 Cf. e.g. 315B (= book 4:88).

31 Cf. also book 2:33: "So far, we have described diligently (however inadequately, considering the dignity of our topic and our [sc. stylistic] insufficiency [tenuitate] to the task)."

details in writing, since they are very remote from the practice of the
ancient Romans. Still, I would rather run the risk of being charged with
incompetence than carelessness. I will thus dutifully report every last detail, so that no diligent man could want more." In this passage, *literis* is
not simply "writing" but specifically denotes "classical (literary) Latin,"
that is, the language that young Venetians would learn from tender age[32]
and that is indeed the language of *De magistratibus* (see also book 1:11
where he notes "[...] have undertaken this task in writing [*hanc rem literis
illustravisse*]."

Syntax and phraseology are also modelled on classical Latin, and especially on the prose of Cicero, whose most elaborate periods serve as
paradigms for the treatise's florid syntax, abundant in complex subordi-
nation and syntactic *variatio* (with prolific use of absolute ablatives). The
same Ciceronian paradigm explains the treatise's linguistic *abundantia*
and *copia verborum*, featuring a profusion of discursive connectives,[33] explicit correlation,[34] long-winded phraseology,[35] emphatic pleonasm,[36]
and resumptive or resuming formulae.[37] For a modern reader unaccus-
tomed to the "copiousness" of Ciceronian standards, the style of *De magistratibus* may be taxing and at times irritating; and yet Contarini's prose
is a carefully constructed artifice, with plenty of ancient models and contemporary parallels, and above all deeply engrained in his ("humanistic") program in *De magistratibus*: to construct a view of Venice through
an authoritative idealized framework.

The Translator's Challenge

It is impossible for a modern translation to maintain the linguistic and
stylistic complexity of the Latin of *De magistratibus* without significant detriment to clarity and accessibility. Since these are the main goals of this

---

32 Cf. book 5:95 "The education of gentlemen has always been, from a very tender age
    until puberty, to spend time under the tutorship of school masters, learning Latin
    according to one's capacity."

33 E.g., *uero, nam, quodsi, enim, sed* but also *ideo, quocrica, quamobrem, idcirco,* etc.

34 Cf., e.g., 317C *et belli et pacis.*

35 Cf., e.g., 268H *nam frequenter evenit ut* [...] *qua ratione fit ut* [...]; 303D *ex his cuilibet
    compertum esse potest;* 314H *qua de causa effectum est ut* [...]; 319B *lege cautum fuit ... ut*
    [...]; 319D *quare facile intelligi potest ... ut* [...].

36 Cf., e.g., 263C *quo effectum esse perspicimus, ut neque adeo diuturna ulla unquam
    perstiterit.*

37 Cf., e.g., 268E *nunc a nobis illud primum omnium statuatur* [...]; 272H *sed eo revertatur
    unde nostra divertit oratio;* 286G *nunc ad rem redeo;* 302 *hoc in loco mihi videor non ab re
    facturus;* cf. also 274E, 276E, 277B, 277C, 279A, 280E.

translation, we have preferred to prioritize clarity over linguistic exactness whenever this would significantly affect intelligibility. This choice, although necessary, is not without consequences, which it is good for the reader to keep in mind. Two examples will suffice to illustrate the point.

At 310E (book 4:80) the original Latin states: *urbani hi quaestores eam pecuniam ex Senatus decreto in usus publicos impendunt, eamque in codices accepti et expensi referunt* (By decree of the Senate, the treasurers of the city disburse money for public use, keeping track of what they receive and expend). A Latin reader would be struck by the classical Latin word *quaestor* instead of medieval Latin *the(n)saurarius, camerlengus* or similar. This use implies that the writer is striving to equate the government of Venice to the government of ancient Rome, and implicitly suggesting that Venice's political system is that of a republic (in the ancient sense). In the present translation this information is lost because, for the sake of clarity, we translated *quaestores* as "treasurers," thereby obscuring the reference to the Roman Republic.

Another example is at 300E (= book 3:65): *consilio coacto magistratus hic Advocatoius accusatoris vice fungitur eosque qui in eo sunt magistratu maxime decet ut accusatores acerrimos agant qualis, dummodo id assequi possint, fuit Cicero in Verrem et in Marcum Antonium, ita tamen ut maledicta caveant, neque extra causam maledicendo vagentur.* Here the syntax of the original Latin is extremely complex, reminiscent of Cicero's more convoluted sentences. This is presumably intentional: in the passage the writer is citing Cicero as a model of rhetoric, and the copious syntax parades the actual ability to write in Ciceronian style. This intentional syntactic complexity contributes to presenting Contarini as the eloquent champion of the Venetian Republic, just as Cicero was in the Roman Republic, as well as associating himself with the great humanist writers. A literal translation of the passage would read something like this:

> Once the Council has assembled, this officer of the Avogaria takes on the role of the prosecutor, and it is most appropriate that those who are in that Office act as most severe prosecutors in a similar way to Cicero against Verres and Mark Anthony (provided that they are able to do so) yet with the provision that they refrain from insults and thus stray beyond the case.

This version would have preserved the syntactic complexity of the original and its allusive potential, but would have been much less accessible to modern readers than the one contained in these pages:

> Once the Court of the Forty has assembled, the state attorney takes on the role of the prosecutor. It is fitting for those in that office to act as severe

prosecutors, in a way similar to Cicero against Verres and Mark Anthony –
provided that they are able to do so. Yet they refrain from insults and do not
stray beyond the case.

For these reasons, the copious syntax and phraseology of the original have generally been pruned or toned down: repetition and pleonasm have been reduced, as well as complex syntax and unidiomatic
phraseology. Similarly, vernacular terms or English equivalents have
normally been preferred over Latinized forms (e.g., *podestà, capitanio,*
and *chamberlain* instead of *praetor, prefect,* and *questor*), especially when
they belong to the standard terminology of modern scholarship on
the Republic of Venice. This also includes the problematic use of *civis*
for "member of the Great Council," which we have consistently translated as "patrician" in order to avoid confusion with the non-noble
population of Venice, and to maintain the classical imprint of the
original.

Despite these choices, the present translation has not completely obscured the treatise's lexical sophistication and complex syntax. This is
not only because any claim to modify or, worse, "improve" on the original
style is absurd and dangerous, but above all because lexical sophistication and complex syntax are indeed important features of *De magistratibus*'s programmatic effort at being embedded in the classical tradition,
as idealized by humanist writers and thinkers.

Consequently, at times the reader will find lexical choices that aim
to preserve the classical patina of the original. An example is from the
fourth book (76 [=307B]): "After the institution of the Republic, the
dominion of the Venetians began to expand into the region of Venetum, which willingly and voluntarily went back to its old masters in a
restoration of sorts [*postliminium*]" The word *postliminium* and its Roman
concept have been preserved in the final version, instead of being substituted with some neutral periphrasis. Similarly, the original *copia verborum*
has been reduced, although not as much as could have been done. An
example is from the closure of the first book: "Let us now proceed to
that constituent part of the Republic which, having a sort of monarchic
appearance, is in full accord with the popular component, not unlike
a well-tuned diapason, where the low note corresponds to a high one
according to a certain interval, and eventually coalesces, with the mediation of other magistracies, into the single choir of our excellent Republic." Given the emphatic tone of the "grand finale," we have preferred
to maintain the paragraph as a single sentence, as in the original Latin,
rather than break it into two or three sentences (as we have done in several other passages).

In conclusion, this translation is a rendition of Contarini's *De magistratibus* in modern English but not a complete rewriting of it in a simple modern style. The present translation will therefore require a certain degree of effort from the reader – though assuredly be less than the effort the original treatise would have required (and expected) from its contemporary readers.

THE REPUBLIC
OF VENICE
De magistratibus et republica Venetorum

BOOK 1

The City and the Great Council[1]

I have often noticed foreigners, people wise and learned, who, upon arriving in Venice and seeing the greatness of the city, are so struck by admiration, almost astonishment, that they say they have never seen anything more magnificent, and this shows in the expression on their face. Yet they do not admire the same thing. Indeed, for some it seems a matter of infinite marvel, scarcely credible to behold, that such an abundance of goods from the shores and regions of the earth are carried constantly to this one city, and exported from here by land and sea to people far away. Others admire the number of residents in the city, and the concourse of almost every nation, as though this single city of Venice were the common market of the world. Others wonder at the extension of its territory and domain, which reach far across the world. But most of all, those of a more educated and acute mind wonder at the singular location of the city, so convenient in every respect that they think it is the work of immortal gods rather than of men; it is for this reason in particular that they think the city of Venice is superior to all others, whether in our time or ever before. And this is not surprising. If you look at the past and present age, you could easily find some cities that you might compare with this city of ours. Indeed, more than a few cities in earlier centuries have surpassed the city of Venice in the extent of their dominion, their number of people, and the abundance and magnificence of their material things. However, never in human history has there been a city founded on such an opportune site. When founding a city, most people thought it sufficient to choose a place that enemies would find inconvenient or hard to access in case of invasion or siege. For this reason, many cities were founded either in elevated and steep places, with rough and uneasy access, or in marshy and remote areas. Other people, following a different line of reasoning, deemed

---

1 Titles have been added to reflect the topic of each book. All the footnotes are the editor's, and are meant to clarify events, personalities, and places cited by Contarini and to give a deeper context to his narrative, without overwhelming what he has to say.

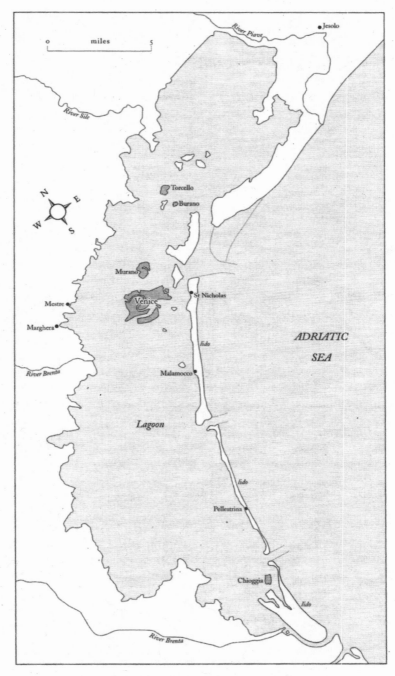

Map 1. The Venetian Lagoon. From Roger Crowley, *City of Fortune*
(London: Faber and Faber, 2011).

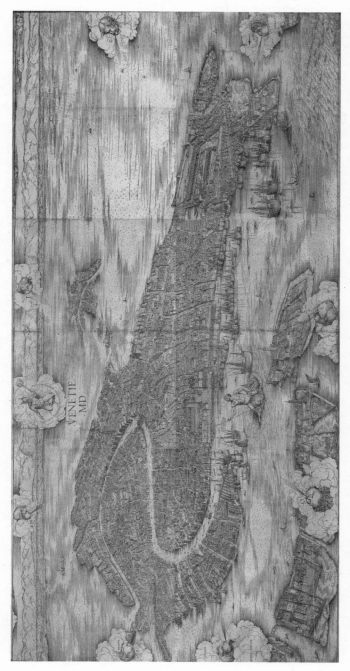

Map 2. A View of Venice by Jacopo de' Barbari. © 2018, Photo Archive – Fondazione Musei Civici di Venezia.

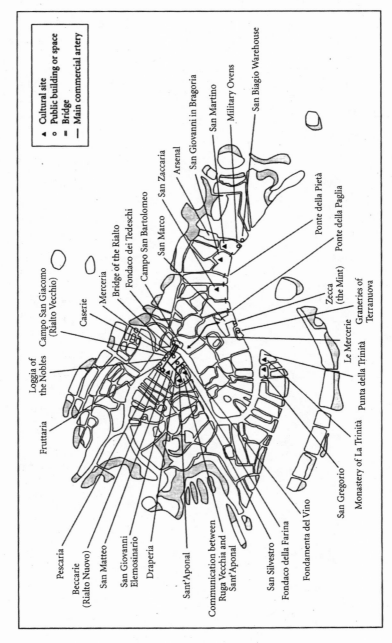

Map 3. Venice: Public Buildings and Facilities. © CROUZET, "Venice triomphante," Elisabeth Crouzet-Pavan.

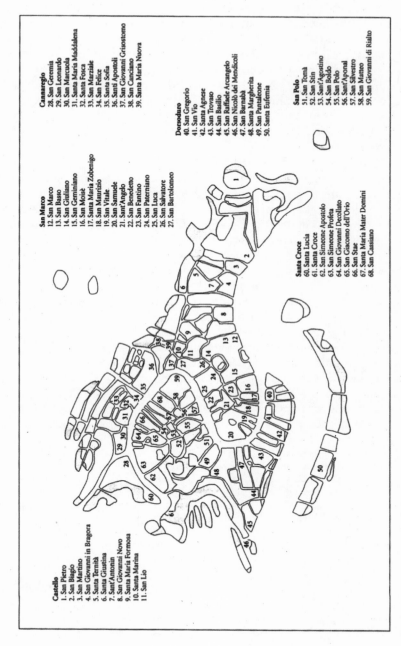

Castello
1. San Pietro
2. San Biagio
3. San Martino
4. San Giovanni in Bragora
5. Santa Trinità
6. Santa Giustina
7. Sant'Antonin
8. San Giovanni Novo
9. Santa Maria Formosa
10. Santa Marina
11. San Lio

San Marco
12. San Marco
13. San Baso
14. San Giuliano
15. San Geminiano
16. San Moisè
17. Santa Maria Zobenigo
18. San Maurizio
19. San Vitale
20. San Samuele
21. Sant'Angelo
22. San Benedetto
23. San Fantino
24. San Paterniano
25. San Luca
26. San Salvatore
27. San Bartolomeo

Cannaregio
28. San Geremia
29. San Leonardo
30. San Marcuola
31. Santa Maria Maddalena
32. Santa Fosca
33. San Marziale
34. San Felice
35. Santa Sofia
36. Santi Apostoli
37. San Giovanni Grisostomo
38. San Canciano
39. Santa Maria Nuova

Dorsoduro
40. San Gregorio
41. San Vio
42. Santa Agnese
43. San Trovaso
44. San Basilio
45. San Raffaele Arcangelo
46. San Nicolò dei Mendicoli
47. San Barnabà
48. Santa Margherita
49. San Pantaleone
50. Santa Eufemia

Santa Croce
60. Santa Lucia
61. Santa Croce
62. San Simeone Apostolo
63. San Simeone Profeta
64. San Giovanni Decollato
65. San Giacomo dell'Orio
66. San Stae
67. Santa Maria Mater Domini
68. San Cassiano

San Polo
51. San Tomà
52. San Stin
53. Sant'Agostino
54. San Boldo
55. San Polo
56. Sant'Aponal
57. San Silvestro
58. San Matteo
59. San Giovanni di Rialto

Map 4. Venice: Venetian Administrative Divisions. © CROUZET, "Venice triomphante," Elisabeth Crouzet-Pavan.

that nothing is better than a site that is convenient and accessible for the trade that a city needs to sustain itself, both for basic necessities and for enjoying a refined lifestyle. However, very few peoples can be found who have strived to care for both things. Even fewer have tried to bring them both about, and I know of none who have succeeded in each respect.

But the site of Venice, thanks to some divine plan rather than human contrivance, beyond the imagination of all who have not seen the city, is not only secure from attack by land and sea, but is also in the most suitable position for amassing an abundance of commodities for its citizens, both from the sea and the mainland, as well as for maintaining trade relationships for all kinds of merchandise with almost every nation.[2] It is located in the innermost recess of the Adriatic Sea, where a great lagoon spreads out where the sea meets the mainland, fortified by a marvellous expedient of nature. Indeed, about twelve miles from the mainland, the sea begins to become shallow and a stretch of land emerges like an embankment between those narrow shallows. This embankment stands against the waves and the rush of the sea, and makes the interior area so sheltered that when the sea is whipped up by a strong tempest, it is driven backwards and breaks into waves, restricting access for approaching ships. Indeed, unless they are extremely lightweight, ships have to lie at anchor in the places where the sea begins to shallow out. Only once the weather is fair can they finally reach the city, after being guided around by expert helmsmen (or by people expert in detecting shallows) through narrow and intricate channels, where the water is a bit deeper – and this in fact changes and varies almost every day because of the sea tides. The strip of land that emerges beyond the shallows spreads out for about sixty miles and encloses the innermost lagoon. However, it does not form a continuous whole, but is broken in seven places to give access to the interior from the sea. It is about six miles from the mainland.[3]

---

2 Many others over the centuries have drawn attention to Venice's location (see Crouzet-Pavan 2002, chaps. 1 and 2, esp. her discussion of the invention of a city in chap. 2, 10–36; Ferraro 2012, 5, 38–9; Finlay 1980, 16–17, quoting the impression of a French ambassador to Venice at the end of the fifteenth century; and Muir 1981, 14–15). In a review of Filippo de Vivo's *Information and Communication in Venice: Rethinking Early Modern Politics* (2008), Thomas Cohen draws attention to Venice's location at the head of the Adriatic and as an unequalled meeting place for trade, nations, and cultures; he adds that Venice's "geographical position made it something like Berlin at the height of the Cold War: all major powers found it handy to have ears there" (2008, 19). Echoing this point, on the trade of information and early modern Venice's intelligence organization see Iordanou 2016a. See also map 1 of the Venetian lagoon.

3 For the striking relationship between Venice and its environment and the challenge of "building on water" in a comparative context, see Bevilacqua 2009; Ciriacono 2006; Crouzet-Pavan 2000, 2013; Tenenti 1973. On the importance of geography and geopolitics more generally, see Grygiel 2006.

Thus the lagoon of Venice is enclosed partly by the mainland, and partly by this stretch of land and shallows. It was in the middle of the lagoon (in the area the ancients called Rialto, which is called this still) that the city of Venice was founded, while the Huns, led by Attila,[4] were burning and slaughtering the whole region of Venetum, an eminent province of Italy on the border of the lagoon. In the course of that disaster, citizens of famous cities of Venetum – Padua, Aquileia, Oderzo, Concordia, and Altinum – which were superior to the others in nobility and wealth, first took refuge with their families on some islands, or higher ground, that rose slightly above the sea in this lagoon. There they built castles, like safe harbours, where they could escape the stormy turmoil of Attila. At the same time, on that stretch of land mentioned above, several strongholds were founded by the inhabitants of that region gathering there, who in similar fashion had left their native countries, pillaged and ravaged by the Huns, and had searched for a safe place for their wives, their children, and their household gods (*penates*,[5] as I may call them). Afterwards, in the time of the kings Charles and Pepin,[6] they made a common plan to convene in Rialto,[7] which was considered the most convenient and secure place of all. Therefore, with the assembling there of all the people who had managed to escape from the suffering and devastation brought to Italy by that enormous influx of barbarians, Venice grew to the size that we see today.

So it is manifest that the site of the city of Venice is exceedingly secure because of the way the city was constituted, when men fleeing the calamities of Italy founded it for themselves and stayed there with their families, unharmed amid such great distress. Indeed, since the events of those times, which we have not read to have happened to any other city, Venice has remained unharmed by hostile violence. This has lasted for almost eleven hundred years, from the city's beginnings up until the present – although such an opulent city, rich in gold and silver and all kinds of goods, could have attracted barbarians in search of booty from the most distant regions of the earth. Accordingly, those who have reckoned that Venice surpasses the other cities for precisely this reason are not, in my view, mistaken.

---

4 Attila's Huns sacked Aquileia in 452.
5 *Penates* were the tutelary gods of the ancient Romans, invoked in domestic rituals to secure safety of the households.
6 Pepin's failed attack occurred in 810.
7 "The forces of the lagoons had converged to create Rialto" (Crouzet-Pavan 2002, 18). See also how a contemporary of Contarini, Marin Sanudo, described it in context in his praise of the city of Venice, *Laus urbis Venetae* excerpts in Chambers and Pullan 2004, 4–21.

I.

There is, however, something else in this city that I think is by far its most outstanding quality: all those who believe that a city is more than just walls and houses are in agreement with me, holding that above all it is the community and the order of the citizens who can claim this name for themselves.[8] Thus the city is specifically the system and form of government by which men attain a happy life. I consider this marvellous quality to be what makes Venice especially shine, seeming to surpass antiquity. In fact, even if in the past a number of cities greatly surpassed the Republic of Venice in power, territory, soldiery, and glory in war, none can compare with this city of ours in institutions and laws suitable for living well and happily. The result of this, in our view, is that none has ever endured for such a long time.

When I reflect on this, I marvel at the wisdom of our ancestors, their industry, their excellent virtue, and, moreover, their prodigious love of country. In Athens, Sparta, and Rome, there were many citizens who distinguished themselves as men of integrity and devotion to the public realm; but they were so few that they could have not been of great benefit to their country, overwhelmed by the multitude. But our ancestors, from whom we received so flourishing a republic, were all without exception of the same mind in their desire to strengthen and advance the country, almost without regard for their own private benefit and personal honour. That the men of Venice were never ambitious when it came to themselves, and were infinitely more devoted to the well-being

---

8   Frederic C. Lane reminds us that, like the rest of the Venetian patriciate, Contarini "considered citizens only those we call nobles. He felt the need of only a few words to justify the exclusion of the working masses from citizenship, that is, from any share in supreme power, since that was then a universal practice" (1973, 258). Echoing the same, Brian Pullan observes that Contarini confined "the use of the term *civis* or 'citizen' strictly to those who formed part of the nobility, and dismissed the other inhabitants of Venice as 'artificers,' 'mercenarie people,' engaged in '*ars mechanica*,' or 'hired servants'" (1971, 99; see also A. Bellavitis 1983, 2004). Those who could claim the name of citizens for themselves thus were of patrician rank, comprising no more than 2 per cent of the population. The Venetian patricians were "the sovereign people at the heart of the republic" (Pullan 1971, 25). For the changing self-image of patricians by the seventeenth century, see Raines 1991. For an overview of the ranks of patricians and *popolani* as an expression of the social order of the Venetian Renaissance state, see Romano 1987, 1996; A. Bellavitis 1983, 2004; and Pullan 1999. As noted in the Introduction, between the patricians and the *popolani* there was another hereditary order of elite Venetians known as *cittadini originari*, who held bureaucratic posts (see also Pullan 1971, 103–6). For comparative and more philosophical analysis of the changing meaning of active citizenship, see Siedentop 2000, chaps. 1 and 2.

of the country, can be deduced by anyone from this one fact: in Venice there are extremely few, if any, monuments to our ancestors, even though they conducted themselves with distinction at home and abroad. After so many great battles, there are nonetheless no stately tombs, no statues, no naval spoils, or standards seized from the enemy defeated in great battles.

I will cite the example – one among countless others – of my relative, the Doge Andrea Contarini.[9] At the time of the war with Genoa, the most troublesome and by far the most dangerous of all wars, this doge was in charge of our Republic, and he preserved its well-being with extraordinary wisdom and remarkable greatness of mind. He crushed the enemies, who had been winning, inflicting a tremendous defeat; all to a man were killed or taken prisoner. Having saved the country, expanded its dominion, and strengthened the Republic, he ended his days, and prescribed in his last will that no emblem of the doge, nor of our family, was to be affixed to his tomb, which can be seen to this day near the church dedicated to Saint Stephen. Not even the name of such a great doge can be seen engraved there. The result of this is that most people ignore the memorial of this distinguished man and illustrious lord.

I believe this is certain proof that our ancestors were concerned not with ambition and empty fame, but only with the good of their country and the common welfare. Our ancestors established this Republic with this extraordinary virtue of mind. If anyone were to compare this Republic of ours with the most famous of the ancients, one would easily perceive that none like it has existed in the memory of man. I dare say that none so rightly formed and fashioned may be found even in the works of famous philosophers, who created forms of government according to the desires of the mind. For this reason I have deemed that it would be far from unwelcome to foreigners if I set the constitution of such a splendid Republic down in writing, especially seeing that none of the many learned men of these times, who excel in intellect, knowledge of things, and eloquence, have undertaken this task in writing. And although I know for certain that the weakness of my style cannot add any radiance, the topic is so splendid that it will bestow more than enough brightness and dignity on itself and my style alike. Therefore, having decided to write about our Republic so that anyone can easily discern whether it is good or bad, I think it is best to start from here.

---

9 Andrea Contarini was doge from 1368 to 1382. He served as captain-general of the sea in 1379, when he was over seventy years old, and led the republic in defeating the enemy in the Fourth Genoese War, better known as the War of Chioggia (1378–81).

That is to say, man is by nature a civil [or civic] creature, and in truth he cannot live on his own, nay not even live at all. This is clearly shown by daily necessities and the concern for food and clothing. It was for this reason that men originally gathered together in civil society, and have persevered in order to live happily and comfortably – that is, in order to obtain, with mutual help and assistance, the greatest good possible for men in this mortal life. For the same reason, the whole concern of civic institutions is to make it possible for citizens to have a happy and tranquil life. But, as the greatest philosophers demonstrate with assured reasons and self-evident arguments, a contented and blessed life consists in the exercise of virtue. And indeed the exercise of virtue applies both to the duties of war and to the preservation of peace. Yet, while the glory of war and military affairs are necessary for cities in order to preserve their freedom and defend their boundaries – and, of course, those things have great dignity and splendour – nonetheless, common sense rejects the idea that the business of war, which is the main cause for the killing and maiming of men, is to be sought for its own sake and that all other civil tasks must refer to it. Indeed, it would befit a cruel nature, or rather a man who abhorred humanity, to wish for battles, slaughters, and burnings just to be renowned in military affairs, or to be honoured with the name of a supreme captain. Therefore, all distinguished philosophers have agreed on this judgment: war is to be sought for the sake of peace, and the entire function of military virtue and the manifest merit of war must be channelled into the tasks of peace. For this reason, the governor of a republic who wants to be considered worthy of praise – and, in the words of the old adage, to seem to have seen to everything – should apply that moderation and safeguard that system, so that the republic as a whole may appear to be constituted for virtue. He should look more to the practice of peace than the business of war, without neglecting to look after military and war affairs from time to time. Indeed, military virtue is mostly necessary for protecting and extending the republic's boundaries, as long as this happens without injustice.[10]

Once these things we have spoken about have been arranged, it is customary to discuss whether it is more equitable for One, the Few, or the Many[11] to preside over the government of the city, which is the system that many assume should properly be called "republic." It has been excellently shown and wisely said that it is wrong to entrust the government of men to one man, whoever he may be, and that there is a need

---

10 This contradicts Niccolò Machiavelli, who advocated a citizen army.
11 Contarini follows Aristotle in discussing government by the One, the Few, and the Many. Contarini refers to *universa multitudo* – not exactly the "many" or "the majority." See also book 5:94.

for something more divine, upon whom this office depends. And this can easily be seen among many species of animals. For a sheep does not govern a flock of sheep, nor does an ox or horse control a herd of oxen or horses; rather, a much more noble creature guards and governs these brute animals, that is to say, man – and everyone knows that man is superior to beasts.

In a similar way, if one wants the outcome to turn out according to the right intentions of the mind, something more worthy and more divine than man must govern him. But in this world perceived by the senses, one can hardly find anything better and worthier than man, even though he is a multifaceted creature comprised of diverse elements. Indeed, in the lesser faculties of his mind man has a kinship with the beasts, but in the higher faculties he rises, so to speak, to the status of the immortal gods. Among human beings, then, that which is divine in man must rightly hold the place of governor and ruler. This, as common opinion recognizes, is indeed the intellect, a sort of ray of divine splendour implanted in human minds. It will therefore not be a good choice for a republic if government is put into the hands of a single man, who is often troubled by brutish forces and diverted from the path of reason. This task must rather be laid upon an intellect that is unsullied by, and immune from, the flux of the mind.

For this reason, through a sort of divine intervention (since it could not happen in any other manner), it seems that mankind has achieved this arrangement with the invention of laws: that is, the task of governing human societies is entrusted only to the intellect and to reason unexposed to the passions. And if one carefully ponders the benefits of laws, I am sure that this almost divine gift should not be considered inferior to any other. For when laws are enacted, there is first a gathering of many wise men. Drawing on their wide-ranging experience, the discoveries of others, and the examples of the ancients, they determine after prolonged consultation that which strikes them as the best. They cannot be diverted from virtue by animosity, friendship, or any other passion of the mind, since in establishing the laws, what is at issue is not the case of a private citizen, which is what usually happens in forensic judgments. Then, after the laws have been enacted, if anyone is caught acting against them and is punished in accordance with the laws, he cannot rightfully hold a grudge against anyone. Consequently, there will be no need to fear that discord or hostility may arise among citizens, which is the greatest and most dangerous contributor to the ruin of states. On the other hand, when someone is punished by the judgments of men rather than by the force of law, grievous discords and enmities are prone to emerge. In fact, we are almost invariably ill-disposed towards someone who has harmed us. And in this regard, I doubt that nature, the mother of all, has conceded anything greater to mankind than the invention of laws, which the ancients consecrated to the immortal gods.

What seems more remarkable is that Aristotle, the prince of philosophers, in the book called *On the Universe* that he wrote for Alexander, king of Macedonia, found nothing to resemble God the Greatest more than an ancient law in a well-organized city. This suggests that in the opinion of that consummate philosopher, God is equivalent to what an ancient law is in a civil society. And in *Politics*,[12] he says that the law is an intellect without desire, which is to say it is a pure and clear intellect, unaffected by any disease of the passions. Any individual, even one of sluggish mind, would perceive the implication that we have already described as most opportune and fitting: namely, that something more divine than man controls and governs human societies. For if a single person is given the task of governing, much trouble and great danger will result – inasmuch as men endowed with both prudence and integrity are extremely rare, and men generally err in judging because the force of the mind's passions tends to powerfully divert from the right judgment. Even if it were possible to find a man so wise and just, and so steadfast in purpose that he would not be restrained from his duty by any troubles of the mind, one should not prefer the dominion of a man to the primacy of law. For even in this circumstance, because a man's nature is mortal and frail, he would not be able to perform that duty for long, whereas laws can concur with eternity.[13]

I think that these arguments have proved that the highest power should be entrusted not to men but to laws, and indeed that as little as possible should be entrusted to the discretion of a man, in those cases where matters cannot be circumscribed by law. Indeed, it is necessary to establish some guardian or deputy who may govern the republic according to the power of the law. And since not all that is brought to judgment or that requires a consultation is such that it can be circumscribed by laws, this person ought to be an arbiter for these situations. We are now back to the same issue that some might thought to have been solved by the enacting of laws: that is, whether it would be best to put One or the Few or the Many in charge of safeguarding the law, and of pronouncing judgment on matters for which laws are inadequate.

---

12 Aristotle (1962), book 3, 1287.
13 For the importance attached to authority and law in Renaissance Venice, the work of Gaetano Cozzi (1973, 1982) remains insightful; on Aristotle's view of the law, see Harrington 1992, 36. For a recent overview, see Viggiano 2013, esp. 51–76.

Many hold that monarchical power is preferable to other systems, and I would tend to agree that, at least considered *per se*, the governance of one man who could truly and rightfully claim kingly dignity is the best system of all. Nevertheless, considering the tendency of man's nature to succumb to his frail disposition and to the brevity of life, the most preferable means of governing the multitude is not by one individual on his own. Rather, experience, the mistress of all things, eloquently teaches us that it is more fitting to a civil society to be governed by an assembly of citizens. Indeed, we have never read of a monarchy that existed in antiquity, nor observed any in our age, that has not shortly fallen into tyranny. By contrast, several republics have persisted for many centuries and flourished in times of war and peace. Clearly the multitude as such is unfit for governing itself, unless it somehow coalesces into one, for there cannot be a people that does not coalesce into some unity. For this reason, even a civil society that possesses various degrees of unity will be fragmented, unless the people are in some way brought together into one.

Therefore, the distinguished philosophers, who have written extensively about the structure of a republic, judge that government should be balanced between the order of patricians, on the one hand, and that of the people on the other. The aim of this balance is to avoid the disadvantages of each system of power, while obtaining the benefits of both. As a consequence, philosophers praise the polity of the Spartans, where the kings, the ephors, and the Senate came together into a mixed assortment, so that it is difficult to distinguish that particular polity's form of government. Yet the philosophers also criticize Sparta for being organized only with regard to affairs of war, without considering the business of peace and pleasure. The result, they say, is that the city, renowned for many celebrated virtues, declined and eventually fell to ruin the moment peace and leisure set in. The same thing happened to the Romans for almost the same reason, and the foremost Roman senators were conscious that this was going to happen. One of these, Nasica,[14] averred that Carthage, though a rival (or rather eternal enemy) of the Roman name, should not be destroyed, so that the Romans would always have an enemy to wage war against, avoiding the situation whereby a state organized for war, with the young men trained to fight, would turn their weapons against one another in the absence of their enemy. Although

---

14 Senator Publius Cornelius Scipio Nasica Corcolum (died 141 BCE) was a political opponent of Marcus Porcious Cato during the period 159–149 BCE. To Cato's insistence that "*Carthago delenda est*" (Cathage must be destroyed), Nasica argued that Carthage must be spared for the good of Rome.

the Senate rejected Nasica's advice, subsequent events showed it that it was indeed the wisest. For after the overthrow of Carthage, civil wars almost immediately broke out, and the most prosperous and powerful empire of all time eventually fell to the ground, reduced to booty for the barbarians.

II.

To come now to the task I have given myself, it is clear that our ancestors who founded the Republic of Venice were endowed with admirable wisdom and outstanding integrity, in that they omitted nothing that pertained to the proper ordering of a republic. First they organized every aspect of citizens' lives and duties, aiming for the practice and exercise of virtue, always with greater regard for peace than for war. Then they applied themselves most vigorously to protecting civil concord from being disturbed in any way, while not neglecting military affairs, which, I believe, were most important for our city. Indeed, the location of the city is such that it is ideal for a naval force, but not very apt for a land force. There is no way to lodge squadrons of horsemen or regiments of foot soldiers in the city, as can be clearly deduced from our earlier description of its environs. Thus, in this city our ancestors applied moderation and balance, combining all respectable ranks, so that this Republic alone includes a monarchical regime, a government of the nobility, and a popular element of citizens.[15] This way, each component seems equally balanced, as will emerge more plainly in the course of the work.

But, to arrive at last at the institution of our Venetian Republic, the highest authority of the whole city – from whose decrees and laws both the Senate and the magistrates receive their rights and powers – is the Great Council, to which every patrician over twenty-five years old is admitted. Several others who have not yet reached that age (but who are over twenty) can also obtain this right by good fortune; we will discuss this matter later on.

Let us make clear, first of all, that it was wise of our ancestors to prevent the common people from being admitted to this Great Council,

---

15 By "popular element" Contarini means the Great Council. Brian Pullan (1963–4, 456–9) notes that the view of a mixed constitution suggested by Contarini here rests on a dubious assumption that members of the Great Council can be considered a popular element; the view, Pullan adds, is not as paradoxical as it seems if we grant that a "political nation could be equated with a small hereditary caste of full citizens" as its sovereign people and if we keep in mind that, indeed, the Great Council had both rich and poor patricians as members.

in which the highest power of the Republic resides. It was no less wise
to make a distinction between members on the basis of nobility of lineage, rather than on degree of wealth, as had become customary in the
ancient republics, and as several ancient philosophers advocate. For although a city is a community of citizens, not all the men that the city
depends on and who live within its walls should be regarded as citizens,
and nor should they be rightly included in the number of citizens. Every
city needs craftsmen and many other people who work for a wage, including private servants. But none of these can truly be called citizens.
A citizen is a free man, whereas all of these workers are under servitude,
either private or public; all the wage-labourers and craftsmen should be
considered as public servants.[16] Consider that a living creature has been
shaped by nature in the same way that a city is organized by men. In a
living creature, there are many parts that are not alive, and yet the creature needs them in order to survive. Likewise, in a community of citizens
there is a need for many men who do not need to be, and do not need
to be reputed to be, part of the city, and nor should they be included in
the number of citizens.

For this reason, it was wise of our ancestors to carefully prevent a situation in which the whole people have the greatest power in the Republic,
which they desired to fashion in the highest degree of perfection. For
the greatest turmoil and popular uproars are often aroused in cities in
which power is held by the common people. We have read that there
are also some republics in which this arrangement has been considered
and even recommended by some philosophers. Yet, they have thought
that they could achieve this if the manner of governing the republic was
defined on the basis of property ownership and family wealth. But they
incurred enormous problems and significant inconveniences.

For it often happens that men from the lowest ranks of the population,
the *popolani*, accumulate great wealth. These are people who endeavour
to increase their patrimony mainly through means and occupations that
are not appropriate to a free man, and who, working without stop, rather

---

16 Contarini echoes here the standard justification, used as far back as the ancient
   Greek city states and as recently as the late nineteenth century (see Bagehot 1867),
   for excluding particular groups of people from political participation. The labour-
   ing classes of early modern Venice, the *popolani*, made up about 90 per cent of the
   city's population. For a re-evaluation of the role of the *popolani* and the relationship
   between master and servant, see the work of Ioanna Iordanou (2016b) and Dennis
   Romano (1987, 1996). On the ambiguities of the office of citizenship in Renaissance
   Italy, see Bizzarri 1916; Kirshner 1973; Najemy 2006, chaps. 1 and 2; Nederman 2002;
   Riesenberg 1992, chap. 5; P. Ventura 1995, and, more generally, Siedentop 2000.

cheapen their spirit to amass riches [to increase their substance]. In contrast, citizens who are noble and receive a liberal education sometimes become poor, either by adverse fate (as usually happens) or because their devotion to liberal studies leads them to neglect the work of increasing family wealth. For these reasons, it happens that foul men, who have nothing in mind other than profit, and are ignorant of the liberal arts, gradually take possession of the republic. But the nobles and those who have received a liberal education, gradually losing their possessions, are deprived of their right to citizenship. From this, turmoil and rebellion inevitably arise, and the republic becomes unsettled.

In order to prevent the Republic from suffering these misfortunes someday, our ancestors, the wisest of men, decided that it would be much better to distinguish civil rights on the basis of nobility of lineage, rather than size of wealth. They did so with moderation, so that not only the men of the highest nobility had this right – for that would have befitted a government of the few, not a republic – but also every other citizen, except those ignobly born. Thus all those who were noble by birth, renowned for virtue, or meritorious towards the Republic, obtained from the beginning the right to participate in governing the city. And if, after that first gathering of citizens, there have been other noble men who have enhanced the Republic with riches or notable service, it is unsurprising that the right to govern the Republic has been extended to them too, which we have also seen in our times. Even a number of immigrants or foreigners have been adopted into the number of citizens, either for their great nobility, their devotion to the Republic, or because they have honoured it with some great accomplishment.

Thus this whole assembly of patricians – this Great Council where the ultimate sovereignty of the Republic resides, and on which the Senate and the authority of the magistrates depends – fulfils the role of a popular authority in this Republic. But the doge, who does not have a fixed term of power, remains in office as long as he lives; he bears the show of royal power, retaining a regal appearance and maintaining the solemnity and dignity of a king. Moreover, the patricians give the doge the respect due to a king, and all decrees and laws, as well as public documents, are issued under the name of his office. But the Senate, the Council of the Ten, and the Collegio of the Elders or chief advisors, who, among ourselves, we ordinarily call sages [*savi*] – that is to say, the college of those who take counsel beforehand and report to the Senate about the Republic – all these display the appearance of aristocracy. And since these are the foremost elements of this Republic, one must first talk about them one by one, before coming to the inferior magistracies.

III.

Let us begin with the Great Council, upon which the whole Republic
depends. All the young men of noble (or patrician) rank who have
passed the twentieth year of age come to the office commonly called
the Avogaria [the office of state attorneys], to which the custody of
the laws is especially entrusted.[17] They present themselves with their
father, or, if their father is deceased, with their mother, or, if they are
orphans of both parents, the closest relative of the family. With two
witnesses (honest men not related to their mother), they confirm that
they are children of the man whom they claim to be their father, and
that they are not illegitimate, but have been born from a legal marriage by a mother who is an upstanding woman. Then the witnesses
take an oath, swearing that they have acquired knowledge of this from
the testimony of the people they knew and from general consent. Af-
terward, the father or the mother or the closest relative states under
oath that the youth has passed his twentieth year. After a clerk has
written all this down in a document, they wait for the fourth day of the
month of December, when the names of all the youths who by chance
have not yet acquired the right of citizenship, and have not passed the
twenty-fifth year of age, are put inside an urn that is brought to the
prince. There the urn is set up in the presence of the [ducal] councillors; there is also another urn nearby in which there are as many
ballots as names in the first one, each written on a separate paper. A
fifth of the ballots are golden, but all the rest are silver. The doge extracts the name from the first urn, and also a ball[18] from the other one.
If the ball is golden, the young man whose name has been extracted

---

17 Three *avogadori*, elected to sixteen-month terms by the Great Council, served as state
prosecutors in the three supreme appeal courts known as the Quarantie; "at least one
state attorney was required to be present in all councils to guard against violations of
the law" (Finlay 1980, xvi–xvii). Dennis Romano notes that "they enjoyed a reputation
as defenders of the law and advocates of judicial and legal equity. In the sixteenth
century they represented the interests of the minor nobles of the Great Council
against the more influential members who controlled the Senate and Council of Ten.
But by the beginning of the fifteenth century the Venetian nobility had begun to
bifurcate, with poorer members depending on minor government offices for a living,
resenting their more prepotent brethren and looking to the *avogadori* for protection"
(2007, 18). Romano further notes that Doge Francesco Foscari, who was doge from
1423 to 1457, rose to prominence in no small part due to the reputation he gained in
his early career as *avogador*. For a recent examination of the ancient magistracy of the
Avogaria, see Setti 2014.

18 The ballots were in the form of balls made of copper or tin.

immediately obtains the right of civil participation and is admitted to the Great Council. If instead the ball extracted is silver, he loses his chance and must wait until the following year, unless he has passed his twenty-fifth year by that time.

For any noble who reaches that age immediately obtains the civil right to participate in public authority by being admitted to the Great Council.[19] Therefore, in this manner, every year a fifth of the young candidates are granted the right to vote with the other patricians. And if it happened that the father or grandfather of a patrician never exercised the right to vote, because he had been away or for some other reason, and his name was never recorded in the common book[20] containing the names of all the nobles, our ancestors did not want the matter to be dealt with solely by the magistrates of the Avogaria, in the interest of avoiding fraud and preventing some ignoble person from stealthily creeping into their congregation of gentlemen. It was therefore specified by law that after hearing an address by the Avogaria attorneys, they would confirm their noble kindred, with witnesses and official documents, to the Court of the Forty. Whether a man is to be admitted to the noble order is debated in a meeting of the Court of the Forty. And in order to prevent anyone from daring to attempt admittance without consequences, in like manner it has been established that anyone who wants to inform the magistrates of his nobility is first required to bring the magistrates five hundred gold ducats, which are deposited in the treasury if he loses the case. Thus we see the diligence of our ancestors in preventing this noble

---

19 As noted earlier, no more than 2 per cent of the population had the right to enter the Great Council. Frederic C. Lane (1973, 254) reports that in 1500 the number of nobles was about 2,500, but as a rule only about 1,400 participated; it is estimated that some forty members never attended (Finlay 1980, 21). Joanne M. Ferraro (2012, 177–8) reports that between 1550 and 1594 the number of male nobles shrank from 2,500 to 2,000; by 1631 there were only 1,666, around 1 to 1.5 per cent, and when the Republic fell in 1797, 1,000 nobles remained. This leads Ferraro to add, "neither restricted marriage nor biology had favoured the endogamous constitutional elite in their efforts to reproduce dynastic lines" (178).

20 "The common book" is the Libro D'Oro in which the names of the two hundred or so noble families of Venice were recorded. The compilation of the book was part of the first serrata [the closing] of the Great Council between 1297 and 1323. For a classic view, see Maranini [1927] 1974. Thanks in part to the research of Stanley Chojnacki (e.g., 2000), we now know that the Venetian constitution and the patriciate were not the exclusive creation of late medieval legislation and that both were recurrently renewed and redefined by new strategies of collective self-definition over the course of several centuries. This new understanding suggests resilience and continuity, but also flexibility and change. See also A. Ventura 1981.

congregation from being defiled. It is for this reason that the patrician citizens who have passed their twentieth year of age do not obtain the right to vote until they have presented themselves to the state attorneys and confirmed under oath with their father, or mother, or closest relative, that they have reached that age, and moreover, until they have confirmed with two witnesses that they are children of the noble man they claim to be their father, and that they are not illegitimate or born of a disreputable woman.

Now I have given a rough explanation of the process by which patrician [citizens] come to have a share in public life. I must note that our ancestors perceived that it would contribute to the attainment and preservation of friendship and harmony among patricians if they gathered together often. Therefore, by both law and custom, the Great Council meets almost every week, and sometimes even more frequently. The main task of this Council is to create all the magistrates. They include not only those who have jurisdiction in the city and enjoy offices in other possessions of the Republic, but the Senate and the Ten, the civilian governors [the *podestà*], the captains, the treasurers of castles and cities that have been joined in league with the Venetian Empire, the governors of fortresses, the captain-general of the fleet, the ambassadors, and the captains of galleys – in sum, everyone who exercises the authority of public power at home or abroad.[21] Likewise, all such laws as pertain to the constitution of the Republic are enacted by the authority of this Great Council, especially during an interregnum, that is, the period following the death of a doge when his successor has not yet been appointed. But I will talk about the interregnum hereafter.

IV.

Now we have to present the whole manner of creating magistrates. At about noon of most festive days, the Great Council gathers in a capacious room, which can be called the hall (or simply the assembly[22]). Here there are ten very long benches, which are naturally almost as long as the hall. All the patrician citizens go and sit in whatever order

---

21 There were about 800 posts elected by the Great Council, about 550 of which were within Venice and 280 on the mainland and in overseas possessions.

22 This is the name used by Lane (1973, 255). Lewkenor (1599, 22) renders it as "session house," no doubt drawing on the British experience. The hall of the Great Council measured about 180 feet long, 84 feet wide, and 47 feet high, with the benches set at right angles to the dais of the doge and Signoria at the head of the hall, to ease movement during voting and the like.

they have arrived, for no one has a fixed seat in the hall, apart from some presiding officers. The latter are the doge, the ducal councillors, and the three heads of the Council of the Forty, who sit on a raised dais and are the only ones with the right to address the Great Council. After these, roughly in the middle of the benches next to the walls of the hall and at a slight elevation, sit the state attorneys [*avogadori di común*], on assigned seats, together with the three heads of the Council of the Ten. Finally, at the farthest point from the platform of the doge are the benches of the old and new auditors, of whom we will speak later. All the other patricians (as I was saying) sit indiscriminately as they wish.

Then, at the appointed hour, the doors of the hall are shut fast, and the keys are brought to the doge's dais and laid at his feet. The grand chancellor,[23] an office that is not of the nobility but that is nonetheless of very great dignity, stands up and, from a raised place, announces in a loud voice the magistrates to oversee the voting for which the assemblies of that day are held. After announcing the magistrates, he immediately goes to the prince's dais, and summons the magistrates who will be leaders of the sessions (as we mentioned above) to come to the prince – or to the councillors, if the prince is absent. When this order is given, the magistrates come up at once and promise under oath that they will devote their efforts to ensuring that the voting laws of the sessions are respected, and that they will not elect a patrician citizen who has broken the law and will punish him with the rigour of the law. After this has been accomplished, everyone returns to his place, except for one state attorney and one of the heads of the Ten, who proceed together to the end of the hall farthest from the prince and take assigned seats. The other state attorneys position themselves on the right side of the hall, while the other two heads of the Ten sit to the left of the Avogaria magistrates. In a similar way, the old and new auditors sit on opposite sides, on the left and right, in the farthest area of the hall from the dais of the prince, so that with the magistrates seated in such a position, they may

---

23 As Contarini implies, the grand chancellor, whose office was instituted in 1268, was
    head of the non-patrician (*cittadini originari*) secretarial class. In John Julius Norwich's
    description, the grand chancellor "was the effective head, not only of the ducal chan-
    cery but of the entire civil service of the Republic ... [and] ranked above senators,
    yielding precedence only to the Doge and the Signoria and the procurators of
    St Mark. Except for the franchise, he enjoyed every prerogative of the nobility" (1989,
    185). For more scholarly description of the office and symbols of the grand chancel-
    lor, see Casini 1991; Lane 1973, 180–1; Muir 1981, 191, 288; Neff 1981.

seem to have been appointed guardians of the whole assembly so that not one patrician can act with impunity against the laws and decrees of the assembly.[24]

After the magistrates have been so positioned, three ballot boxes containing some golden and silver balls are set up beside the prince's dais. They are arranged in this way so that one ballot urn is in the middle of the dais, flanked by the other two. In both there are only thirty gold balls, but countless silver ones. Sixty balls are placed in the middle urn, of which thirty-six are golden and twenty-four are silver. The golden balls are inscribed with certain letters, upon which the nominators draw lots for them at each session in order to avoid any deception.

Once the vases [i.e., the urns] have been set up, [three of] the youngest councillors rise from their seats and go and sit on the edge of the dais next to the three ballot vases, in such a way that each councillor is next to a ballot box. The councillors draw lots and the patricians on whose bench the lot has fallen rise from each side of the hall. Ten rows of seats are arranged down the full length of the hall in which patricians, as we said earlier, sit as they please, and a single lot is used for two rows that correspond to each other on each side of the hall. Thus the members of the bench on whom the lot has fallen are loudly summoned by a herald, and stand up from each side of the hall in the randomly ordered sequence. Following the order in which they were seated, the patricians make their way to the urns, beside which the appointed councillors sit, next to the dais of the doge. Each of them puts his hand inside the urn and extracts a ball. If it is silver, he goes back to the seat he came from, though by a different route. But if he has extracted a golden one, he immediately hands it over to the councillors in charge of the ballot box for inspection. The latter dutifully examine its inscription. This style of marking has been devised in such a way that no one can bring a golden ball with him from home, and covertly put his hand into the vase and pretend to extract it, thereby fraudulently obtaining the place of an elector. Thus the one who has picked a golden ball – by chance, that is – at

---

24 The officials wore coloured robes according to their functions, in sharp contrast to ordinary patrician citizens, who wore plain black robes. Writing in 1611, Thomas Coryat (1905, vol. 1), an English traveller, was astonished to observe in Venice the ease with which patricians mingled with the common people, going so far as to shop for provisions in neighborhood markets and fairs, unaccompanied by servants. The painting of the Schiavoni Quay by Leandro Bassano on the cover of his book helps to convey what Coryat observed. For a comparative view of the style of life of the Venetian patricians and the Amsterdam elite, see Burke 1994, chap. 5.

once proceeds to the middle vase and extracts another ball from there. If this one is silver, he returns to the place he had left without the right to vote; but if it is golden, he goes up the dais, and sits in an assigned seat next to the prince. The second person who has drawn the same lot takes himself to the same place, and the third follows suit, and so on in the same manner until they are nine, making up the first order of electors. They position themselves in an order determined by age, but not by anything else. Here we must not fail to mention the practice according to which the names of those who have been made electors by chance are proclaimed in a resounding voice by the grand chancellor, so that everyone can hear. No possibility is left to any of his kinsmen or anyone closely related to him to seize the opportunity to become an elector. Moreover, access to the order of the electors is open to no more than two people from the same lineage, as our ancestors prescribed with utmost wisdom, so that this elective task may extend to diverse kindred and lineages, and the public office may be as open as possible among patrician citizens. If the lot falls to two people from the same family, that is enough to enable them to share in the exercise of public authority.

But let us return to the point where I diverted the discourse. As soon as this first order of patrician electors is completed, the nine of them leave the assembly and head to an appointed private room. Here they find a chancellor of the Republic, who reads them the instructions that must be observed, according to the law concerning nominations to office. At the same time, the decrees of the Senate and the other laws are read, stipulating that the electoral choices must not be driven by bribes or some bad scheme or fraud.

Afterwards, the nine electors position themselves on the basis of age, with the elders in the worthiest and most important place, for Venetians want no discrimination among patricians apart from that of age, which is never a cause of contention or hostility. This has been noted by the most important of philosophers – by Aristotle in *Politics*, and by Xenophon in that famous work of his, *The Institution of Cyrus, King of the Persians*. Once the electors have positioned themselves in this order, nine balls are put into an urn, with numbers written on them from one to nine. On a long piece of paper, the names of the magistracies are written in the order they are to be voted on. The eldest of the electors draws a ball from the urn. After he notes the number written on the ball, he has the right to nominate whichever patrician he wishes for the office marked on the paper with the number that has been extracted. So it is with the second eldest, the third, and everybody else in succession, so that each elector draws by the lot and is assigned to nominate a person for a particular magistracy, as determined by chance.

Afterwards, the one to whom the first office has been allotted nominates a patrician he wants. The work then proceeds with the selection by the nine electors. If the designated candidate obtains six or more votes among electors, then he is nominated for that office, and his name is written down next to the first office on the long piece of paper containing the names of all the magistracies on which the Great Council is to vote. If he obtains fewer than six votes, which happens very rarely, the same elector proposes somebody else. Then the same procedure is repeated, and so on successively, until someone is proposed who is approved by the vote of at least six electors. This procedure of election is observed for the second, the third, and all the others, until the electors have selected one patrician for every office.[25]

Meanwhile, while these matters are being carried out in a private chamber, the patricians in the hall do not interrupt the allotment that has begun there. Instead, they go to the ballot urns in the random order in which they sat down, drawing out the balls until nine have extracted golden ones from the urns. These make up the second order of electors, who, taking their age into account (as we said), also withdraw to an appointed chamber. Another secretary is there, who, in the same manner as the previous one, reads aloud the decrees of the Senate that must be respected. He then positions each patrician in his place and brings them a paper listing the same magistracies, in the same sequence as the first one, which (as we just described) had been presented to the private meeting of the first order of electors. In the same way, the electors are assigned their lot, according to each one's extraction, and one patrician is nominated by each of them for the magistracies on which the Great Council will vote. Following the familiar pattern, a third group of nine people, forming the third order, withdraws into another room, in which the procedure is repeated. Finally, a fourth group of nine patricians withdraws, and in this way the four groups of electors complete the roster of thirty-six patricians, which was, of course, the number of the golden balls that had been placed in the middle urn. Therefore, of the sixty patricians who had extracted the sixty little golden balls from the first urns, thirty-six become electors, distributed into four groups. As for the twenty-four patricians who extracted silver balls from the middle urn, they return to their seats, hopes frustrated.

---

25 For a discussion of the procedures in the election of office holders and the dynamics of enlisting supporters, gaining nominations, and winning elections, see Chambers and Pullan 2004, 58–9; Finlay 1980, chap. 4; and Maranini 1974.

I am aware that it is extremely difficult to explain these details in writing, since they are very remote from the practice of the ancient Romans. Still, I would rather run the risk of being charged with incompetence than carelessness. I will thus dutifully report every last detail, so that no diligent man could want more.

Let us return to the point where I diverted the discussion. By this stage, four patricians have been nominated to each office [magistracy] by the four groups of electors, one by each group – unless it happens that someone is elected by two or three orders of electors, which occasionally happens, but generally there are four competitors for each office. However, for some magistracies of small dignity and lower rank, only two competitors are elected. For only the first two groups of electors have the right to nominate and elect the competitors for those lesser offices, since the remaining two groups lack this right.

After the competitors have been nominated for all the magistracies in the way we explained earlier, the electors are immediately dismissed: they cannot vote for anyone on that day, nor attend the sessions of the Great Council. The grand chancellor, who (as I said) is not a noble officer but nonetheless has the highest reputation, declares from the dais the competitors for the first magistracy. One by one, he loudly reads out who has been nominated and by which order of electors, as well as the identity of the patrician's nominator and the sequence in which he was nominated.

At this point, I must not neglect to mention that which has been prescribed by law: that is, the patrician elector who is responsible for the nomination and election of a competitor is considered as his guarantor. Imagine it so happens that the nominated individual defeats the other competitors, thereby fulfilling his ambition and obtaining the office he seeks. But let us imagine further that while he is in that office, he takes away some public funds for himself, is convicted of embezzlement, and is not able to make restitution. In such a case, the patrician responsible for his nomination is called upon to compensate the treasury. Thus, after the grand chancellor announces the competitors for the first office, and immediately after the naming of it, if any competitors are present, they leave the assembly with their relatives and closest connections and go to an appointed room, where they wait for as long as that office is being voted on. Once this is completed, the grand chancellor urges everyone to comply with the divine and human law, and to vote for the candidate who seems the best and most worthy for the Republic.[26]

---

26 This exhortation accompanied every election, even if it was common knowledge that
    it was not always practised.

Then he names the first competitor, that is, the one chosen by the first order of electors, for whom they proceed to vote. At once some young men stand up, as many as necessary to take care of each order of seats in pairs.[27] In their hands they carry some urns, constructed with extraordinary craftsmanship. The exterior of the urn is green, the interior is white, and both are covered by a single lid. When a person puts his hand inside, he can place his ball in whichever urn he prefers, while no one else can tell which one the vote or pebble has been put in, even if he sits next to it and watches carefully. And voting is not carried out with balls but with ballots made of linen, so that there is no way to determine, from the sound they make when they fall into the urn, how the ballots are cast. For our ancestors believed that it would be of the greatest service to the Republic if judgments were made freely; so they went to great lengths to ensure that the votes were as secret as possible.

Therefore those young men, each with his contrivance of urns joined together, go to their respective rows of seats, and present the urns to the patricians in the order they are seated. Then every man shows his ballot, places his hand under the lid, and drops his ballot into the urn he wishes. If he wants to vote in favour of the nominee, he drops it into the interior portion, which is white; if he wants to vote against, he drops it into the external one, which is green. Each bench or row of seats votes together, following the procedure and method explained above. In a very short time, the whole assembly of patricians has voted. The urns are brought to where the doge sits, and here the collected votes are cast into two large vessels. The votes that have been collected in the green ballot boxes, which are votes against the competitor for that office, are put in a green vessel. To be counted, the ballots are brought to the row of councillors, in the midst of whom the prince is seated. The votes in the white vessel, which are in favour of the competitor, are counted by the councillors who sit on the right of the doge. Those that have been collected in

---

27 These young men were known as the *ballottini*. At one point they were literally young boys, but their work illustrates the challenge that Venice faced in finding methods that would protect the political process: "*Ballottini* were ... a problem in maintaining honest elections. Originally, men from the supreme court were entrusted with circulating the urns, but because they displayed an unjudicial partiality towards their friends, the task was given in 1467 to non-patrician youths of less than fifteen years of age. Apparently the innocence of youth did not long survive acquaintance in pursuit of office, for in 1492 secretaries, beginning long apprenticeships in the chancellery, were put in charge. Predictably, this too failed to eliminate abuses" (Finlay 1980, 202).

the green vase, which are the ones who are against, are examined by the councillors seated to the left of the prince. The public secretaries stand near the councillors and tally the votes.

While the votes for the first competitor are being examined, the patricians vote in the same manner for the second competitor, the one selected by the second group of electors. In the same way, the votes are then brought to the councillors to count them and the secretaries for writing down the results. Thus they proceed to the third competitor and finally to the fourth, if the competitors are that many. After the votes are counted, the patrician who obtains the highest number, provided that this is more than half, is proclaimed elected by the grand chancellor. When the voting is completed, the Great Council is dismissed. But if none of the competitors for that office has obtained more than half of all the votes, all these competitors are considered invalid and the election is postponed to another convocation. Once voting for the first office is completed, the names of those elected in the second office are proclaimed. Those competitors withdraw to a private chamber with their kinsmen and close relations. But those who have been excluded, that is, the kinsmen and close relations of the first competitors, are allowed to return to the hall. In exactly the same way as before, they vote for the competitors for the second office, and the votes are counted by the councillors. The patrician with the greatest number of votes is considered elected, provided that their votes add up to more than half of the total. The same procedure is observed for the third one, then for the fourth one, and afterwards for all the remaining sessions or assemblies. Once voting is completed, the names of the electors are read out in a loud voice by the grand chancellor and then the Great Council is dismissed.

The sessions of the Council may not be prolonged after sunset under any circumstances. If they are interrupted by sunset, the patricians who have already been elected are immediately proclaimed, but the remaining nominees are set aside. Having been excluded by time, they cannot avail themselves of the opportunity given to them by good fortune and by the classes of the electors. This custom was not established without an excellent reason. If the matter were prolonged into the night, it would not be easy for the presiding officers to keep such a great number of citizens on duty and to prevent them from committing any illicit acts under cover of darkness. Thus our ancestors, wise men who appear to have given thought to everything with prudence and diligence, established that it was not permitted to extend voting after sunset, or to bring any lamp into the hall in any way while the sessions were in progress.

V.

This is the whole procedure of holding sessions. I must not fail to mention that the offices are distributed among patricians in such a way that two members of the same family, or even two close relatives, cannot serve in the same office. And in like fashion, as we pointed out earlier, two kinsmen or close relatives cannot by chance be candidates in the same elections. This has been established for an excellent reason, that is, that the right of public power should be shared among several people and not restricted to a few who are related. For if the latter were to obtain power, they could easily plot something together and upset the Republic. It is inevitable that a good number of people, if deprived of honours, would feel hostile towards the Republic and concoct a rebellion. There is clearly not much hope for a Republic's longevity when many or a large part of its citizens do not approve it. And, moreover, there is nothing more proper for a Republic than the sharing of public power among a great many people. It is not fitting for a Republic to consist of citizens who, despite being largely equal among themselves, obtain honours on unequal terms.[28] For those who place public power in the hands of a few kindred can easily establish that form of government of the Few that the Greeks call *oligarkhía*. Therefore, in the Republic of Venice, the magistracies are distributed among patrician citizens in such a way that all families and lineages participate in the honours and duties of the Republic. At the same time, the system is set up such that not just anybody governs and carries out public responsibilities, but rather only those who excel in honesty and prudence.

This first institution has some of the quality of a popular government; the second, that of the government of the nobles. It therefore is clear that all the principal forms of government are mixed together in this single Republic. Indeed, although the Great Council has some appearance of a popular authority, nevertheless one can see that it is a form of popular and patrician government. For it is a popular thing to elect the magistrates by lot. Indeed, in such a political system, the just and the right are measured only by arithmetical calculations, considering (they say) that since every member of the patriciate is a single, free individual, and since equal things are due to equal individuals, every member of

---

28 Finlay recalls that "equality in the Great Council was regarded as the guarantor of liberty in Venice" and notes the observation of a patrician merchant and diarist, Girolamo Priuli, who observed that "in the Great Council patricians fought with the ballots and not with blood" (1980, 74, 61).

the patriciate should benefit from the Republic in equal right and equal profit. And Venetians believe that there is no reason why one patrician should attain magistracies less than another. And since not every man can govern at the same time, but only in turns, they think that the matter should be entrusted to fate, and that those so favoured should govern.

The opposite happens in a government of the Few, which is different from a polity of patricians. In such a system, they think that since unequal things are due to unequal people, and the rich are superior to the other citizens because of their family wealth, the highest honours are also due to them. And in both of these views they are mistaken, and greatly deviate from the right path of reason, although still relying on an appearance of it. They are right in stating that equal things are due to equal people, and that unequal things are due to unequal people. But they are patently wrong in their judgments – that is, in measuring equality only on the basis of number, and in measuring inequality only on the basis of wealth. For those who are equal in number are in part equal but not completely so; and those who are unequal in wealth should not be considered completely unequal. Since civil society has been constituted for citizens to live well, virtue is the only appropriate basis for discrimination. Those who excel in virtue should, in the same way as the unequal and more superior, obtain the highest honours in a state. And equal honours should be given to people who are equal in virtue and civil zeal. This is the method, this is the norm of the patricians.

Thus, as it befits a popular government to resort to chance in the constitution of electors, so it befits a government of the patricians to consider as more appropriate the individual who is judged worthier in virtue by the judgment of the Great Council, and to reject those who have been considered less meritorious. From this I think it can be easily understood that in this procedure of nominating and voting, we find a form of patrician government mixed with the appearance of a popular government – and yet with such a balance that the component befitting a government of patricians plays a more decisive role than that befitting a popular system. For chance plays a decisive role only in the constitution of the electors, and the worthless men of the state participate in its power and thus have equal right with the noble citizens. But nothing is left to chance in the conferring of honours, and everything depends on choice and judgment.

At this point, I cannot omit the mandate by which, in those votes for offices requiring men who are endowed with extreme valour and zeal, the Senate creates a fifth nominee to join the four nominees that I talked about above. For at the same time that those orders are nominating the competitors they wish in the private chambers that are designated for that task, if the sessions are held for any of the magistracies that I mentioned above, the Senate assembles in a smaller hall. There, each senator may nominate the patrician he wishes for one of those specific offices, and they then proceed to the election. The one who has obtained the most votes is proclaimed elected by the scrutiny of the Senate, and becomes the fifth competitor in the Great Council. Therefore it is quite plain that in our Republic aristocratic government has a greater role than popular government.

At this point, however, I have explained the voting system in sufficient detail. Let us now proceed to that constituent part of the Republic that, having a sort of monarchic appearance, is in full accord with the popular component, not unlike a well-tuned diapason, where the low note corresponds to a high one according to a certain interval, and eventually coalesces, with the mediation of other magistracies, into the single choir of our excellent Republic.[29]

---

29 Stephen D. Bowd (1998, xviii) recalls that Contarini used corporal and musical metaphors, among others, to suggest the harmony in the body politics.

BOOK 2

The Doge

There is no one who does not know that the doge in Venice displays the outward features of a king and assumes the very image of a monarch. So far, we have described diligently (however inadequately, considering the dignity of our topic and our insufficiency to the task) the Great Council, which represents the form of a popular estate. Now we will explain why our wise and virtuous ancestors wanted a prince at the helm of the Republic. We will then expound on the origin and nature of this princely institution.

I repeat what is well known: that is, a city is a kind of civil society, sufficient unto itself for those things necessary for pursuing a good and happy life. Obviously, society is either linked together to form a certain unity – and who could doubt this? – or else it is bound to come apart and disintegrate. It has happened that cities of considerable grandeur and wealth have collapsed in a short time because of discord and civil strife, and have been utterly destroyed. Unity can only be properly contained in an individual, who presides over the multitude of citizens and all the magistrates (entrusted with certain functions), and who gathers that scattered and disjointed multitude together into one body. This was noticed by the great philosophers and researchers of nature, and is true in both the structure of the universe and the microcosm or little world, that is, the living being.[1] They observed that in this world, diverse motions, as bestowed by each one's nature, are contained by a single divine and eternal motion; that all causes are contained by one cause, first

---

1 Karl Appuhn (2009, 71–4 and chap. 6) recalls that the idea of nature constituting an appropriate model for human beings and human activity goes back to Socratic philosophers and was given new currency in the thirteen century by Saint Thomas Aquinas. By the fifteenth century the idea of *imitatio naturae* had become widely accepted by humanists throughout Italy. Contarini makes an effective use of the concept to justify excluding the common people from constitutional and governmental rule in the Republic.

among all; and, lastly, that in a single living creature there are many very different members, whose functions are various and diverse, but that are all enclosed and held together by one soul and one member, the heart. In almost the same way, it is impossible to hold together multitudes of citizens for long, unless they recognize the authority of some individual, upon whom depends the common good of all and the preservation of civil unity, and to whom the actions of each citizen, both private and public, refer for their ultimate and primary aim. Otherwise, the polity will fall to pieces, breaking into its different parts. Although no one in particular may be blamed or accused for this outcome, such a collapse is not surprising, when each one tends to care only about his own individual interest, and the common good is entrusted to no one in particular.

Consider, for instance, the officers responsible for the provision of grain.[2] They devote their energies to importing an abundance of grain into the city from all areas. In doing so, however, they may bring down the market price of wheat, and the result of these two things together is detrimental to public revenues. In a similar way, the officers of the fleet, our most beautiful possession, will endeavour mightily to build as many galleys as possible, to equip them with first-rate war-like and nautical instruments, and to spend public monies collected for this use. But because of this assiduousness, the city's public revenue may not be enough for repairing towers and castles, and for paying salaries for the garrisons. The Republic is thus bound to fall to pieces and its structures disintegrate: not through the wrongdoing of its citizens, but rather because of their dedication as everyone strives to discharge his own particular responsibilities in the most overzealous way possible.

From such unfortunate circumstances, it follows that it is important to entrust the care of the common good into the hands of one particular individual – someone who does not have one specific responsibility, but who is to govern and oversee the function of everyone, steering them towards the common good and the cohesion of the Republic. I do not think that it is beneficial for a city to assign this task to several people. For, as Aristotle says,[3] what is common to the greatest number gets the least care, and if something is done wrongly, it is not possible to hold one person accountable before the others – especially considering the

---

2 As part of the Council of Ten at a later time, Contarini had a direct hand in the selection of magistrates in charge of grain supplies (Gleason 1993, 66–8). For an in-depth analysis of the complex arrangements for the supply of grain and the prevention of famine in Venice over centuries, see esp. Pullan 1963–4 and Faugeron 2014. See also book 4:83–4, notes 15 and 16 on the same pages.

3 *Politics*, book 2, chap. 3, p. 44.

competition and rivalries that usually arise among peers. Now, if a person is charged with this task and holds the office on a temporary basis – for a year or a semester, but not as long as he lives – he will probably do well as long as the Republic also does well during his time in office, without much concern for how events will evolve afterwards. For this reason things generally end badly, which can be easily demonstrated by examples taken from the many republics that have this type of government in our times.

It was therefore with the utmost wisdom that our city endowed the constitution of the Republic with a form of royal governance, tempered by the laws in such a way that, after removing all kinds of impediments and dangers that could threaten the Republic,[4] and having adopted the benefit and advantage that a royal government usually brings, it seemed that nothing was left lacking. We now have a most free Republic with a monarch presiding who bears the title of doge. As long as he lives, he presides over the Republic and takes special care of the common good, which is the chief thing that holds cities together (as I think we have demonstrated with good reasoning). He does not have any specific function, and yet there is nothing in which he must not take part. He is to ensure that every patrician citizen and all magistrates discharge their duties, and he is to direct them in such a way that they all – as it were – play together in some sort of harmony for the common good. In this way, no function is detrimental to the commonweal and exerted more than necessary out of excessive zeal, or overlooked because of negligence.

The task of the prince is to be, so to speak, the lookout post of the Republic: to keep watch over all activities, and especially over those entrusted with public authority. And if he notices anyone neglecting his

---

4 For Frederic C. Lane (1973, 267), Contarini's claim that the doges gave Venice the advantages of a monarch without its disadvantages "was a bit of nostalgic wishful thinking." While it is true that the doges lacked executive powers, Lane notes that they could, and at times did, function as political leaders using persuasion, not command. There is a growing literature in support of Lane: see, e.g., the diaries of Marin Sanudo in Labalme and White 2008, chap. 2; Bouwsma 1968, 62–4; Muir 1981, chap. 7; and Romano's (2007) in-depth portrait of the life of Doge Francesco Foscari (1373–1457). Charles I in England, then, revealed that he did not quite know about the doge's influence and power when he apparently noted, in a conversation with James Harrington, that the king must be something more than a doge (cited in Pocock 1992, iii). Muir's characterization of the doge as a paradoxical prince is more to the point (1981, chap. 7; see also Cozzi 1970 and King 2014, 140–50). Jack Rakove's (2002, 32) research on the creation of the presidency in post-revolutionary America suggests that the task of establishing a national executive on republican principles posed "the single most perplexing program of institutional design" faced by the framers. That task continues to raise constitutional challenges in the twenty-first century.

duty, he must summon him to the presence of the full College[5] and reprimand him verbally. If the matter requires it, he must also convene the state attorneys or the chiefs of the Council of the Ten, and order that the misdeed be assessed and the culprit punished appropriately according to the judgment of the Collegio. In addition, the doge himself, if he so wishes, may assume the authority of a state attorney of *Avogaria di común* or of a chief of the Ten, and address the ducal council [the Signoria] about a particular person's crime and the punishment that should be inflicted. We will explain how this usually happens below, when we deal with the judgments of crimes. For the doge has the power to join any of the courts as a colleague of the responsible magistrate, and to have a right equal to that of the other chiefs, so that he can advise everyone, particularly for this reason.

Yet this power is restricted by the laws in such a way that he can do nothing on his own.[6] When he sits with the other magistrates, he does not wield more power than any single one of them in a given office. Moreover, the authority of magistrates is so restricted that no one, however eminent, can decide anything significant, except by decision of the ducal council. (We will speak more about this matter in due course.) In addition, in any council, the prince only has the right to one vote, like everybody else. Likewise, the prince abides by the same rights and restrictions as everyone in the Great Council, such that he cannot vote for a candidate who is a kinsman or a relative. From what I said, it is clear that the doge of Venice has been deprived of every capacity to abuse his position and act as a tyrant. And thanks to a most ancient and long-standing practice, going back to the earliest origins of the city up to these times, this state of affairs has been established on such a solid basis that Venice has little fear of the doge conspiring against the freedom of the Republic.

On the other hand, since anyone would refuse enormous toil and great mental anxiety unless they received some kind of reward, the prince is compensated with the bestowal of exterior princely honour, and princely appearance. His attire is regal, for he always dresses in purple or golden

---

5   To anticipate what will become clearer later, the College was the Collegio, involving members of the Signoria and the *sapientes* or *savi*. The Signoria consisted of the doge, the ducal council made up of six members (one from each district or *sestiere*, and elected each for an eight-month term), and the three heads of the Council of the Forty (three courts of the forty judges). The *savi* consisted of sixteen members elected for a six-month term. See the glossary of terms, Appendix B.

6   The challenge of creating and applying restrictions on the authority of the doge is ably conveyed by Romano (2007) in his portrait of Doge Francesco Foscari during the tumultuous years from 1423 to 1457. See also the sources in note 4.

cloth. His head is covered with a linen veil as a royal diadem, and he wears a purple cap on top, adorned with a golden band. The part of this that covers the back of the head rises in the shape of a horn. The prince has a seat on a dais, and this dais is of a royal sort. All citizens, both private individuals and those who function as magistrates, address the doge bareheaded and standing up, while he is seated – a special sign of honour in this age.[7] He does not rise up for any person. All public documents are issued and sealed under his name. All ambassadors, *podestà*,[8] magistrates, captains, and whoever else who writes to the Senate address their letters to the doge. The proclamation of edicts, laws, and decrees of the Senate: all are done under his name. All coins, both gold and silver, are minted with the name and image of the prince.

Finally, to put it briefly, everywhere you can see the signs of a king, but never of his power. Nobody of sound mind would dare deny that in the Republic of Venice this has been established with exceeding wisdom, in the same manner as everything else. For the duty of the prince, burdensome in other respects, is compensated with the reward of honour, which is the only prize of virtue, as is commonly said and the great philosophers have shown. Among these, Aristotle said in his *Nicomachean Ethics*[9] that since those who manage an office with rectitude and integrity are not concerned with their own advantage, but with that of others, there is no way to grant them their just reward, other than by having them surpass all others in honour. Moreover, and most importantly, the dignity of this prince causes the other citizens to greatly fear being reprimanded by him, and hence carry out their duties with greater zeal.

I.

Six councillors are joined to the doge, from the six districts the city is divided into, with each district choosing one councillor.[10] They hold office for eight months, always accompanying the doge and attending audiences with him. No document is sent forth without the consent and signature of four councillors, yet this does not apply to letters distributed to the public. The documents they sign are the only original documents, written by the secretaries and kept by them after the copies are circulated.

---

7 The doge was supposed to doff his *corno ducale* only to the pope, emperor, or king.
8 A Venetian governor also known as a rector.
9 See especially book 4, 1123b15, where Aristotle discusses honour.
10 The districts or *sestieri* were originally organized in 1171 in order to coordinate tax collection for military action against the Byzantine empire. Each district was further subdivided into administrative divisions; see map 4.

On this point, one cannot fail to mention that the documents, given out not by decree of the Great Council but by order of the doge and his councillors, generally deal with matters of small importance and so carry very little authority. It is useful to recall that legal authority and power is attributed only to an individual council, and that no single magistrate can wield a large amount of power by himself. But we will talk about the councillors below. For now, let us return to our discussion of the doge.

As it is generally the case that private means are not enough to preserve the dignity and the honour of the position, the treasury grants the doge 3,500 gold ducats each year.[11] In order to prevent an avaricious person from converting that money into family property, thereby neglecting public dignity and utility, some duties are assigned to the doge that he must fund at his own expense, thereby looking after his own dignity and the advantage of the Republic. And if he neglects these in order to save money, a heavy fine is imposed on his heirs. This way, if he tries to increase family wealth to benefit his heirs, the doge actually inflicts great damage on them. Besides this, the true inheritance he would pass on to his posterity would be ignominy and disgrace. The doge maintains many servants who do not carry arms, and he always wears purple garments. He lives in a house magnificently adorned with tapestries. He has an abundance of objects made of silver, and other such princely things. Every year he organizes four banquets, lavishly and sumptuously prepared for sixty or more patricians. This was an ancient custom of the Spartans and Cretans, whose republics were illustrious, which our ancestors adopted in a less ostentatious form. Indeed, since the frequent gathering of citizens contributed significantly to securing their reciprocal goodwill, both the Spartans and the Cretans set up a number of public feasts at the expense of their treasuries, where citizens would convene. There, everyone could easily be introduced to everybody else, a common practice that bound them one to another in a close relationship. But since this involved gathering people as if into a single body, it was inevitable for disorder and commotion to break out during those feasts. And since each of those who had the responsibility for the feasts wanted to treat the citizens lavishly for his own advantage, public finances suffered great damage. So when this custom was introduced in Venice, the whole matter was entrusted to the doge with certain amendment and moderation.

Four times a year, patricians are invited by the prince to a luxurious banquet, yet the event does not arouse envy. They do not all come

---

11 This was a relatively large sum of money. For a comparative scale of annual wages and salaries *circa* early sixteenth century, see Labalme and White 2008, 541–3.

together as a single mass, but only those whom the prince has invited, in addition to the ducal councillors, state attorneys, the heads of the Forty, and the heads of the Ten, who always attend. All other patricians come by formal invitation. The four banquets are organized in such a fashion that the more senior and distinguished patricians are invited in winter on the day consecrated to Saint Stephen the Protomartyr.[12] Early in the morning they gather in the ducal palace, where the prince lives, and they accompany him in solemn procession to the Basilica of Saint Mark, where they attend mass. Once this is over, they go with the prince back to his palace, where they feast together. In the month of April, on the feast of Saint Mark the Evangelist[13] – whose sanctity the Venetians especially revere, and whom they adopted as their patron after the relics of his body were translated to Venice[14] from Alexandria, a famous city in Egypt – patricians of lesser years and status are invited by the doge, and, following the same procedure and hearing mass, they partake of the customary banquet.

On the feast of the Ascension,[15] a market day in Venice, the prince invites patricians who have reached manhood. In the same manner as noted earlier, they accompany the doge from his ducal palace early in the morning, and together they board a boat that has been constructed in a most sumptuous fashion, which the Venetians call the *Bucintoro*.[16] After they have come out of the lagoon and the open sea can first be seen, the prince, according to a privilege of some early popes who conferred the honour on this Republic as a reward for its great number of valorous and illustrious deeds against Christianity's common enemies, throws a ring into the sea and declares, in almost these very words, that with that ring he marries the sea "in a sign of true and perpetual dominion."[17] These words are followed by a ceremony conducted by the Patriarch

---

12 The day after Christmas.

13 April 25.

14 The year 828, according to tradition.

15 The feast of the Ascension marks the day when Jesus Christ ascended into heaven, and is celebrated forty days after Easter, the day of the resurrection from the dead.

16 The *Bucintoro* was the doge's private barge. The peculiar name is thought to be based on an archaic word for boat, *bucio*, and the word for gold, *d'oro*. The first such boat was constructed in 1277; the last one built in 1728 was destroyed by Napoleon's soldiers, who chopped it to pieces in order to salvage the gold leaf. For a colourful description, see Wills 2001, 50, 56, and chap. 7.

17 The origins of this ceremony are uncertain, but it attained its final form sometimes during the late twelfth century. It continued until the end of the Republic itself. For various descriptions of this marriage, see, e.g., Ferraro 2012, 31; Muir 1981, 119–34; Norwich 1989, 55, 116.

of Venice.[18] After this ends, they sail to the church dedicated to Saint Nicholas,[19] an ancient church built on the shore that divides the sea from the lagoon. There Holy Mass is celebrated, and once this has duly concluded, they board the boat again, return to Venice, and accompany the prince back to the palace to feast together.

The fourth banquet pertains to the young patricians who, on June 15, a day dedicated to the martyrs Vitus and Modest, go in solemn procession with the doge to the shrine of these saints, which is located beyond the Grand Canal that divides the city in half and is spanned by a bridge built on boats to save time and prevent an almost infinite detour. They visit the shrine, attend mass, and finally accompany the prince back to the ducal palace where a lavish feast is offered. Dancers, mimes, and excellent singers are often invited to entertain guests. Sometimes plays are intermixed with the other entertainments, which capture the rapt attention of the audience. This ancient custom is still observed in the Republic of Venice in a similar fashion, albeit with moderation. By this means, patricians of almost every order – though always equal with equal – take part in the banquet and share in the dignity of the doge. And it seems that this has been sagely established to render the patricians most favourably disposed towards each other.

On the other hand, since the noble citizens cannot be honoured with a banquet every year, and to prevent anyone being left out or forgotten, it has been ordained, according to an old law and custom, that during the winter five sea ducks[20] are to be sent to every citizen who has the right to vote in the Great Council. This is also a great way for the doge to win

---

18 The patriarch is the ordinary bishop of the archdiocese of Venice. Originally he was the patriarch of Grado, before the patriarchate was relocated in Venice. The patriarchate of Venice is one of three such bishoprics in the Catholic Church of the Latin rite. The Basilica of San Marco remained the private chapel of the doge.

19 The reference here is to the church of St Nicolo' di Lido, built to house the body of St Nicholas of Myra (the basis for the figure of St Nicholas), translated to Venice around 1110. There is a church in Bari dating to about the same time. Saint Nicholas was the patron saint of all those who went to sea; hence the importance attached. For more information see Lane 1973, 13–15; Muir 1981, 97–101; Norwich 1989, 78–81.

20 Maria Stella Florio (2009, 177) wonders why Contarini should write about the doge's gift of the five sea ducks "when already in 1514 the gift had been replaced by cash, silver coins called *oselle* for distribution on St Barbara's day (December 4)." Florio further notes that Contarini should have known – as Giannotti did – that the replacement had been established by law in 1521 and that all the details had been implemented by 1523. This leads Florio to speculate that Contarini might have started working on the book at an earlier date than that thus far noted and that he did not have an opportunity to revise the manuscript later (178). Muir (1981, 254–5) notes also that the change from animal to money gift was part of a general updating of the doge's image.

the love and goodwill of the noble citizens. These expenses consume a great part of the annual funds that the treasury disburses to the doge. Therefore, even if greed might tempt him, the doge cannot stain with dishonour the dignity and nobleness of his office.

We have clarified the power and authority of the prince. At this point, it is worth relating the origins of that institution and the procedures followed for his election.

II.

Since the earliest origins of the city, the most noble citizens of the province of Venetum convened at this lagoon on the Adriatic Sea, where later the city of Venice was founded. They made their dwellings in areas close to the place they had left, Aquileia, Altinum, Concordia, Oderzo, Padua, and many other great and rich cities destroyed by the violence of the Huns, who wrought enormous disaster in Italy under Attila's leadership. About twenty-two settlements were founded, partly on that stretch of land that encloses the interior lagoon, partly on some higher grounds emerging from the lagoon. In the beginning, those settlements were not sufficiently fortified and none had a sufficient number of ships of its own to be able to resist pirates and brigands. Since their towns shared the same fate in not being sufficiently protected, in time they realized the advantage of joint action in countering the incursions of pirates, making common provisions for sharing supplies of wheat, wine, and all crops necessary for sustenance, and, above all, for the security of their own homes. Since each town had initially chosen one person among its citizens to take charge and be its leader – whom they called the tribune – it was collectively decided that on fixed days those tribunes would assemble and make decisions regarding the common interest of all. Later, the practice taught them that since this function did not fall to any one person, and since many difficulties ensued from this fact, it would be very advantageous if the responsibility for the common welfare were entrusted to a single individual whom others would recognize as their prince.

It was therefore decided by the consensus of all the settlements to elect one doge or prince. In the beginning, his seat was established in the settlement called Heraclea, located in the innermost part of the lagoon on an island next to the mouth of the river Piave, which in our times has been joined to the mainland by the river sediment. But later that place no longer seemed appropriate, since it was in a remote region of the lagoon into which pirates would often gain access, and before the news of this calamity would reach others, pirates would descend upon the inhabitants of the settlements unaware, or destroy their goods. They thus established that it would be better if the prince left Heraclea and moved to Malamocco, a settlement located in the middle of the stretch of land, where it was easy for the doge to learn beforehand of impending attacks planned by pirates, and to respond, with little effort, wherever it was necessary. Finally, at the time when Pepin[21] was threatening death and enslavement to those incipient and – as it were – constituent elements of Venice, everyone withdrew to Rialto from all the settlements, and the seat of the prince was also transferred to that place. With the gathering of the inhabitants of the settlements, Venice grew to the size we see today.[22] Since those origins of the city, with constant continuity, one doge has been head of the Republic of Venice. The first princes had considerably more power. But with the benefit of experience, the power of the prince was gradually abridged through customs and laws, and to this we now turn.

III.

In the beginning, the procedure for electing a doge upon the death of the preceding one was simple. As men of integrity who were free from ambition, our ancestors recoiled from accepting such a demanding charge. Rather, they proceeded by general acclamation. The one reputed to be the most honest and wisest was proclaimed the prince. With time, as the city and its population grew, it was deemed unsuitable for the Republic to entrust such a great matter to the recklessness and fleeting favour of the people. Then, it came about that eleven men of the highest repute were elected to choose a doge. As individual ambition also grew, to some extent, in proportion to the growth of the city, they established new and unusual parliaments and devised a complex procedure for electing the prince. We will briefly explain this, so that nothing is missing in the work we have begun.[23]

Following the death of a prince – after the funeral rites are devoutly and honourably solemnized – the ducal councillors, who in the interregnum

---

21 As noted in book 1, note 6, Pepin's unsuccessful attack occurred in 810.

22 Of about 125,000.

23 As Dennis Romano notes, "the procedure for electing the doge was not a perverse joke or a mere flight of fancy: it was carefully designed to reduce the danger of factional interference in elections by incorporating a generous element of chance. The several rounds of lottery made it difficult for anyone to guarantee that he or even his allies would have a place in the nominating committees. Chance served to underscore the essential equality of all members of the Great Council" (2007, 37).

period after the death of the prince retire to the ducal palace assigned as his dwelling place, summon the Great Council. In this first gathering after the prince's death, five patrician citizens are elected, according to the council's procedure described earlier, and these citizens must scrupulously examine the actions of the dead prince and annul, by decree of the Great Council, anything that he has done contrary to law and customs. If he received bribes from anyone and refrained from making the prescribed expenditures, the five must report it, and the heirs, as commanded by law, are fined by the Great Council. This fine is pecuniary in nature and the amount of money is confiscated from the inheritance of the prince and deposited in the treasury.[24]

In the same Great Council sessions, five other patrician citizens are elected. They withdraw into a private chamber adjacent to the hall and do not leave until they decide what seems appropriate to remove from, or add to, the power of the prince. Once they settle the issue, the Council gathers again, after which the five come out of the private chamber – for only now are they allowed. Each reports his opinion about the responsibilities and duties of the doge. The discussion is open to all patricians, who decide by ballot the best course of action for the Republic. Once the power of the doge has been determined, that decision is included among the laws that the new prince must observe. On the following day the patricians proceed to those intricate sessions by which princes are usually created.

All patricians who have passed their thirtieth year of age convene in the Great Council. By an ancient custom of the Republic, those who are younger are not admitted to these proceedings. Then all the patricians are counted, and as many balls as the citizens who are present are thrown into an urn. Of these, thirty are golden, and all the others silver. This urn is placed on the dais of the hall, where the councillors sit. A young boy stands beside that urn to extract the balls. Patricians are summoned, one row of seats at a time, and they all proceed towards that urn in the order in which they are seated. No one places his hand into the urn, as normally happens in the other assemblies; the boy extracts one ball for each. Those who have been allotted a silver ball leave the assembly at once. The grand chancellor in a loud voice announces the one whom chance has favoured with a golden ball. At once, the chosen one leaves

---

24 The idea behind this was that public officials should not profit monetarily as a result of their office, while serving the common good, something that does not happen in today's world, when political offices tend to become sources of economic wealth and inequalities.

for an appointed private chamber, while members of his family and close
relatives stand up from their seats and withdraw to a part of the hall.
There they are counted, and as many silver balls as there are family and
close relatives are removed from the urn as they leave the hall. In this
way thirty people to whom golden balls have been allotted by chance
are selected from the whole assembly of patrician citizens. Once this has
been done, the Great Council is dismissed.

After everyone has left, the thirty people return from the private
chamber and again draw lots in the presence of the councillors, to select
nine electors favoured by chance. The selected electors then retire to
a private chamber where they close themselves in and allow no one to
be admitted, not even a servant. Nobody is allowed to talk to them and
they cannot leave that place before they elect forty men. No one may be
considered elected by them if he has not obtained six out of nine votes;
no one can be elected with four voting against him. As soon as the nine
have elected forty men, they inform the councillors, through the guardian or porter who acts as an intermediary, that they have carried out
their task. Unless it is late in the day, the councillors summon the Great
Council. Once all the patricians have reconvened, the official document
containing the names of the electors is produced. The grand chancellor
steps onto the dais and loudly announces the forty appointed patricians.
When they hear their names, each of them stands up from where he was
sitting, approaches the dais of the councillors, and then withdraws to an
appointed private chamber. But if any of the selected patricians is absent,
he is immediately sought throughout the whole city by a councillor or
one of the heads of the Forty. When the nominee is found, he is led by
the same magistrate to the hall and then to the private chamber to join
his colleagues. During these elections in particular, to prevent lobbying
(for our ancestors considered elections to be inviolable), he is forbidden
to approach or speak to anyone. With the forty designated citizens gathered together, the Great Council is dismissed.

Then these forty people come out of the private chamber and approach the councillors in the assembly hall. Following the same procedure of drawing lots that we have explained, twelve are selected and
the remaining twenty-eight are excluded from further proceedings.
These twelve, in turn, elect twenty-five men, each of whom needs to
obtain eight votes, for no one can be elected with fewer votes than
that. Once this is completed, they inform the councillors by way of the
intermediary. If enough time remains they convene the Great Council,
and, in the same manner as before, those twenty-five men are summoned without forewarning. By the same method of drawing lots, nine

men are selected, and the other sixteen leave. These nine men nominate forty-five men, requiring six votes each, who in the same manner, once the Great Council is assembled, are announced by the grand chancellor and brought together in a private chamber. These forty-five patricians are reduced, using the same random procedure, to eleven, who then elect forty-one patricians, all from among the most senior senators. As soon as these forty-one are announced, they withdraw to an appointed hall, where they are charged with electing the doge. The laws do not admit two members of the same family or close relations into this class of electors, a constant practice among the Venetians for all of their offices.

Our ancestors, wise and virtuous men, wanted such a cumbersome and complicated process to ensure that the multitude would not be completely deprived of the power to elect the doge. For the electors of the first stage are chosen by chance, which renders equal all patricians. Next, they combine chance with election, yet in such a way that election prevails over chance. Indeed, chance cannot favour anyone who has not been approved by the judgment of the first stage. In the next stage, chance is abandoned, for it is established that the choice of those electing the doge should not be left entirely to the arbitrariness of chance. Thus neither is the multitude completely deprived of choice, nor is this responsibility granted to the uninformed populace, in which favouritism, rather than the judgment of wise and virtuous men, prevails. Moreover, since there are no fixed electors of the prince, and the entire matter depends on the judgment of those who have been favoured by chance, no space is left for ambition. For it can easily come to pass that the patricians who have been excellently canvassed[25] will not obtain any power.

Now to return to the main topic.

---

25 A not-so-veiled reference to *broglio,* the Venetian term used to describe lobbying, electioneering and, generally, intrigue and the selling of votes. As can be expected, and was noted in the Introduction, Contarini does not directly address this issue. "The *broglio* presented politics as it was: the jostling for position, the pursuit of ambition, the dispensation of favours, the petitioning for largesse" (Finlay 1980, 27; see also Muir 1981, 37). Descriptions of *broglio* can be found in, among others, Labalme and White 2008; Chambers and Pullan 1992; and Raines 1991. Much of the literature on the so-called myth and anti-myth of Venice has drawn attention to this phenomenon. For *broglio* as part of a broader intellectual history of political practices and the changing meaning of corruption, see Buchan and Hill 2014, 84–7, and North, Wallis, and Weingast 2013, xi–xiii.

IV.

Once the forty-one electors of the prince have been nominated, they convene in the hall in which the Senate usually gathers, without saluting or speaking to any man. There, first of all, Holy Mass is religiously and piously celebrated, and the electors all lay their hands upon the altars and promise by oath to God the Almighty and the Republic that they will elect the doge they deem to surpass the others in integrity, love of country, zeal, and wisdom. Once the priests have gone away, the electors close themselves into the chamber and do not send for any attendants or other servants. Then three of the eldest among them sit as leaders next to a table arranged for this task, on which an urn has been set up. Each elector writes down on a piece of paper the name of the man whom he nominates as doge and places the written paper into the urn. Once all the pieces of paper have been placed inside, one of them is extracted – the first paper that came by chance into the hand of the person extracting it. The nomination is read by the chiefs, and the person whose name is drawn – if he is present, as normally happens – leaves the hall at once. Then, if anyone thinks that this patrician is not apt to bear the weight of such a great position, or that for some other reason it will not be useful for the Republic to have him as doge, he stands up and, after a modest introduction, he freely expresses his opinion about that citizen and expounds on the reason why he thinks that making him doge would be against the interest of the country. Once he brings his speech to a close, the chiefs call in the nominated person and the most senior of them summarizes the charge that is laid against him, though without naming the accuser. For all of the electors have themselves been previously bound by oath to perpetual silence. The nominee then responds to the charges as he wishes. Then he leaves the hall again, and if the first man or anyone else still wishes to contest or accuse him with new arguments, he is given the opportunity to do so. The nominee is then called back again and responds to the accusations; the procedure is repeated in the same fashion until the accusers have said all they have to say.

Finally, they proceed to the vote. Before our time, if the nominated person had obtained twenty-five votes, there was no further reckoning of the competitors, and he was proclaimed doge at once. But in our time, during the sessions in which Andrea Gritti,[26] a most distinguished senator, was made doge, the procedure was changed. For although it is still

---

26 Andrea Gritti served as doge between 1523 and 1538. Before becoming doge at the age of sixty-eight, Gritti had been a grain merchant and, possibly, a spy in Constantinople and had led a colourful life there. He was fluent in, among other languages,

the case that no one can be elected prince without obtaining twenty-five votes, nonetheless the procedure does not stop with the first who has obtained that number of votes, as was the case before. Instead, the electors proceed to the others, so that if anyone has exceeded that number of votes, he is proclaimed doge, and not the one who was initially elected with the minimum number of votes.

Once they have voted for the one whose name came out first, another nomination is extracted from the urn, and everything proceeds as before, and so for the third, the fourth, and subsequently all the others. If no one reaches the required number of votes, then, if the day is not too far spent, the sessions repeat with the same procedure. The electors are not allowed to leave, or to meet or talk to anyone coming from elsewhere, before twenty-five of them have agreed on the election of a prince.

Once he has been nominated, the councillors are immediately summoned to the Senate chamber where they salute and pay homage to the new doge. After this, the news spreads through the city, creating excitement everywhere. All citizens rejoice and humbly pray to God the Greatest and Almighty that this will bring happiness and good fortune to the Republic. The members of the family and the relatives of the doge rush to the hall to congratulate him. Coins are minted featuring the name of the prince and his profile is imprinted on them. Everything necessary for the celebration is prepared. Meanwhile, the doge and the electors are robed in the same place. Once everything is ready, they depart from

---

Greek, Latin, and Turkish. According to Frederic Lane (1973, 270), he was more influential than any other man in reanimating the fighting spirit of the Venetians after the Agnadello defeat in 1509 (on the trauma connected with this defeat, see Muir 2000; Sanudo in LaBalme and White 2008, 10–11; see also the Introduction). Contarini gives no hint here that he worked closely with Doge Gritti, especially between 1528 and 1535. Elisabeth G. Gleason (1988, 268) notes that Contarini does not tell the reader that this doge, in spite of his military exploits and patronage of art and architecture, was not popular and that his election was the result of a remarkable network of alliances among a closely knit inside group of nobles. One reason Contarini did not address what Gleason notes may have been that he shared the doge's pro-French sympathies and his policy of promoting Venice as the cultural and intellectual centre of Europe. For a more general discussion of Gritti's efforts, see Bowd 1998, chaps. 6–9, and Finlay's (2000) sketch of Gritti as "Fabius Maximus in Venice." The painting of Doge Gritti by Titian, now housed in the National Gallery of Art, Washington, DC, is generally regarded as one of the finest of all Titian's portraits, and captures Gritti's strong personality. For a conference in Instanbul in 2011, I stayed in a hotel whose meeting space was called "Gritti Hall": that Gritti's name still adorns a public space in modern Instanbul may be taken as a proxy measure of his continuing fame in that city.

the hall and proceed to the nearby Basilica of Saint Mark, a majestic and richly decorated church.[27] They first worship God and then ascend a podium built of porphyry. The most senior elector addresses the people, announces the election of a new doge, and praises him modestly. At that point, the doge gives a speech, and after a short and prudent self-introduction, he promises and vows to observe all such things as befit a virtuous prince, with great care for the welfare of the Republic, without concern for his private interest. He vows that he will, above all, perform the duty of sacred justice and endeavour that everyone is treated equally; and he vows that he will not spare his family wealth, nor himself from taking up any toil and not even from giving his life, in the interest of the Republic, and even to his own detriment.

Finally, he entreats God the Greatest and Almighty, Saint Mark (under whose protection the city of Venice is placed), and all the saints to show him favour, and to assist him in the good management of such a great office. His words are received by the people with a great applause. After the doge concludes his speech, everyone descends from the podium, and they place the doge in front of the main altar of the church. Here he lays his hand on the Gospels and solemnly swears to God and the Republic that he will not eschew any of the responsibilities that are bestowed by law on the doge of Venice. Once this is done, the electors, who until that moment have remained with the doge, depart from him. But the doge steps onto a wooden platform, taking with him the relative he holds most dear. Our mariners [of the Arsenal], who are held in high esteem, lift the platform onto their shoulders and carry the doge around the whole square of Saint Mark, amidst great applause. From the platform, the doge throws coins minted with his name. There is no fixed amount of money to be thrown; rather, the measure is set according to the abundance or scarcity of family wealth, or to the disposition of the prince. The populace eagerly collects the money that is thrown. Finally, once the sailors go around the square and reach the stairs of the ducal palace of the prince, they put down the platform, from which the prince descends. It is customary for the robe worn by the doge and the silver urn that had contained the money to be given as a gift to the mariners who carried the platform on their shoulders.

---

27 For an overview of the importance of the church and its rich assemblage of mosaics, sculptures, and reliquaries in Venetian political, ceremonial, and religious life, see Maguire and Nelson 2010 and Muir 1981, passim. As noted earlier, the Basilica of St Mark, the most important church in Venice, was the private chapel of the doge and not of a bishop (see also Lane 1973, 12).

The doge climbs the stairs of the ducal palace and is received by the councillors who were being robed there, and who crowned him with that head-covering explained earlier as being the mark of honour of the prince. This is the sequence of the whole celebration. On the following day the Senate gathers in the hall and the doge gives a speech, thanking God and the senators for elevating him to that office and honour. He promises to spare no effort in advancing the interest of the Republic, giving an oration similar to the one he gave to the Great Council after his election.

Let this conclude what we say about the prince or doge of our Republic. Next, we will briefly mention a few matters concerning the councillors, which will be enough to illustrate the power of their offices.

As noted previously, six councillors sit beside the prince, one from each of the districts [*sestieri*] into which the city is divided. Three of these[28] are on the nearer side of the Grand Canal, which divides the city in half; three others[29] are on the far side. A councillor from each city district is elected by the same methods with which all the magistrates are elected, as we have amply explained above. Their office extends for eight months and shares responsibility with the prince in all things pertaining to the Republic. According to an ancient custom, the whole procedure of the sessions is put especially into the hands of the councillors. If a matter must be reported to the Great Council and ratified by its authority, the issue is decided by the councillors, as they were the only ones holding that responsibility. However, they are sometimes joined by the heads of the Forty, who would not have the right to report on their own. This power is not conceded to any other magistrate, with the exclusion of the doge. If it pleases them, the councillors can also report any matter both to the Senate and to the Council of Ten. However, the task of summoning and reporting to the Senate is especially entrusted to the *savi*. In the same way, it is a duty of the heads of the Ten to summon the Council of the Ten and report to it. We will deal with this topic below. Yet councillors are endowed with greater authority, insofar as in the Senate they are equal to the preconsultors, and in the Council of the Ten they are equal to the heads of that council. They sit together with the doge for eight months and perform the duties that I have explained. And for

---

28 These are the districts of San Marco, Castello, and Cannaregio. It may be worth mentioning that Cannaregio was the district in which Contarini and his family lived.

29 These are the districts of Dorsoduro, San Polo, and Santa Croce. See also Crouzet-Pavan 2013, esp. 35 with a map of the *sestieri*, and Lane 1973, 98–9. See also the maps in this book.

four months they attend (or rather preside over) the Court of the Forty, to whom the most important causes are entrusted and judged, as will be explained in its due course later on.

We have described (perhaps with scarce elegance, but at least with accuracy) the Great Council, which in this Republic resembles a popular order, and the prince, who possesses the outward show of a king. The work I have embarked upon now requires that we explain the other parts of this government that represent a regime of the patricians.[30] In the city of Venice such a government is clearly superior to the others, as we will thoroughly explain in the following book, God willing.

---

30 As noted in book 1, Contarini refers to the patricians of the Great Council as citizens; here he alludes to the often rich patricians of the Senate, referred to by Sanudo and others as the *primi di la terra*, the first ones of the city, the aristocracy of the patricians. See also Appendix B; Crouzet-Pavan 2002, 209; and Finlay 1980, 26 and passim.

BOOK 3

The Senate, the Council of Ten, and the Courts

In order to keep itself on the right course, every human institution needs to imitate nature,[1] the mother of all things, which has ordered the basic structure of the world so that the things that are deprived of sense and intellect are governed by those endowed with reason. The same may also be observed in that interaction of men which we call a city.[2] Elders are superior to the youth in wisdom, since they are not as exposed to the mind's passions and have the benefit of having experienced more aspects of life over a longer span of time. For this reason, Aristotle says in *Politics*: "In each Republic that intends to emulate the cleverness and wisdom of nature, the elders should be in charge of the highest public interest, while the task of the youth must be to do whatever the elders have ordered. And since this regulation follows the course of nature, the youth cannot censure the directives of the elders and thereby excite any sedition, since in discrimination based on age there is no room for envy or complaint, seeing that the youth certainly hope to obtain compensation in their turn from those younger than them."[3] All republics (or at least those with any commendable reputation) reveal the value of Aristotle's opinion on this matter. In these cities, a council of elders (called a senate, from the Latin word *senes*) was in charge of the government and public affairs.

In this regard, if the matter were not already sufficiently well known, I could mention not only the laws and customs of the Romans, but also those of the Athenians, the Spartans, the Carthaginians, and many other

---

1 As mentioned above, *imitatio naturae* was very much part of the conceptual world of Venetians. On this point, see also book 2, note 1, and book 5, note 10.
2 In his study of the social foundations of the Venetian Renaissance state, Dennis Romano (1987, 10) draws on modern social science to characterize the city of Venice as "a network of networks."
3 Book 7, chap. 14.

cities. In the same way, in our Republic we have the Senate and the Council of Ten representing the order of patricians, which is, as I said, the part of the Republic that combines the orders of the king, the people, and the patricians. The latter constitute a kind of middle level that joins the extremities: the popular[4] level of government represented by the Great Council, and the royal level constituted by the prince. In the same way, as Plato says in *Timaeus*,[5] the extreme elements, earth and fire, are joined together with the intermediate elements. Similarly, in the consonance of the diapason, the extreme voices are harmonized with the intermediate voices of the diatessaron and diapente.

I.

To continue on the path I have begun, the Senate has 120 legitimate senators; and since many magistrates obtain senatorial status ex officio, in our time more than 220 people have the right to vote in the Senate. The legitimate senators are created each year by the whole assembly of patricians that, as I have often said, is called the Great Council. This office, however, is not vacated in the same way as all the other offices. Rather, if chance allows and the Great Council so decides – as generally happens – the same people can remain in that post every year. We expounded the electoral procedure earlier when we were explaining the organization of the Great Council sessions. Thus, six senators are elected in every session during August and September, with a set of ten separate votes electing a total of sixty patricians. Sixty more are added or registered together with the others, and all are elected together in particular assemblies. On the 29th of September,[6] the Senate is summoned, and each senator and whoever else has the right nominates patricians for the Senate.

On the following morning at nine o'clock,[7] patricians gather in the hall of the Great Council. The names of the citizens nominated by the

---

4 Recall what meaning Contarini attaches to "popular": see also notes 8 and 15 in book 1 and note 30 in book 2.

5 The reference is too vague to be able to assign it to a specific passage in *Timaeus*.

6 It may be recalled that on this day the liturgical calendar of the church celebrates the feast of St Michael, the archangel who fought for justice against Satan and his evil angels. This feast is the most ancient of all the angel festivals in the church.

7 The original Latin says "three o'clock in the morning," for in Contarini's time the twenty-four-hour clock began near sunset. Hence, taking into account seasonal differences in the time of sunset, ranging from about 5 p.m. in winter to 8 p.m. in the summer, night hours started differently, so that 3 a.m. can be taken to be mean roughly 9 a.m. in our own time. Before 1797, the Venetian calendar year began on 1 March. See also Labalme and White 2008, xxi–xxii.

senators the day before are read out by the secretary [the Grand Chancellor], after which the nominations are collected in an urn and drawn by lot. Next, the Great Council votes for each of these sixty nominees. Those who obtain more votes than the others, as long as they have more than half, are enrolled in the Senate for that year, under the proviso that no more than two people from the same family may be so enrolled. Among the legitimate senators there can only be three people from the same kin. This law demonstrates exceeding wisdom on behalf of the Republic. Indeed, no more pernicious plague could creep into the Republic than one of its constituent parts prevailing over the others. Where justice is not observed, it is impossible to maintain harmony in civil society, which is normally achieved when the many offices of the Republic work together as one. A mixture dissolves if one of its elements is more dominant than the others, just as a consonance becomes dissonant if one instrument or voice is amplified more than is appropriate. Analogously, if one wishes a city or Republic to continue to exist, it is paramount to ensure that no part is made more powerful than the others, and that all have a share in public authority as much as possible.

It was therefore an extremely good decision of our ancestors to sanction, as a long-lasting provision of our Republic, that there should be no places in the Senate or other offices for men from the same family – no more, that is, than is demanded by equality. No less wise is the procedure of electing the Senate, according to which 60 senators have to be elected using the usual method of assemblies (i.e., by a combination of chance and choice), but 60 others are to be added by a different method in which nothing is left to chance. If chance played the same role for all, it could easily happen that foremost patricians[8] would not be elected, and that this neglect would be detrimental to the Republic. It was decided, therefore, to have an election of 60 senators not by lot but by choice, and to hold such an election every year. Thus the Senate consists first of 120 people, of whom 60 are called by the proper name of senators, and the others are called adjuncts, or as members of the Zonta,[9] whose sessions take up a whole day. On equal terms with these Senators, the doge, and the ducal councillors, there are the Ten and the Court of the

---

8 As noted earlier, what diarist Marin Sanudo referred to as "*primi di la terra*" (prominent patricians, literally "first of the land"), while the Great Council remained the "*Signor de la Terra*" (Crouzet Pavan 2002, 209).

9 The Senate was thus composed of four groups: 60 ordinary senators, 60 extraordinary senators (the *Zonta*), the Court of the Forty (Quarantia criminal), and about 140 magistrates who entered by virtue of their offices.

Forty (who act as judges of capital cases and the more serious crimes),
the magistrates of the Salt and Supply of Grain, the procurators of Saint
Mark,[10] and several other officers. In our time, the total number of Senators exceeds 220.

The whole business of governing the Republic belongs to the Senate.[11]
Whatever has been decreed by the authority of the Senate is considered
sacrosanct. The Senate discusses and deliberates about making peace and
waging wars. The revenues of the Republic are collected and expended on
its orders. If the situation requires it, new taxes and tithes are both levied
on the citizens and collected under decree of the Senate. If the Republic has decided that some new officer is to be established *pro tempore*, he is
elected by the Senate. Moreover, the Senate has the authority to choose,
at any time, ambassadors to foreign princes, and to create the Collegio,[12]
those officials who have the right to summon the Senate and to report to it.

---

10 The procurators of Saint Mark were nine men originally elected for life by the Great
    Council. The procurators acted as treasurers for the government and as fiduciaries
    for private individuals. The doge was generally chosen from among this number. For
    a study of the office of procurators, Mueller 1971 remains useful.

11 In time, the concern for protecting the security of the state diminished the authority
    of the Senate and increased that of the Council of Ten. Contarini's contemporary
    Marin Sanudo recognized this dynamic situation in his lifetime when he described
    the Counci of Ten as "a severe magistracy of the top nobles [*primi*] of the city" (in
    Cozzi 1973, 303, and Chambers and Pullan 2004, 54–6). Elisabeth Gleason, Contarini's modern biographer, observes that "despite [Contarini's] description of the
    Senate as the heart of Venetian government he actually endorsed a strict hierarchy
    that confined supreme executive authority to a small elite of thirty-two men: the
    Council of Ten, its advisory board (*Zonta*) of fifteen, the doge and his councillors.
    Contarini's stands shows that he prized efficiency and order in the day-to-day workings of the government and did not fear that the Council of Ten might become
    tyrannical" (1993, 66). In brief, the authority of the Senate may have remained sacrosanct, but exigencies of security between the fourteenth and sixteenth centuries
    gave more power and repute to the Council of Ten even though its jurisdiction was
    restricted (Cozzi 1973, 303). See also book 3, note 18, and refer to the discussion in
    the Introduction.

12 The College or Collegio was the steering committee or cabinet of the Senate, which
    set the agenda and made proposals to that assembly. To anticipate what Contarini
    details shortly, the College elected by the Senate was composed of "sages" elected
    for six-month terms: five members of the *savi agli ordini*, responsible for maritime
    affairs; five members of the *savi di terraferma*, responsible for military affairs on the
    mainland; and the six-member *savi grandi*, responsible for general governmental affairs, who were the highest members of the Collegio (Finlay 1980, xvi). Elisabeth G.
    Gleason reminds us that Contarini's period of participation in the inner and highest
    councils of Venice began with his assumption of the office of *savio grande* on 1 April
    1530 (1993, 63).

Aristotle[13] named these people the "preconsultors;" our men call them by the more assuming name of "Sages" [*savi*] – a name that we, too, have deemed it best to use on occasion, so as not to seem averse to common parlance.

The sessions of the Senate, in which both the ambassadors and the *savi* are chosen, leave less room to chance than those described above, that is, elections in the Great Council. Every senator nominates the person he wishes, and then the Senate votes on all of the nominees. A nominee who obtains more votes than the others, as long as it is more than half of the total, is elected. If at times the needs of the Republic require that some public office be assigned to someone against his will, every senator notes down the name of the person he considers most suitable on a piece of paper, and then he casts it into an urn prepared for this purpose. These are then extracted by a secretary and read aloud, after which the senators vote on each. The one with the most votes is proclaimed elected, as long as the votes add up to more than half. This method has been devised so that no one, fearful of incurring the enmity or hate of another citizen by designating him for some office that he could clearly perform well but would be displeased to have imposed on him, might therefore refrain from nominating him,[14] thereby harming the Republic in the service of a private interest.

Now we have to review the way in which the Senate takes counsel and decides and sanctions what is to be done, and how the decrees of the Senate are usually made. It did not escape our ancestors that, if each senator could indiscriminately express his opinion without that responsibility being specifically assigned to particular offices, there would always be great disturbance in the assembly. In addition, experience has shown that what all equally care for, all will equally disregard. Therefore our laws have established that sixteen citizens are elected by the Senate, who are commonly called "sages"[15] [*savi* or *sapientes*] because they seem to be

---

13 *Politics*, book 6, chap. 8. Aristotle also observed that in some states the holders of this office are called *probuli*, or preliminary council, because they initiate legislation.

14 Contarini alludes here to a practice among legislators and public officials of his time with which modern students of comparative politics from Canada to China are familiar: to designate someone whom one does not like for an office that the person does not wish to have or be "promoted" to. Still, Maria Stella Florio (2009, 27n108) suggests that this practice in Venice does not mean that many patricians tried to avoid public office, as some historians of Venice such as Donald E. Queller claims.

15 Following his years as ambassador to Charles V, Contarini was elected and served as one of the six *savi di terraferma*, responsible for military affairs on the mainland. In 1530, as stated in note 12, he assumed the more prestigious office of *savio grande*, which made him one of the highest-ranking members of the College, the steering committee or cabinet of the Senate (Gleason 1993, 62–3). See a general description of the *savi* in Chambers and Pullan 2004, 43–5, and the glossary of governmental terms in Appendix B.

better informed than everybody else. Following Aristotle, we can rightly call them preconsultors, because they take counsel in advance regarding the matters that the Senate must review. These have the right both to summon the Senate and to report to it. They hold office for six months.

These *savi* are grouped in three ranks or committees that differ considerably from each other. In the first order (*savi grandi*) there are six senators, eminent patricians who surpass their fellows in experience, dignity, and reputation.[16] Their main task is to give counsel and advise the Senate about the administration of the Republic, including on questions of war, peace, and matters equally grave. In the second order [*savi di terraferma*] there are five patricians, who, despite having the same power as the first order to report about every matter to the Senate, are nevertheless subordinate to the first ones in dignity and reputation. Their responsibility, above all, is the care of the soldiers who are maintained by the Republic and who serve under the captain-general of the army. There are also five senators in the third rank [*savi agli ordini*], entrusted with looking after maritime concerns. Apart from this, they do not have the right to report to the Senate on other matters. When Venetian maritime affairs flourished under our ancestors, this post was held in high esteem. However, as the importance of maritime affairs waned and the interests of our people turned to the dominion of the *terraferma*, this office began to be held in low esteem, to the extent that in our age it is young people, almost adolescents, who are elected to it.

These sixteen citizens, whose gathering has customarily been given the specific name of the Collegio by the Venetians, meet in the early hours of the morning with the doge and the Signoria [ducal councillors]. Until nine o'clock they receive private citizens who have some business either with the Republic or with some other magistrate. They deliberate about these cases together, or, if the matter seems to require it, they report to the Senate about them. At about nine o'clock, private citizens are dismissed from the hall, and without delay the letters sent to the Senate are read by an official who belongs to the Chancery of the Republic. Afterwards, unless interrupted by the ambassadors of some prince asking to meet with the doge and the Collegio, or by some business of importance that cannot be delayed, the *savi* withdraw to a chamber to take counsel. After they have gathered and everybody is seated, the patrician who is the head of the Collegio (for each of them in turn holds that administrative role for seven days) establishes the agenda. He

---

16 Contarini was in time to become a *savio grande*. See Appendix C, "Principal Events in Gasparo Contarini's Life."

asks each person for his opinion, in the following order. The sages of the first class, eminent patricians, are always first asked for their opinion. After them come the five we have placed in the second rank. Finally, if the subject concerns maritime matters, the sages of the third class express their opinion, though if the item under consultation does not pertain to sea matters, these latter hold their peace.

In every meeting, the first to express his opinion is the one who has presided over the previous seven days, after whom speaks the eldest one by age, and then all the others according to seniority. The last of all to express his opinion is the head for those seven days, who has established the subject of deliberation and has questioned the others. Finally, after the matter has been duly deliberated, whether they have all come to a consensus or divided into two or three different ones (as the minds of men differ), they report to the doge and Signoria before they summon the Senate. The position of everyone is presented; if the doge or any of the ducal councillors wants to assent to or favour one of the opinions with his authority, or conceives a new one, they discuss the matter once more and finally put all the opinions in writing. This is the task of the secretaries of each of the three ranks.

After they [the full Collegio] have taken counsel concerning the business to be decided by the authority of the Senate, they summon the Senate. They read out the letters that are of some importance, or that have been handed over to the prince or the sages after the dismissal of the last Senate. Afterwards, matters deliberated by the Collegio are read out, whether they are in agreement or not, in almost the same manner in which Plato[17] apparently shows how the appeals of the people used to be made among Athenians. Nobody apart from those who are called *savi*, as I said, has the right to report to the Senate and have his opinion ratified by that body's authority, with the exception of the doge, the ducal councillors, and the heads of the Forty, about whom I will say more below.

Once all opinions are read in the Senate, the chief of the first order of sages for that week speaks, if he so wishes. Otherwise, the most senior patrician speaks, or the one who is willing to speak and has been allowed to do so by the others. The speaker goes up onto a raised platform specially built for this purpose [the *renga*] and addresses the Senate. He puts forwards reasons that support his view, and, in the modest and grave manner that befits a man of the senatorial rank, refutes the contrary reasons. After he has finished speaking, another sage stands up, who disagrees with the first; he defends his own opinion and refutes the previous

---

17 The reference here is too vague to be assigned to a specific passage in Plato's work.

speaker. Then the third stands, if there are so many opinions, and puts forward the reasons consonant with his thinking. The procedure is carried out in this sequence until everyone who wants to speak is included. The senators may not speak until all the *savi* who wished to exercise their right to do so have finished. After the *savi* have given speeches and arguments in favour or against as long as they want, the other senators are given the opportunity to speak. If a senator wishes to oppose, defend, or put forward a new position, he is given the opportunity to do so. Yet no senator has the right to argue before the Senate concerning the opinion of which he himself is the author. It normally happens that if the judgment of that senator seems to be in the interest of the Republic, a member of the Collegio or a councillor or a chief of the Forty brings it up in the Senate. Once the matter has been sufficiently discussed and deliberated upon, the Senate decides – by the vote of all who are in that order – which opinion it approves. Yet they do not walk to the side of the hall that represents that opinion, or withdraw to the opposite direction, according to the practice observed by the Romans and handed down by history; nor do they express their opinion openly. Rather, they decide the matter with urns and votes, using a procedure similar to that which, as I explained earlier, is observed in the meetings of the Great Council.

The secretaries of the Senate bring forth as many urns as there are opinions about which the Senate is taking counsel and hearing arguments. In addition, a green one is brought forth to collect the votes of those who oppose all the opinions, and a red one in which the senators who are still uncertain cast their votes. Each senator casts a ball into the urn corresponding to the opinion that he commends. If he rejects all the opinions, he casts his ball into the green urn, and if he is uncertain and in doubt, into the red. The councillors count the balls. The winning opinion is that which obtains more than half of the senators' votes. If no opinion obtains more than half of the total, the opinion approved by the fewest number of people is rejected. The votes for the others are then repeated. With the same procedure of shelving the least voted-upon opinion, the debate is reduced to two, one of which will necessarily obtain more than half of the votes. This opinion is then pronounced a decree of the Senate. Once one matter is concluded, the senators take up another. Unless it is not too late in the day, the same method is observed for all of them.

And if there is an ambassador of some prince who has arrived in the Republic, he is received by the doge, and the whole Collegio. They request time to consult, and dismiss the envoy. As the matter is deliberated by the *savi* as described above, the Senate takes counsel. First, the doge announces what the ambassador has requested, and then the opinions of all who have the right to report to the Senate are read aloud. They decide to answer the ambassador's request following the same procedure by which a decree of the Senate is made. The envoy is summoned and the answer of the Senate is read to him, and then he is dismissed. This is essentially the entirety of the points that seem to pertain both to the degrees of the Senate and to the whole procedure and order of taking counsel in the Senate.

At this point we have explained all the components of government parts that concern the Great Council, which in the city of Venice has the form of a popular order, and those that pertain to the doge, whose appearance in this Republic somewhat resembles that of a king, and finally the whole procedure of holding the Senate. It seems appropriate now to talk about the Council of Ten.

II.

The Council of Ten has the greatest authority among the Venetians over the safety of the Republic.[18] We have to relate the origin of this council at some length, so that the whole point of the office may be more readily understood. With a kind of divine foresight, our ancestors anticipated that, as in a human body, countless dangerous diseases follow from the putrefaction of bodily fluids, sometimes even leading to death; so too in republics, sometimes citizens can cause the Republic distress by aspiring to rule wrongfully rather than obeying the laws – either because they are driven by ambition and lust for power, or are oppressed by debt, or also because, being aware of their crimes, they fear punishment. Among people of this sort we find Catiline, Sylla, Marius, and lastly Julius Caesar, who succeeded in becoming a tyrant and completely overturned the republic. Also in some Greek polities (and certainly very distinguished ones), history records that there have been many citizens of this sort. In our times, it is evident that almost every city in Italy, whether it is

---

18 Elisabeth G. Gleason (1988, 267, and 1993, 62–4) recalls that Contarini tried to
be elected to the Council of the Ten several times but it was only in the 1530s that
he succeeded. He was a member of the Council of the Ten from September 1530
through August 1531, and again from September 1533 to August 1534. He was one of
the three heads of the Ten for October and December 1530, March and June 1531,
October and December 1533, and March 1534, and served five times as one of its
inquisitors. Sometimes, as noted by Gleason and as can be expected in the practice
of governance, Contarini's action as a high official deviated from the general description
he gives here. It is worth recalling Gilbert's point that Contarini's "treatise was intended to show how men ought to act in politics rather than how they did act" (1969,
113). See also book 3, note 11, and the discussion in the Introduction.

governed by a popular order or even by one of its own patrician citizens, eventually falls into the tyranny of some faction of its citizens. For this reason, our ancestors decided that they had to try with all their might to prevent their Republic, splendidly organized and governed by excellent laws, from being afflicted by some such monster. In their view, they should fear nothing so much as an internal enemy and hostility between citizens. Since they realized that in the polity of the Spartans the Ephors had the highest authority, in Athens the Aeropagites, and in Rome the Decimvirs, who also established the laws, they believed that they would benefit if, imitating those examples under different circumstances, they instituted an office with the highest power in this city of ours.

This office would have the special task of ensuring that no dissension arose among patrician citizens that could lead to an insurrection, and that no faction or pernicious citizen could plot a treacherous attack against the Republic. And if an unfortunate plague of this sort were to secretly creep into the city, this office would have the power to inflict punishment and prevent the Republic from suffering any damage. But such a power could not be conferred on just a few people without risk, nor inspire fear if conferred on too many. In order to avoid both disadvantages, they therefore created the Council of the Ten.[19]

Members of the Ten hold office for one year and are then obliged to vacate it, so that one who has been in that office even just one more day in a given year must stand down from the post, not only for that year but also the following one, and they cannot take part in the sessions of the Ten. The doge and the ducal councillors were added to the Ten, so that this council with great power and authority consists of a total of seventeen patrician citizens. Of these Ten, three are elected by lot each month, and are called the "heads" of the Ten in our native language. They have the right to summon the Ten and report to it; they have a private chamber set aside in which they meet every day; and they also appoint attendants, doorkeepers, clerks, and guardians, so that no other court or office is approached with greater deference. Anyone who has business with the Ten goes there. They also read the letters addressed to the Council and report to it about them. However, in order to avoid

---

19 It is worth noting that the Council of the Ten was originally set up in 1310 as a temporary measure to complete the suppression of the failed Querini-Tiepolo conspiracy. The Great Council established the Ten as a permanent body in 1334, and Cozzi (1973, 303) observes, quoting Sanudo, that some of the most dramatic events in Venetian history were linked to it: the execution of Doge Marin Faliero and of Count Carmagnola, the chief of the Venetian army, and the deposition of Doge Francesco Foscari (see also Romano 2007, chap. 4).

the intervention of the Senate without good cause, a single head of the Ten does not have the right to report on his own; instead, two who wish to report a matter are required, or four councillors. And for the same reason, so that nothing can be modified by very few patrician citizens without good cause, it was established that if someone wants to abrogate an existing decree, for this to be so recognized it has to be approved and ratified by two-thirds of the council who voted for it.

The Ten also observe the practice of not admitting a defendant to their meeting while they are passing judgment on him, nor an attorney or a pleader to defend his cause – a right that is nevertheless allowed to defendants when they plead their case in front of another office. They observe the following procedure in conducting trials. The defendant is given an audience with the heads of the Ten, and his words are recorded in writing. But when the case is brought before the Council, the same heads and judges who are present both plead on behalf of the accuser and the defendant. And the most important matter is always decided with moderation of judgment.

Originally, the Ten only devoted their efforts to preventing the occurrence of anything that could harm the Republic and civil harmony.[20] Later, certain extremely grave crimes and great offences were also entrusted to the severity of this court, as in the case of someone minting counterfeit money or practising sodomy.[21] And in our own time, the authority of the Ten has expanded to pass judgment and fix punishment on the most wicked of men who would dare to swear against God or the Blessed Virgin.[22] Moreover, it has been established that matters of the highest confidentiality pertaining to the highest interest of the Republic are also referred to the decision of the Ten. They do not decide, however, any matter of tremendous importance unless by the decision of the whole Senate. They also administer a large number of financial businesses.

Therefore, in order not to entrust authority over so many important affairs to fewer patricians than appropriate, the *savi* of the first and second ranks also take part in the Council's activities, like the state attorneys and

---

20 Civic harmony was an important community value, even though we know from the history of Venice that Contarini "exaggerated the stability of the Venetian republic and projected it too much back in time" (Pullan 1971, 9). Civic disharmony was indeed evident in Contarini's time (Queller 1986), but it was not powerful enough to topple or alter the republic (e.g., Romano 1987, 4–6, and 2007, esp. chap. 4).

21 On this topic, Patricia H. Labalme's (1984) article remains important.

22 The Virgin Mary played an important role in the self-definition of Venetians. See esp. Muir 1981, 92, 138–45, 152–3; Wills 2001 refers to the Mark and Mary partnership in the Venetian identity.

the procurators of Saint Mark, whose office is held in high esteem. Besides these, fifteen senators also serve as "adjuncts" [the *Zonta*] to this council, though not all of these have the right to vote. Those who do vote are the aforementioned seventeen, and the fifteen associated with these, for a total of thirty-two people. The others, although they participate in all deliberations, are debarred from voting. The fifteen adjuncts [of the *Zonta*] are not usually elected by the Senate or the Great Council, but are chosen among senators by the Ten – who, however, are neither kinsmen nor closely related to them. Nowadays, the fifteen associates are elected by the Great Council.

Experience, the master of all things, has shown the Council of Ten to have provided great benefit to the Republic. In fact, 210 years ago, Doge Marino Falier,[23] who was plotting to become a tyrant and was about to cause great trouble to the Republic, was immediately restrained by the authority and wisdom of the Ten, and paid the price for the temerity of his crime. Under the sentence of this Council he was condemned to capital punishment, together with the many distinguished citizens who had conspired with him for the destruction of freedom, and he was marked with perpetual ignominy. In the area of the ducal palace where the paintings of the doges hang, with praise for the deeds each accomplished for the Republic, there is no painting of Marino Falier. There is only an engraving with short verses declaring that this doge (to quote it literally) was struck down by the executioner's axe because of his crimes. This conspiracy would certainly have been fatal, easily bringing about the destruction of the Republic, if it had not been immediately suppressed by the authority of this Council. Several other citizens who, driven by ambition, had promulgated dangerous laws to gain popular favour, were immediately restrained by the severity of the Ten and punished by the Republic for their temerity and hubris. The outcome of this has been that, with the favour of God the Almighty and thanks to the strength of the authority of this Council, no such plague has overrun our city.

By now we have described the most important components of the Republic, which constitute almost the whole government. But in order to complete the work we have embarked upon, we will also speak about the other magistracies that administer justice and public finance, and that oversee the governors of the cities under Venetian rule, and the captains of the fleets and the army. Finally, I will describe which institutions are in place to hold in check resentment on the part of the common people for lack of participation in the governance of the Republic. We will also

---

23 Marino Falier, doge from 1354 to 1355, had a distinguished career that made him "appear the perfect leader." What could have led him to such ignoble death baffled Petrarch as it continues to baffle modern historians (Lane 1973, 181, 183).

show that training and exercising for war among the youth has not been neglected, as many believe.

III.

Before I proceed to explain the organization of these arrangements, I think it is not out of place to draw the reader's attention to the fact that the method by which the Senate and the Council of the Ten deliberate – which I explained above – clearly reveals a mixture of the legal system of the popular order with the government of patricians. On one hand, the fact that the Senate cannot decide anything unless the *savi* first report it to the Senate itself is a feature of the regime of the patricians. On the other hand, that the *savi* do not have power unless they consult with the Senate, and have their opinion confirmed by the authority of the Senate, is certainly a practice of a popular government. Therefore it is not just in our Republic taken as a whole, but also in each of its components, that one will discover (if he is right in his assessment) this mixture and blend that I mentioned earlier, by which those systems of governance have coalesced into the characteristic single form of our Republic. But let our discourse go back to the point where it digressed.

First of all, we have to explain that part of government which pertains to justice. That system, usually administered by judges, is divided into two parts. One part deals with criminal cases, including the penalties that must be inflicted on criminals who have committed some great offence against the fatherland or against some citizen, or who have been impious towards the immortal gods. The second part deals with judgment of civil cases. There are, therefore, two types of judges in Venice, one who presides over civil cases and the other over capital crimes. We will speak first about capital crimes.[24]

Some offences are considered less important, either because of their nature, or because of the condition of those men who commit them. But many offences are considered more serious and of greater importance on similar grounds: that is, because of their very nature, or because of the high rank of those who commit them. For this reason, two types of magistrates have been established for trying these capital crimes. The more serious cases and the more significant crimes are referred to the first type of magistrate, and the less consequential ones to the second. One will find

---

24 The research of Stanley Chojnacki (1972), Guido Ruggiero (1980), and James E. Shaw (2006) on the Venetian justice system and its dynamics in dealing with various forms of crime gives depth to the topic explored here by Contarini. We will return to their works in the following books.

that in the Republic of Venice all judgments are divided and organized most excellently according to the manner that we have just expounded. We discuss first the more significant, and then turn to the others. Apart from the offences entrusted to the censorship of the Ten (as we explained above), all the more serious crimes are usually settled with the reports of the state attorneys [*avogadori*] and followed by sentences of the Court of the Forty, with punishments fixed according to the case. These Forty are commonly called Quarantia criminal, or the criminal judges. We first deal with the *avogadori* and then consider the appeals court itself.

In earlier times, the office of the Avogaria possessed extraordinary authority. Then as now their main responsibility is custody of the laws, i.e., preventing the impairment of any aspect of the law. For this reason, those who occupy that office have almost the same faculty or capacity to impose a veto that the Tribunes of the Plebs used to have among the Romans. But those tribunes had that veto power in order to preserve the freedom of the people of Rome, whereas our officers [state attorneys] have it to protect the strength of the laws. Therefore, it would not be unreasonable to call them the tribunes of the laws. However, to avoid ambiguities (which is a great concern of ours), we will not depart from the common and accustomed terms. While the tribunes used to report to the people or plebs, our state attorneys report to the Forty regarding minor cases, to the Senate regarding serious ones, and to the Great Council regarding the most significant, if they deem it appropriate. For this reason, in earlier times the authority of this office was great. Nowadays, however, since the power of the Council of Ten has greatly expanded,[25] the authority of the state attorneys has diminished, and their reputation has dimmed.[26] Even if the state attorneys do not have any authority for determining measures against the people prosecuted, except in some cases of little importance, their office holds a power of veto in reporting cases, and in prosecuting acts again the laws, since it is their duty to devote themselves to the preservation of the Republic more than the others. All the other cases are decided by the Council.

At this point I think it will not be irrelevant, seeing that this method is not followed anywhere else as far as I know, for me to explain the system of capital judgments that are made with the state attorneys. At the same time, I believe, we will make the nature and authority of the Avogaria clear. After a criminal offence has been put before the officials of the Avogaria, if

---

25 Largely as a result of the events surrounding the Cambrai war, which, it will be re-
    called, sought to do away with the *terraferma* dominion of the Venetian republic. See
    also Gilbert 1973 and Muir 2000.
26 For a recent overview of this ancient magistracy, see the work of Cristina Setti (2014).

the matter is thought to deserve their oversight, then all of them, or even just one (for there are three people charged with this office), immediately interpose a veto, and the person whose name has been referred to them is prosecuted. Afterwards, they report on the crime to the Council chosen by the state attorney who interposed the veto, although generally they consult the Council of the Forty, which is in charge of the judgments of capital crimes. There the case is read out and debated, and they, Quarantia criminal, determine if the defendant should be imprisoned and summoned to trial, or if he may plead his case as a free man. Next, the defendant is summoned by decree of the Quarantia criminal, or arrested by the guards of the Avogaria. Whether free or under arrest, he pleads his case. They interrogate him about his crime. He answers, and the witnesses on both sides are cited. What he says spontaneously, or what he is coerced into saying under torture, as well as what the witnesses have declared in favour of or against the defendant, are all put into writing for the record. Once the whole case has been recorded in the public book, a copy of everything that has been written is given to the defendant. A period of time is set in which he can inform the officers of the Avogaria, and the advocates that he has appointed, about the case; these parties diligently examine everything that might serve as a defence for the defendant, and devise ways to refute the charge and the pieces of evidence against him. Finally the trial begins.

At this point I must not fail to mention an ancient custom that has continued into our own time. If by chance someone who is prosecuted possesses little family wealth, so that he is unable to sustain the expenses of hiring advocates to defend his cause, the Republic pays two advocates to hold this office and defend that poor person. In such a way, the law prevents anyone from being punished without the cause being pleaded. After the defendant thinks nothing more is required for his defence, the state attorneys of the Avogaria call the Quarantia criminal, and a day is appointed for the trial. Once the Court of the Forty has assembled, the state attorney takes on the role of the prosecutor. It is fitting for those in that office to act as severe prosecutors, in a way similar to Cicero against Verres and Mark Anthony – provided that they are able to do so. Yet they refrain from insults and do not stray beyond the case. One who indulges in insults appears to act as an enemy and a bad man, rather than plead the case of the Republic. And in this respect, the situations of Venice and Rome differ vastly. In Rome any citizen could serve a summons to another, and accuse him most harshly in front of the judge. But in Venice no private patrician citizen has this prerogative. By the law of the Republic, that prerogative belongs to the officers of the Avogaria.

In this regard, it must be said that our ancestors imitated nature and cared for harmony among citizens with more wisdom than the Romans did. For one who has committed a crime has first and foremost offended the laws and the Republic, and so their penalty should be paid above all to the Republic. The officer who is a custodian of law is the one who must by law demand requital from the criminal and strive for this with all his might. By contrast, the duty of the private citizen is to forget the offences committed and pardon the accused one without difficulty. Moreover, no private citizen can assume the role of the prosecutor without incurring the extreme resentment and enormous hatred of the person he has summoned, and discord among citizens easily arises from this. Therefore, our ancestors wisely avoided this trouble by laying the task of making accusations at the feet of the magistrate, who performs his task driven not by private hostility, but by the ordinance of the law. As a result of this, it is almost unheard of for any of the Avogaria magistrates to be reprimanded for inveighing against the accused with vehemence. Rather, one who discharges his duty with harshness obtains great praise among patrician citizens. But let us go back to the system of judgments introduced earlier.

Once the Quarantia criminal has gathered, an officer of the Avogaria acts as prosecutor, and presents a rigorous case against the prosecuted. First he presents the crimes and offences, then he reinforces the accusations using witness testimony and corroborates them with plausible hypotheses. After he has concluded his indictment, the case is pleaded by the advocate appointed by the defendant. Afterwards, if an Avogaria officer or attorney wishes to interrogate the defendant again before the judges passes a sentence, he has the opportunity to speak. Similarly, the advocates of the defendant may respond and refute the crimes. In the same way, both sides may go back and forth until one side, either the defendant or that officer of the Avogaria upon whom the role of speaker has fallen, declares that he does not want to argue any further. Once this is done, the defendant and his advocates leave the court. The Avogaria attorneys and their secretaries shut themselves away in a private chamber with the judges but no one else. The state attorneys first report to the judges about the conviction of the defendant, and if they deem that the defendant should be punished, they ask for the sentence, without fixing a determined penalty. This is essentially the practice followed by the Athenians, where judges gave sentences in two stages. At the first stage, they either acquitted or condemned the defendant. At the second stage – if he had been condemned in the first – they establish the penalty, as can be clearly evinced from Plato's *Apologia of Socrates*.[27] We, too, make use of a similar sequence of judgments and an almost equivalent procedure here.

---

27 *Apologia of Socrates*, 36b.

First, the state attorneys report on the conviction of the defendant. The judges proceed to vote, for among the Venetians the councils decide every matter with a vote. Three urns are carried in: one for the conviction of the defendant, another for his complete acquittal without penalty, and the third for the votes of those still uncertain about which decision to make. The urn for the conviction of the defendant is white; the second, for the acquittal, is green; and the third is red. Cases may be conducted with the Forty as judges (as is normally the case), or the Senate may be consulted (which seldom happens, usually only in the more serious cases), or the Avogaria attorneys may report to the Great Council (which happens even more rarely and only in the most serious cases). But in all of these cases, the procedure is for each judge to cast a linen ball into the urn he prefers, so that no one can discern his vote.[28] Afterwards the votes are counted by the chief of the respective council. If more than half of the votes are for the acquittal of the defendant, he is immediately declared absolved, and the measure proposed by the state attorneys is rejected. But if more than half of the votes are for conviction, they immediately declare him condemned. If neither of these has obtained more than half of the votes, because many judges are still uncertain, they declare the trial adjourned and the judges and defendant are given a fixed date on which the case is to be heard again, with the state attorneys acting as prosecutors and the advocates once more refuting the indictment. After the proceedings [of the second trial] end and the plea is completed, judges are polled again. If nothing is decided even then – that is, if neither side obtains half the votes as a result of some undecided judges – then the trial is adjourned and the Court of the Forty is summoned for a third time. A date is set for the trial to be repeated yet again. At last they proceed to vote, but this time there is no longer a third option for those who are still uncertain. Unless the votes are equally divided, the defendant is either condemned or absolved. If he is acquitted, he does not have any further business, as I said before. If instead he is found guilty, the Court determines the punishment to be inflicted. Both the state attorneys and the president of the council of the judges present motions about the type of penalty. Usually the officers of the Avogaria propose the penalty that looks the most severe for that type of crime, for it is their duty to incline towards severity. But it is customary for the others, that is, the councillors and the heads of the Forty, to propose lighter penalties, unless the crime is so terrible that there is no room for mercy, or the state attorneys have acted with more leniency than is appropriate

---

28 Contarini is in effect describing a linen ballot to be cast in a tripartite urn so that the sound would give no hint where it fell.

to that office. Once all the opinions have been presented, the penalty inflicted on the defendant is decided in almost the same fashion by which a decree of the Senate is usually passed when the opinions of the *savi* are at variance (as explained above). At this point, however, if I were to repeat the description of this procedure and inappropriately bore the reader, I could rightly be considered foolish. It is enough to say that the sentence pronounced by the judges is one that has obtained more than half of the votes. At this point I will not digress much if I describe two practices that have been most wisely handed down by our ancestors.

The first practice is that our ancestors did not want any magistrate or patrician to be the arbiter in any matter or judgment without a summons to court; rather, they decreed that in any circumstance, the supreme right and judicial power belong to legislative bodies or councils. The other practice is no less beneficial than the previous one: it was stipulated that judges would not give their sentences orally or state openly what they think, but would instead decide what they deem best in secret, with a vote. In my opinion, both practices are most wise. Indeed, the fact that the highest authority is not granted to any magistrate is a very prudent custom. For, besides the fact that it is dangerous to entrust the highest responsibility on any matter whatsoever to just a few patrician citizens, it also means that the city cannot complain about a few patrician citizens if the trial in question ends badly. And no less wise is the statute [or practice] according to which decrees and judgments are made secretly. For in a system of secret polls, judges express their judgment more freely than if they had to give sentences openly and orally. If that were the case, they would sometimes be led astray from the path of justice because of ambition, or they would scruple to give offence to a friend or patrician who has done them some service, or they would fear the resentment of the more powerful. Moreover, it also allows each judge to follow his own judgment and not depend on the authority of another judge, which could happen easily if the person who initially expressed a sentence had a reputation for being endowed with great wisdom and sound judgment. For this reason, the most distinguished philosophers[29] have not failed to mention this type of judgment either.

---

29 Contarini, who knew his Aristotle by heart, probably here has in mind Aristotle
    in *Politics*, book 3, chap. 15, where Aristotle asks whether it is best to be ruled by
    the best man or the best laws. He notes at 1236a32 that individuals are liable to be
    overcome with anger or other passions when passing judgment, and it is best not to
    leave judgment in the hands of the few. I owe this reference to Jonathan Montpetit,
    a doctoral graduate student in political theory, Department of Political Science,
    McGill University.

IV.

Let me return to the topic at hand. Having described the method of judgments, I will now go back, as planned, to discuss the forty judges of capital cases. Our city has established that the Court of the Forty is where the state attorneys make motions on the capital cases, as well as decide on the punishment of convicted criminals. Therefore the Avogaria magistrates do not consult the Senate – and more rarely the Great Council – except in the gravest of cases, where the outcome of the judgment concerns the Republic itself. But all capital causes are referred to this Court of Forty, whose sentences carry legal validity and from whom there is no possibility for appeal. These magistrates serve for eight months, after they have already spent sixteen months judging civil cases. There are indeed three courts [Quarantia] in the Republic, each consisting of forty judges. Two hear civil cases, and the third deals with capital cases, which is the one we now deal with. The magistrates are organized in such a manner that as soon as the capital judges have completed their term, they are reduced to the common rank, and forty other patrician citizens are appointed in the sessions of the Great Council. However, these judges do not accede straight away to judging capital cases; it is the Court of the Forty, which in the previous eight months was in charge of domestic cases, that now succeeds to consider the capital cases. The civil domestic judges are replaced by a third group of forty men, who in the foregoing eight months had been assigned to foreign cases, and the newly appointed judges succeed to their position. Thus, in turns, the same judges decide on civil cases, both domestic and foreign, and on capital cases, and they are involved in these judgments for the duration of two years.

These three courts of judges have their own particular denominations. The first, to which the foreign cases are referred, is called "New Civil Forty" [Quarantia civile nuova]; the second, which is in charge of domestic cases, is called "Old Civil Forty" [Quarantia civile vecchia]. The third, which renders judgments on the life and death of offenders, is called "Forty of the Criminal" [Quarantia criminal]. These forty men serving as "Criminal" judges, besides having the highest authority in the judgments of criminal or capital cases, are also admitted to the Senate and have the right to vote in that rank. Moreover, they have three chiefs at the head of their court, who are randomly selected every two months, and who in turn always sit together with the doge and the [ducal] councillors. These chiefs share the power to report to the Senate about any matter they wish, and also to the Great Council, by the procedure I mentioned above. And it is not without reason that these forty younger men are mingled

with the senators, who are generally elderly men: in this way the natural
lack of enthusiasm of the elderly is balanced by the ardour of the young.
These young men are present in much smaller numbers than the elders,
but there are as many as needed to demonstrate and add some traces
of ardour to the decrees of the Senate, which, at times, when discussing such matters, is extremely necessary. In addition, by conceding the
senatorial authority to the men of the Forty, the administration of the
Republic can appear to be shared in some respect by patrician citizens
of inferior rank, such as those who hold the office of the Forty Men. In
this way our ancestors seem to have made use of a kind of popular legal
practice. Indeed, a fixed remuneration has been allotted to patricians
on the three Courts of the Forty for each day they meet.[30] Therefore
it is extremely rare for rich citizens to apply for this office, and, if they
do so, they are likely to be rejected. But patricians of poor means, who
are nonetheless honourable men, have easy access to this office.[31] Thus
it happens both that the indigence of honourable men is cared for in
some respects, and that the administration of the Republic is entrusted
not only to rich and illustrious citizens. Such an arrangement would be a
feature of a regime of optimates [patricians] and the dominance of the
Few, although in small respect, the patricians of inferior rank share in
the governance of the Republic – a practice typical of the popular order
of the Many. From this it is evident to anyone that in every part of the Republic, as we said at the very beginning of this work, our ancestors strove
above all to combine that mixture of a popular order[32] with a regime of
the optimates, and yet with such a well-designed balance that elements
of the patrician regime are in greater number. I think that I have said
enough about both the officers of the Avogaria and the Forty judging

---

30 They were in fact the only magistrates to receive a regular salary for their work.

31 Brian Pullan notes that Contarini "had every reason to be acquainted with the problem of noble poverty" (1971, 229). Pullan goes on to note that Contarini was also
aware of the potential for poor nobles to be exploited for electoral and related *brogli*
by politically ambitious patricians due to one simple fact: that "no matter how ignobly
poor, a nobleman over twenty-five enjoyed a vote in the Great Council which elected
to the highest magisterial offices; and as Sanudo wrote censoriously in 1519: 'if anyone want honour, he now has to give money to certain poor noblemen, known as the
Swiss.' Considerations of this kind may well explain the high priority which Contarini
accorded to the poor of noble origin or *poveri vergognosi*" (230–1). In his earlier book
De officio episcopi, Contarini had written on the spirit of charity and made several practical recommendations on the subject of poor relief, which, he argued, should first be
bestowed on persons of high social rank, that is, the poor of noble origins. See also
Pullan 1960, 1964.

32 I.e., the patrician members of the Great Council, including the poor nobles.

the capital cases, who have been assigned to deal with more significant crimes, either for the type of offence or the status of the offenders.

Now time requires me to touch briefly on some inferior officers in charge of punishing offences and illegal acts that are less important, either because of their nature or the status of those involved. These officers are of two types. The first type have jurisdiction over capital cases, and the second do not; their power extends to dealing with the basest of men and prostitutes. These are ordered to be whipped or thrown into prison, according to how their crimes are assessed.

The office that can inflict capital punishment is more powerful, and this again is divided into two distinct types: judges who investigate crime and those who summon the defendant to trial and pronounce the sentence. The judges of the first type – that is to say, the heads of the Lords of the Night Watch [*signori di notte*] – conduct the preliminary investigation of the defendant's case and put down in writing what the witnesses have said, as well as what the defendants have confessed to the judges, either spontaneously or under torture. Finally, they refer the whole case to the judges of the Proprio.[33] These magistrates differ from those of the first type, and they pronounce sentence when the case involves a capital charge. For if the crime is of minor importance, so that it is deemed enough that the defendant should be whipped or kept in prison for a few months, then the heads of the Lords of the Night deal with the whole case and do not consult the Court of the Forty – regardless of whether they wish to throw someone in prison or summon him to trial. Not even an attorney of the Avogaria holds this right: he must first consult the Forty and rely upon the authority of a ruling of that council. And this, it seems, has been established not without an excellent reason. If the Forty were to be consulted for every crime [misdemeanour] whose defendants are miserable men, this would create extraordinary congestion in the administration of the Republic and the guilty people would be given more licence to commit crimes, thanks to a greater prospect of impunity. Therefore, as a way of making judgments of this sort quicker and shorter, the heads of the *signori di notte* are given this power as well, which the state attorneys lack.

There are six heads of the Lords of the Night, and six are also in that lower office that has the power to punish the basest men and the pettiest crimes. Those who hold this office are called the heads of the city's

---

33 As Patricia H. Labalme and Laura Sanguineti White (2008, 547) describe this office, it is "one of the oldest courts in Venice, with jurisdiction over dowry restitution, intestate succession, divisions between brothers and some property disputes." See also Glossary of Terms.

districts [*sestieri*], since from each *sestiere* (the whole city being divided into six *sestieri*),[34] both a head of the *signori di notte* and a head of the *sestiere* are elected. We usually employ the same practice as in the election of the ducal councillors, as we surely did not fail to mention earlier. Moreover, the duty of each office is to conduct vigils in their own *sestiere* on alternate nights. In turn, the head of the Night and the head of the *sestiere* (together with armed guards and sergeants) take turns patrolling their own *sestiere* until cockcrow, to prevent the perpetration of illegal acts under the darkness of night, which usually offers men more opportunities. This way, no burglar breaks into houses, or no thief prowls the streets and assaults anyone. In the beginnings of Venice – the origins of the city – both of these positions were held in great esteem. Subsequently, with the addition of new offices to the Republic as required by circumstances and convenience, their reputation and authority have dwindled. After greater power was transferred to new offices of magistrates, the little and more sordid affairs have remained the responsibility of older positions, as if to obscure the scum. At this point, though, enough has been said about the officials who decide the capital cases. In the next book, we will talk about the officials who decide civil cases.

---

34 For an elaboration, see Crouzet-Pavan 2002, 203, and 2013. See also earlier references in books 1 and 2.

BOOK 4

Magistracies of the Republic

In the Republic of Venice the practice has always been that no single magistrate possesses sole and final authority in important cases. This authority was deliberately assigned to a body of magistrates, or, in the common manner of speech, to councils. Furthermore, in civil law cases where the amount in question exceeds fifty-five gold ducats, judgment does not rest with a single magistrate. In fact, judgments can be appealed to the auditors of the civil cases, who are called in the vernacular "Old Civil Forty" [Quarantia civile vecchia], and to the councils of the Forty mentioned earlier.

I.

In order to clearly explain the whole system of civil cases, we begin by considering the auditors first. There are two types, the "new" or "recent" auditors [*auditori nuovi*] and the "old" auditors [*auditori vecchi*].[1] The "old" acquired their name because of the antiquity of the office, since this office is much older than the other, which was introduced in the Republic many centuries after the foundation of the city, when the city acquired dominion over the *terraferma*. In the judgments of civil cases, which are debated and decided by civil judges, these old auditors have almost the same authority held by the Avogaria magistrates. In most affairs, if the laws appear to be obstructed in any respect, the old auditors have the power to interpose a veto. Thus, when the civil judges pronounce a sentence against someone, this person is allowed to challenge their judgment and appeal to the auditors. The case is brought to their court, where it is disputed by the

---

1 Drawing on the work of a host of historians, Patricia H. Labalme and Laura Sanguineti White (2008, 546) identify the new auditors as "supervisory magistrates who traveled throughout the Venetian dominion, receiving appeals and judging the sentences of Venetian governors," and the old auditors as "intermediaries between courts of first instance in Venice and its lagoon, on one hand, and appellate tribunals, on the other." See also Appendix B, "Glossary of Terms."

contending parties. Then, if it does not exceed the total of fifty gold ducats and the judges agree on the sentence, they can resolve the matter without the Council of the Forty. But if the judges disagree – even if just one of them opposes it – the case is then argued in front of a minor council, composed of the auditors and three other judges who deal with decisions regarding found property. These minor causes are judged here. But if the whole case exceeded a total of fifty gold ducats, it was not possible before our time to bring the matter to the Court of the Forty unless one of the auditors had interposed a veto on the sentence given by the judges, and it had been referred to the judgment of the Forty. In our day, however, the person sentenced by the initial judges is allowed, after three months, even if none of the auditors has issued an injunction, to serve a summons on his adversary and appeal to the Court. This law has greatly diminished the authority of the auditors. But it still has some influence on settling the case, when they do interpose a veto. For there is no need to wait for three months, and their veto serves as a kind of prior verdict. If an auditor has interposed a veto, he serves a summons on the initial judges, and the Court of the Forty convenes. Previously it was the case that both magistrates would plead and defend their respective sentences before the Court.

Gradually, laxity led to the practice that not only do the initial judges whose sentence has been vetoed not plead, but they are not even present when the case is brought before the Forty. On a day appointed by a secretary, they formally reply that whatever the law requires should be ordained. On the other hand, the practice has been preserved until our time by which the auditors first report to the Forty about the case in which they have pleaded and on which they have interposed a veto. This practice, though, has largely fallen out of use, and only the advocates perform this duty and defend their clients' cases. As a result, the dignity of the office of the auditors, long pre-eminent, has been completely diminished and obscured today.

These Forty judges of civil cases observe almost the same procedure that is usually observed by the Forty of capital cases, as explained above. The only difference is that, in cases where the lives and properties of the defendants are at stake, the judges do not establish a fixed time for pleading. By contrast, in civil litigations a period of time is prescribed beyond which they cannot extend their pleas. In fact, only an hour and half is allowed for pleading. In the judgments of these civil cases, they do not report various opinions, so that the Court selects the one it prefers, in the way that usually happens when determining punishments for criminals and men of negligible value, as explained above. They only report whether the sentence given by the previous judges should be confirmed or repealed, and they report the repeal if any auditor has interposed an injunction. But if no veto has been interposed and the case has been referred to the Council without opposition, then once the case has been pleaded by both sides, the heads of the Court decide not on its repeal, but on whether to confirm the sentence given.

The judges proceed to vote under oath. In the familiar manner,[2] three urns are brought in. The green one is for repeal of what has been reported, the white for approbation, and the red is intended for those who are still uncertain and want the case to be deferred. No measure is considered decided unless more than half the judges have repealed or approved it. And if the judges are still uncertain and no judgment is made for either measure, they defer the case to another day, at which time almost the same procedure is repeated. And if on that day judgment still remains undetermined, the Court gathers for a third time, and the proceedings are once again repeated. Once the pleas for both sides end, the judges proceed to vote, but now there is little to no consideration for the undecided judges. Unless the votes end up tied, the judges decide on one side or the other: whether the given sentence should be repealed or confirmed. If the sentence is repealed, the pleader is not deprived of the right to repeat the trial, for in cases of a repeal nothing is established – the sentence is simply rejected. But after the confirmation of the sentence given by the prior judges, there is no longer room for an appeal, and the trial on the same issue cannot be repeated, unless something new emerges that is relevant to the case.

What has been said up to this point about the old auditors is sufficient. Now let us briefly talk about the newly created auditors [*auditori nuovi*]. This magistracy was not established in our Republic until Venetians began expanding onto the mainland bordering on the lagoon.[3] One can

---

2 As described in book 3.

3 This expansion to the *terraferma* is generally dated with the acquisition of Vicenza in 1404 and Padua in 1405. The expansion continued under Doge Foscari (1425–54) to include Peschiera, Brescia, and Bergamo. The most wealthy city of the Venetian empire seemed to be Brescia, which also turned out to be "Venice's most loyal city" (Bowd 2010). Historians disagree as to why Venice sought to extend its rule to the *terraferma*. Some historians (James Grubb and John Law, and Dennis Romano, for example) argue that it was an almost inevitable reaction to the aftermath of the war of Chioggia and the move was haphazard, "a not premeditated step ... an ad hoc response" (Romano 2007, 13–14), while others (for example, Gaetano Cozzi) see it as a deliberate and permanent strategy of conquest. For a contrary, negative view of the expansion, the work of Domenico Morosini, *De bene instituta re publica*, remains a good point of departure: see Finzi 1969 and Cozzi 1964,1970. For thoughtful reviews of the different interpretations, see Venturi 1979 and Appuhn 2009, 7, 75–7. Appuhn is persuasive, to me, when he notes that Venice's relationship with the *terraferma* is not easy to characterize for it "was emphatically not that of an imperial metropole to its colonial possessions" (7).

appeal to these judges concerning the judgments of the *podestà*[4] and those of the other magistrates who administer justice outside the city over the people who have come under our alliance [rule]. The old auditors could not handle both types of cases, that is, those inside and outside the city. For this reason this office acquired a new name, the office of the new or recent auditors. After the institution of the Republic, the dominion of the Venetians began to expand into the region of Venetum, which willingly and voluntarily went back to its old masters in a restoration of sorts [*postliminium*].[5] For, as we explained at the beginning of the work, the noblest men of the Venetum region, who had fled the barbarian invasion and the devastation of Italy, took refuge in our lagoon and founded this magnificent city. They gave it the plural name of *Venetiae* because of the number of people, and also in order to show posterity that the flower of the nobility of Venetum's cities had convened there. Thus, when the dominion of Venice increased to an enormous size in a short amount of time, a single office did not suffice for both domestic and foreign cases.

Therefore this new office was established, along with a new Court of Forty. Appeals to sentences made by judges outside of the city are also referred to these magistrates' benches, so all cases of this type are decided through debate. The magistrate and the Court follow the same procedure and method usually observed by the old auditors [*auditori vecchi*] and the older Court of Forty that adjudicate civil cases. Only one other right has been granted to the new auditors: in cases that do not exceed the total value of forty gold ducats, they can review a prior sentence that is being appealed and, if they so determine, they can repeal part of it and allow another part, as long as they reach common agreement. For this reason it has been arranged that foreigners (who, in the tradition passed down to us by the greatest philosophers, should be given particular attention) could avoid delay and conclude their lawsuits without excessive costs. The old auditors do not have this right. Indeed, they need either to approve a sentence, or to wholly reject it. Thus, whereas the new auditors can oppose part of the sentence, but not the rest, the old auditors can either oppose the whole of it, or leave it all as it is. In this way the lawsuits

---

4 A Venetian governor also known as a rector.
5 Contarini is describing the annexation of new territory to Venice as it were a restoration of lost property through the metaphorical reference to a notion of the ancient Roman law system, the *postliminium*. The legal term denoted the restoration of civil rights, or the recovery of property, temporarily lost or suspended during exile, capture, or analogous circumstances. I owe this point to the translator, Giuseppe Pezzini. For contrary views of annexation, see sources in note 3 and Grygiel 2006, on the constraints that land annexation posed to the geopolitics of Venice as a maritime republic.

of foreigners are settled in a shorter period of time than the cases of Venetians – although the cunning of advocates and jurists (which leaves nothing aside that is morally improper) may limitlessly protract any lawsuit, just as usually happens elsewhere in the world where judgments are not made arbitrarily, but follow constituted rules.

II.

Having explained the judicial system, a few things remain to be said about the magistrates who handed down the initial sentences in the civil cases, and from whose sentences appeals are made to the old auditors and the Council of the Forty. There are six benches of these judges, divided according to the type of case and the people involved. The various types of litigation concern commerce and merchants, houses and estates in the lagoon, properties and fields on the mainland, and matters of contracts. As for the litigants, they may be either citizens or foreigners, or cases of foreigners and citizens together. Finally, orphaned wards are sometimes the objects of litigation, and widows pleading the recovery of their dowries after the deaths of their husbands. Thus, in order to avoid confusion between judgments of such different kinds and thereby avoid impediments of one kind or another, various benches of judges have been appointed, so that – as far as possible – each person might appear for his litigation before the proper judges, according to the type of business and litigation involved.

Litigation [or lawsuits] pertaining to the houses or estates within the boundaries of Venice – i.e., those situated in the lagoon – are decided by the judges who are called "judges of properties" [*giudici del proprio*], and these are also the judges who are approached by the widows who want to recover their dowries from their deceased husbands' heirs. The judges of properties have acquired their name and appellation because our ancestors believed that only that which was situated within the lagoon was the property of their citizens so it is not property easily transferable to foreign ownership. And they decreed that possessions situated on the mainland, whether fields or houses, were to be called "mobile" – that is, things that could be easily taken away from owners against their will, and were more directly vulnerable to loss. If a quarrel arises about estates on the mainland, the parties can approach the "judges of the procurators" [*giudici del procurator*]. These judges also handle the matters of orphans under the care of their tutors. It is for this reason that these judges have acquired their name, for in Venice the curators and tutors are usually called procurators. Similarly, if a lawsuit deals with commercial enterprises and trading, they approach the benches of the judges who are

called the "consuls of the merchants" [*consoli dei mercanti*].[6] The judgments of the latter follow a more abbreviated procedure than the other
civil magistrates, so as to avoid prolonged litigations that would hinder
and delay the affairs of busy merchants.

If a litigation is between foreigners, or a citizen serves a summons on a
visitor, one needs to go to the "judges of foreigners" [*giudici del forestier*].[7]
All other cases concerning a contract in which someone claims that
someone else owes him something come to the "judges of the petitions"
[*giudici di petizion*]. These hold the role of the *podestà* of a city. In addition, there are minor cases, whose judgments are under the purview of
the "judges of movables" [*giudici del mobile*]. Besides these offices, there
is also another one that decrees, in the case of any item that has been
found that previously was hidden or lost, whether that object belongs to
the treasury, to some private citizen, or to the person who found it, and
this office decides about all other similar cases.

III.

Since we have described the system of judgments, we need to move on to
those magistrates who look after the treasury or who have been entrusted
with the administration of public revenue [*carmelenghi di comùn*]. It might
seem to some that these are more numerous than necessary, since fewer
magistrates could suffice for the whole business of the treasury.[8] But in
this regard, we must point out that our ancestors used extreme care to
prevent fraud from being perpetrated in the administration of public
finances, since the treasury, like nourishment, is responsible for overseeing the needs of every part of the Republic. If it runs short or is lacking,
the Republic itself would run short or be lacking. For this reason, they

---

6 Labalme and White (2008, 547) described the *consoli dei mercanti* as follows: "Magistrates having administrative and judicial competence in commercial disputes, including maritime matters, insolvency, exchange rates, private banks, insurance contracts,
   brokerage fees, and the production of woolen goods, silk and soap." The *consoli dei
   mercanti* were foundational institutions for the smooth work of trade and profit, as
   Contarini notes. More recently, Roger Crowley (2011) and Jane Gleeson-White (2011)
   offer vivid accounts of the importance of bookkeeping, trade, and profit for the sustenance of life and well-being in Venice as well as for the creation of modern finance.
7 *Giudici del forestier* was one of the oldest courts of law of the Republic of Venice. For an
   appreciation of the complexity of this world in law and practice, see Calabi 1999 and,
   more recently, Fusaro 2014.
8 In fact, the work of the *carmelenghi di comùn* was aided by other, more specialized magistrates in revenue (*governadori dell'intrade*), expenditure, accounts (*magistrati sopra i
   conti*), and controller of finance (*proveditor sora i danari*).

decreed that if a patrician were convicted of embezzlement, he would be perpetually branded with ignominy, and this would be noted every year. On the day appointed by a magistrate of the Avogaria, the Great Council is summoned, along with the gathering of all patricians. The names of those who have been condemned for that offence are read aloud, so that whoever dared to commit such a great crime pays the penalty of eternal shame. But let us not diverge too much from the topic.

The magistrates in charge of the treasury are of two classes, as are the public finances themselves. The money deposited in the treasury comes from either public revenues or dues; but in certain cases, when the income of the Republic does not seem to suffice for expenses, levies are imposed on patrician citizens on the basis of their wealth.[9] Inevitably, this is not a rare occurrence, given the wars, either on land or the sea, that have often afflicted our city. Our possessions have been attacked by the Turks, whose assaults we have sustained for many years – not without enormous losses – containing a most violent enemy that raged against the whole Christendom. Christian princes, who at times were jealous of the greatness of the Venetian empire, have also conspired for our ruin. This happened fifteen years ago, when almost all the Christian princes entered into a league and conspired for the destruction of our domain.[10] Divinely favoured, we checked their attacks, and the situation, though it had almost collapsed, was restored to its former state.

Since public money is divided into two classes, magistrates in charge of it are also divided into two types. Some are in charge of the money collected from citizens, while others are in charge of the revenues and dues of the Republic. These tributes are levied on goods that are exported and imported. Some are collected from the cities that are part of the Venetian empire. The dues of the city are far greater than anyone could ever imagine, both because of the abundance of merchandise and the gathering of merchants, and because of the multitude of people who live in this city. As the types of merchandise and goods differ, so too do the magistrates established to oversee them, according to how best they

---

9 This was the system of forced loans that dates back to at least 1207. Dennis Romano (2007, 75) notes that since these imposts were not technically taxes but loans to the state, shares in this funded debt paid interest and came to be treated like any other forms of property. A detailed analysis of the strengths and weaknesses of the system of forced loans can be found in Gleeson-White 2011. See also comments by F. Gilbert quoted in note 11.

10 A reference to the War of the League of Cambrai (1509–16) in which, as noted earlier, Venice managed to withstand the alliance made up principally of France, Spain, the Papal States, the Duchy of Ferrara, and the Holy Roman Empire.

seem to the officials in charge of arranging and levying taxes. It would be
tiresome to list them one by one; it would cause annoyance rather than
pleasure. For this reason, I will omit the magistrates that are not permanent but who are appointed as the situation requires.

In short, the duty of these magistracies is to prevent public money
from being either misappropriated by fraud or lost through negligence.
Controversies pertaining to this class of money are judged and handled
by them. They immediately remit all the money that they collect to the
governors of public revenues [*governadori dell'intrade*], as these magistrates are called. But since this responsibility is enormous, it is usually
conferred only on distinguished patricians. In order for such citizens
to willingly serve in this office and not refuse it, great benefits and high
authority have been added to this burdensome duty. These magistrates
nominate the attendants, the messengers, the guards, and all the other
officers of this type, who receive salaries from the treasury. The remaining money is remitted to the treasurers of the city [*camerlenghi de común*],
the office that receives the public money handed over by any chamberlain and magistrate. This applies to the collection of public money outside and inside the city. By decree of the Senate, the treasurers of the city
disburse money for public use, keeping track of what they receive and
expend. Such a duty is laborious and requires a considerable amount of
toil; it is customarily entrusted to younger patrician citizens who are distinguished by nobility of birth and integrity of conduct. This is done in
order to avoid public money being converted into private wealth. Treasurers have been accorded senatorial rights, almost the same as those
held by the elected senators.

The money levied on the wealth of patricians when the Republic is
in dire straits has yet another specific magistrate. Sometimes a Senate
decree is issued about the collection of money from private wealth in
such a manner that no mention is made either of the restitution of that
money, or of any other interests that may be granted as restitution to the
citizen from whose private wealth the state has taken a portion. This,
nevertheless, happens rarely. More commonly (or rather, always), the
Senate makes provisions to avoid such disregard of private wealth, unless
the situation requires otherwise.

When a decree of the Senate is promulgated for the collection of
money from private sources, and an appropriate time is fixed for payment, each patrician within that time period pays the sum he owes according to his wealth. The governors of revenues [*provveditori dell'intrate*]
remit it to the treasurers of the city. More often than not, the Senate's
decree regarding the collection of money from private wealth is made
in such a manner that, after a fixed period of time, it is returned to the

citizens with allowance for profit and interest. To that end, some fixed taxes are assigned to this, but before our time, a decree of the Senate on collecting money from private wealth made no mention of restitution, and nor was a fixed time established for that to occur. But the magistrate called the "prefect of loans" [*prefectus mutui*] – a name that has remained up until the present – received money from each patrician and recorded it in his books. Until the money was returned, five gold ducats for each hundred that had been collected, in lieu of taxes, were paid each year to the creditors, with taxes assigned to this purpose. In this way, during past wars, the exaction of money was easy and it was usually made from private wealth.[11]

One should not consider it unjust that citizens who had depleted or greatly diminished their family wealth for the sake of the Republic in times of need would be repaid from public revenues. As the parts must attend to the safety of the whole, so nature makes it evident that the whole takes care that the parts do not suffer great detriment. Instead, the whole, according to its strength, sees to it that the parts are unharmed and provided with nourishment, thereby restoring their strength and protecting their safety. In our own time, the debt of the Republic's levied money was so great that, as I said, almost 300,000 gold ducats were spent every year on interest disbursed to patricians. Payment was suspended in recent years because of the grave situation of the Republic. At last, four years ago, under the report of the distinguished senator Domenico Trevisan, wise and most honourable, and Senator Andrea Gritti,[12] under whose auspices as doge the Republic is currently governed, the Senate decreed that there should not thereafter be payments of yearly interest, and that money collected from patricians in that way would not be recorded in public ledgers. Lest patricians imagine themselves completely defrauded, however, numerous taxes and land possessions in the district of Rovigo[13] have been set aside for the reimbursement of their capital and the interest owed to them on it. I myself executed the greatest part

---

11 Felix Gilbert (1973, 288) suggests that Contarini may have been too optimistic: he notes that "tax morality in Venice, as in other city states, was low and the war [Cambrai] did not better it. One way to force payment was to publish names of delinquents in paying taxes, and when that was done the list of delinquents included some prominent and wealthiest members of the ruling group such as Andrea Gritti and Domenico Trevisan."

12 We met Gritti in book 2; and see also previous note.

13 The so-called Polesine of Rovigo, an area of the delta of the Po river, that Venice took possession of around 1484, after the War of Ferrara. The duchy of Ferrara continued to claim the area and, between 1508 and 1511 during the War of the League of Cambrai, annexed the territory, only to return it to Venice after the war.

of that task, while I was holding the office assigned to reduce and, if possible, extinguish this debt of the Republic. (Below I will say a few things about this.) This way, the majority of that great and almost unbelievable public debt was reduced, and the assets of private citizens were satisfactorily attended to, still in such a manner that the common good of the Republic continued to have priority over private interest. This is the norm that has been handed down from our ancestors until our times. But let us return to where our discourse digressed.

The chiefs of loans exact the money collected for the needs of the Republic from wealthy private citizens [patricians]. They receive it and record it in their books, and finally they remit it to the treasurers. The same chiefs exact from the treasurers the sum of money that used to be disbursed every year to patrician citizens instead of revenue. They used to record in their ledgers the money that they received and expended. At that time, money collected from patrician citizens as decreed by the Senate, and that must be reimbursed to them over a given period, was exacted and reimbursed by its own special magistrate. Nowadays, that entire task is entrusted to the Governors of Revenues [Governatori delle Entrate]. Besides these, there is another financial magistrate whom we absolutely cannot fail to mention, who devotes his energies to meticulously searching for patrician citizens who owe money and or who have not paid the amount charged to them according to their wealth. He confiscates their assets and eventually auctions them off. In addition to these, there are many other financial magistrates who seek indebted patrician citizens and examine their reckonings in public records, in order to prevent any fraud from being perpetrated against the public revenues and treasury. I will deliberately skip these magistrates in order not to bore the reader, for they are not relevant to the description of the Republic's government that I set out to provide.

IV.

Besides these magistrates, there are many others whose offices benefit the city and contribute to its citizens' living well and happily, and thus must not be omitted from our work. The first to enter our picture are the commissioners of gold and silver coins [*provveditori sopra ori e argenti*], which account for the transactions of Venetians both with foreigners and amongst themselves. Then there are the supervisors of the provision of grain, and the supervisors of the city's health [*provveditori alla sanità*], without whom it is impossible to live. In addition, there are the supervisors of the immense shipyard of the Arsenal, and also the urban officers [*pioveghi*] who have the responsibility of repairing streets, bridges, and other such structures; and these are most necessary. Finally, there is a most distinguished office, which the Venetians call "the procurators" of San Marco, which is the most beneficial office in our city.

There is no need to say much about the commissioners of the coins. Their duty is to prevent the silver and gold from being minted with less perfection and purity than the law establishes, and to make certain that the ducats weigh what is prescribed by law – a matter to which we have always given the most scrupulous attention. The Venetian ducats have always been, and still are, held in great value among barbarian nations, to say nothing of the Christian countries. For whereas all the other princes have minted silver and gold of lesser purity in order to more easily meet their expenses, our princes have, with great determination, always maintained the quality inherited from their ancestors.[14]

Magistrates in change of the provision of grain [*provveditori alle biave*] are most necessary to the city, since almost no grain is harvested from Venice itself, surrounded as it is by the vast lagoon and the city bursting with people.[15] Great care must be taken in the provision of grain, in order to avoid having the people – whose welfare our ancestors took into great consideration – struggle with the scarcity of grain and fall into famine. Three masters, holding office for sixteenth months, oversee the provision of grain to avoid the city falling into famine during the year. Their task is to ensure that the city never suffers a scarcity of grain. If it happens that they have reasons to fear this, they go to the doge and the Collegio, and discuss the matter with them to decide on a useful way to procure a plentiful supply of grain. Sometimes they work to establish a fixed payment from the treasury for those who transport wheat to Venice from the more distant provinces. Occasionally, they buy wheat at public expense from merchants who promise to deliver a certain quantity of grain within a fixed time and from particular provinces. If they do not bring the supply as promised, they are punished with a monetary fine. The Republic also sells cheaply what it has bought at a heavy price, in

---

14 In fact, the Venetian gold ducat was a sort of "world" gold standard from the 1300s to 1797 when the Republic was suppressed by Napoleon (Lane 1973, 148; see also Chambers and Pullan 2004, 461; Gleeson-White 2011, 50, 55).

15 For an in-depth analysis of the food industry, including the provision of grain, that served to nourish people in Venice, see Faugeron 2014. The importance of this study for Venice and more generally for economic history is emphasized in its introduction by Elisabeth Crouzet-Pavan. In his popular account of Venice as a city of fortune, Roger Crowley (2011, 147) sums up the more scholarly accounts this way: "Venice, the landless city [that] had always lived on import, had an unsurpassed understanding of food supply."

order to attend to the welfare of the people and to the lack of provisions, even if this sometimes causes considerable loss to the treasury.[16] There are many laws and excellent practices for the provision of grain. If I were to review them here one by one, I would digress from the topic much longer than is appropriate.

Next, there is the office tasked with looking after the health of the city [Magistrato alla sanità]. Its main duty is to prevent infectious diseases from creeping into the city. And if ever a disease does creep in unnoticed, which sometimes happens,[17] the health magistrate applies himself to preventing it from spreading further. Some very spacious houses have been built in the lagoon, three miles away from the city, and close by are some most luxuriant gardens.[18] When a common person exhibits the first symptoms of disease, he is immediately brought with his whole family to these houses. Those who have had any interaction with a sick person need to abandon their homes so as not to infect others, and withdraw to other public housing built outside the city for this purpose, in an area far away from the previous place. Here they are retained for forty days. If during this period they remain healthy, they are allowed to return to the city and their homes. Great care is also taken with the household furniture, to avoid anyone's being infected by contact with it. Moreover, the Sanità office makes sure that nothing that is rotten or that can harm public safety is put on sale. Finally, the office sees to it that living in Venice is healthy.

This class of officials was established not long before our time. Previously, the city was often struck by pestilence, to the extent that at a certain point almost everyone would leave their homes because of the raging disease, and withdraw to the nearby mainland. But since this responsibility was assigned to this new magistrate, and with the protection of divine favour, there has been almost no pestilence. Obviously, sometimes some houses are infected, which cannot be avoided when a large

---

16 At one point, after the completion of this work, Contarini supervised the grain trade as a head of the Council of Ten. See also book 2:34 and note 2 on the same page.

17 Stephen D. Bowd notes that Contarini makes no reference to the serious outbreak of typhus and plagues that struck the city in 1528–9 (1998, 160). Joanne M. Ferraro notes that there were fourteen outbreaks of plague in the roughly seventy years between 1456 and 1528; the plagues of 1575–7 and 1630–1 were particularly ferocious, each decimating between 25 and 30 per cent of the population (2012, 145, 157, 177). For a very informative study of plague hospitals and the specific social, political, and comparative contexts in which they operated in Venice, see Jane L. Stevens Crawshaw 2012.

18 There seems to be no available historical evidence to support Contarini's claims of "spacious houses" and "luxuriant gardens."

multitude of men from all parts of world flock together. Yet thanks to the care of this magistrate, and the help of God, the disease has not been able to spread further.

V.

Now we have to talk about the magistrates of the immense shipyard the Arsenal.[19] This is not only a great ornament to the city of Venice, but also adds considerable lustre to the whole of Italy. It is a gigantic workshop, most worthy of admiration, conveniently built in an area of the city close to the open sea. It was created by excavating three docks, or, if you prefer, compartments. Inside these, the sea enters through a single opening wide enough to fit and accommodate large galleys. The entrance is fortified with towers on both sides, joined by a bridge of beams and grid gates that are kept shut unless it is necessary to lead galleys in and out of the shipyard. There is no other way to access the interior of the shipyard except by passing through this portal. The first dock inside is the smallest of the three, but it is still very large. It is constructed in the guise of a warehouse, with roofing and walls encircling it on all sides. The galleys are hauled there from the sea, and, if circumstances do not require their

---

19 The Arsenal (from the Arabic *Dar al-Sina*, place of industry) was established in 1104. By the time Contarini was writing, the Arsenal had more than doubled in size (to an area covering twenty-four hectares) and was probably the largest industrial plant in the world, with a high degree of specialization, division of labour, innovation, and entrepreneurship. The Arsenal captured the imagination of Europeans over time, most probably aided by Dante's reference in his *Divine Comedy*. Dante visited Venice in early 1321, and the visit inspired him to evoke the image of the Arsenal in the twenty-first canto of the Inferno, to explain the punishment reserved for swindlers, the immersion in boiling pitch. Dante's visit to Venice is generally viewed as the cause of his death: in his travels Dante contracted malaria that killed him in Ravenna in September 1321 (see www.venetoinside.com/hidden-treasures/post/the-footsteps-of-dante-in-venice/). For modern accounts of the importance of the Arsenal for Venice as a maritime and commercial republic, and the environmental expertise that Venetian artisans and skilled craftsmen used to harness timber to build its great naval and merchant ships, see in particular Appuhn 2009; Trivellato 2008; Davis 1991; Lane 1966a, 1973; and the by now classic studies by Giorgio Bellavitis 2009 and Ennio Concina 1984. Appuhn may be worth quoting: "in contrast to the aristocratic knowledge being produced by northern European institutions, Venetian bureaucratic expertise had a decidedly republican flavor. The Venetians were by no means egalitarian – only the patrician officeholder could mount the rostrum in the Ducal Palace to deliver reports and receive applause – but to a far greater extent than other early modern states, Venice actively sought to take advantage of the technical skills and knowledge of artisans and skilled craftsmen" (2009, 204). For more general accounts of technology and artisanal guilds, see Epstein and Prak 2008, 1–24, and Trivellato 2008.

use, they remain intact and undamaged there for many years, protected from the wind and storms. In the same hangar, new ships are built, and old ones are repaired. This is an exceptional work, a great source of lustre, and most useful for shipbuilding.

Beyond this dock, there is another interior one, of greater size, constructed with an encircling hangar [roofing], with the same roofing described above. This area usually holds two galleys if the bays are wide or just one if they are narrow. The third dock is no smaller than the second; it was added to the previous one not long ago, and is enclosed by splendid walls. Many hangars or canopies have been built inside it, although they have not yet been completed in every part; they [workers] are working with great zeal in order to give the final touch to that construction. One enters these three compartments in succession on a single route. They are enclosed by a single wall with several towers, where guards keep vigil at night to prevent damage from afflicting such a remarkable work, whether due to the fury of arson, the scheme of a criminal, or some other cause, as may happen. Within the walls there are vast halls filled with sailing-gears, where shipwrights have their workshops for all types of things that pertain to ship work. Metal is cast here for the manufacturing of artillery and a great quantity of powder is produced for artillery use.

To make a long story short, there is nothing that pertains to ship work that is not found in the shipyard. Here one can observe a great multitude of workmen, each doing his own job. There are many rooms of considerable size, holding a vast quantity of weapons for war – that is to say, artillery and cannonballs. There is also a great amount of sails, oars, and every sort of gear stored there, each in its own chamber. In this way, if the Senate mobilizes the fleet, all that is necessary can be ready and prepared. An office is in charge of all the equipment and works, which is what we began by describing.

Everything that pertains to ship work is managed by this magistrate and the attention of his office. He chooses the craftsmen, both those working with wood and with metal, and all the other workmen who must be admitted to perform their services. He takes utmost care that no one fails to attend to his job. Public money is disbursed to this office to sustain the expenses of the shipyard, but not before consultation with the Collegio and a report of the expenses to the treasury [i.e., *carmelenghi del comùn*]. At the time of our ancestors, who held maritime affairs in great esteem, this office was greatly admired. In our age, the dignity of this office has diminished, and has almost entirely disappeared. Thus, in a crisis, if something requires particular attention, the Senate puts other patrician citizens and senators in charge of the shipyard – men of the highest reputation, who are given authority over the previous magistrates while retaining their assistance.

VI.

Our last task is to review the procurators of Saint Mark, which apart from the doge is the most distinguished office of all.[20] Procurators have no fixed term, but their term of office is for life. Perpetual senatorial dignity is attached to this post, accompanied by the right to vote with elected senators. Moreover, the procurators, exceptionally among other magistrates, have acquired another important privilege. Senior patrician citizens do not have precedence over others except in certain places and in certain seats; by contrast, this honour is granted to the procurators in every circumstance. Indeed, wherever they sit, they are always accorded precedence, and always honoured with a more dignified seat, just as if they were performing the duty of their office wherever they are. One of their duties is the tutelage of the orphans, who, being underage, cannot manage their own affairs and have not been assigned a guardian after the death of their father. These magistrates are appointed by the Republic as public tutors of a sort.

They are called procurators of Saint Mark because their duty requires outstanding faith and exceptional integrity. Their office is entrusted to patrician citizens who have gone through almost all the steps of a public career and who are of manifest probity. In office, they obtain the perpetual right to administer to the Republic, like soldiers who have earned a reward for a lifetime of service.

In earlier times, the reputation of this office was so great, not only in Venice but also in other nations, that many foreigners – not to mention natives – named procurators in their will as guardians of their heirs and of their whole family wealth. A great quantity of the money that is disbursed to the poor is entrusted to their good faith – so that, in our times, great resources are administered by this office and distributed at their will to the benefit of the indigent. The office was first established to prevent the inheritances of patrician citizens who were killed in foreign nations while defending or expanding the Republic, or who

---

20 Chambers and Pullan 2004, passim, and Labalme and White 2008, passim, draw on the diaries of Marin Sanudo to present sketches of the election and activities of some procurators in Renaissance Venice.

died abroad while trying to increase their wealth with business or commercial enterprise, from being fraudulently misappropriated or stolen from their underage heirs in the absence of a will. The result has been that this care is publicly entrusted to patrician citizens whose probity is evident to all.

In the beginning, three patricians exercised the office of procurator. As the city grew, three others were added, yet divided so that the earlier positions are responsible for the young wards living on the nearer side of the Grand Canal that flows through the centre of the city. Similarly, three procurators look after those who have their home on the farther side of the Gran Canal. Thus the first looks after one half of the city, and the second after the other half. Besides these, there are another three who are patrons of the magnificent and majestic church dedicated to Saint Mark the Evangelist, under whose protection the Republic of Venice has been blessed with good laws, and its dominion has grown to the size of an empire. The name of this class of magistrates derives from this last type of procurators, procurators of San Marco, inasmuch as it is considered to be of a most noble rank.

I do not have to add anything about the structure of this church [Saint Mark] – the plenitude of marble and columns, the porphyry and jasper stone, the mosaics and gold-plating, which cover the ceilings and all the vaults, and have been laid on the very floor.[21] There is almost no one who does not know this from having seen it, or has not heard its fame. These three procurators are charged with the upkeep of the church, in case some parts deteriorate in any way, as well as with supervising its clergy so that they venerate God with the devotion and solemnity required by the eminence of the city and the dignity of its patron, Saint Mark the Evangelist.

These are, in my judgment, the magistrates who above the others must be considered the most essential for living well and happily. For the care of minting money should never be neglected, since the commerce of citizens depends on it, as well as the solicitous provisioning of grain. Nor should one give any less care to the health of the citizens, and to the repair of the streets, bridges, and similar kinds of structures. These are tasks common to every city. Other concerns are, however, more characteristic

---

21 For a discussion of the role that the church of San Marco (with its rich collection of mosaics, sculpture, metalwork, and reliquaries going back to Roman and Byzantine times) played in the political, ceremonial, and religious life of the republic, see Maguire and Nelson 2010.

of Venice; that is to say, the concern for sea matters and the protection of orphans, since many citizens perish abroad while others end their days in public affairs or commercial activity. Thus, the magistrates devoted to these tasks are publicly instituted. If one pays careful attention to the way the Republic is constituted, it is clear that our ancestors did not neglect anything for the sake of the common good.[22]

---

22 A point he also made, among others, in his repeated references to Aristotle through-out, and in book 2 when discussing who should be charged with caring for the com-mon good.

BOOK 5

Magistracies beyond the City, the Army, and Civic Institutions

Now that we have expounded almost the whole system of the Republic's government, and examined the institutions of the city, it will not seem inappropriate or unrelated to my work if I discuss the magistrates outside the city – that is, those who govern the cities that have joined our alliance.[1] We will then turn to the command of the army, and finally to the institutions of citizens who are not of noble rank. Once I describe these institutions, I will give the final touch to the work.

I.

Four magistrates are in charge of the more distinguished cities to have entered into the league with the empire of Venice. Though one *podestà* administers justice to all, deciding on the civil litigations and proceedings against criminals, he does have some legal experts as assessors and avails himself of their counsel. Besides him, there is a captain [*capitanio*] who is in charge of the soldiers who live in the city or the countryside nearby. The *podestà* has no authority over these soldiers; only the captain has. The latter is responsible for the fortress, the walls, and the city gates, as well as the taxes and all the revenues of the city and the countryside alike. There are one or two chamberlains. Their office administers, pays, and exacts public money, and holds the records of public accounts. A chamberlain does little without the orders of the *podestà*, and sometimes he acts with the order of both the *podestà* and the captain. This system of administration is more practical than putting the civil authority and

---

1 Lewkenor refers to these cities as "under the subjection of the state of Venice" (1599, 126). The judgment of modern historians tends to be more nuanced than that of Contarini, Morosini (ed. Finzi), and Lewkenor. For the general context, see Chittolini 1991 and Cozzi 1982; more directly, see, e.g., Bowd 2010; Mallett and Hale 1984; Muir 2000; O'Connell 2009; and Romano 2007, passim. See also notes 3 and 5 in book 4.

the administration of the treasury in the hands of the same person, for in such a system it would be easier to embezzle funds from the treasury. Money that remains over and above the charges of the province is brought to the treasury in Venice, which – as we said above – receives the public monies collected from all areas.

The fourth magistrate in each city is the guardian of the castle. In some places, there is just one; in others, several. They command the soldiers who defend the castle, and are in charge of the weapons, provisions, and artillery stored there for defending against enemies. The authority of the guardian of the castle is not absolute, and he is subject to the command of the captain-general, to whom the authority and power over things like this are assigned. But in the minor towns and cities there is no captain, and there the *podestà* fulfils both roles. In the villages, frequently found in the countryside around the major cities, there is only a *podestà* who administers justice, with no magistrate other than him. The treasurers and captains of the principal cities have jurisdiction over the whole countryside.

It is possible to appeal to the new auditors [*auditori nuovi*] regarding the sentences the *podestà* gives. At one time the state attorneys had veto powers to set aside the capital sentences of the *podestà*. But since the judgments were frequently protracted and the criminals did not pay for their crimes and misdeeds, the Council of the Ten passed a law according to which the state attorneys would no longer have the right to veto sentences pronounced by the *podestà* with the assistance of the legal experts that normally accompany them (as I explained above).

I have said enough about the officers who staff the institutions of the Republic both inside and outside the city. However, one has to take into account not only the making of peace, but also of war. As Plato says in the *Statesmen*,[2] those who completely neglect war will not be able to preserve peace for long. Those who instruct future generations about the direction that the constitution of a republic might take recommend that citizens should be trained for both tasks. While performing their functions well under the laws and customs of their fatherland, they gain the skills for making war and for living peacefully at home; they embrace both activities so as to channel the virtues and skills of war into the tasks of peace, which is a more important matter. Such is the force of nature that it covets what is convenient to itself, resists what is contrary, and strives as much as possible to protect itself from injury. And this is most clearly evident in the nature of the living being, which is the most perfect of all.

---

2   This is the dialogue by Plato commonly translated in English as *Statesman* (in Latin *Politicus*), lines 304–10 (Jewett translation).

Every living being has been endowed with an appetitive faculty, by which it pursues what is consistent with its nature. Besides this, each one has been given an irascible faculty (which Plato placed in the heart and the breast),[3] so that any living being, driven by the spurs of that virtue, repels what is contrary and uncongenial to its nature. The civil man must nurture the virtues of both parts (the seeds of which nature has sown in the hearts of men), bring them to maturity, and thus be ready to make both peace and war. This concern was not neglected by our ancestors, as some people tend to think.[4]

Since the city was built from the very beginning on the sea, for many years it shied away from extending its reach to the mainland, and from getting involved in land wars. Instead, it directed all its energies to maritime warfare. And in this it achieved notable exploits, both in defending its liberty and in taking revenge on its enemies. History records many great and glorious deeds of the Venetians, who have triumphed in defeating their enemies and vanquishing their fleets. From these triumphs it would be easy to show that in earlier times Venetians greatly surpassed others in maritime affairs.

Finally, after a long time, the judgment of the higher council [in Venice] was won over by the entreaties of neighbouring nations, who could no longer tolerate the tyranny of their petty rulers,[5] which they had suffered for many years. The Senate turned its attention to *terraferma*, expelled the tyrants, and, while the citizens were rejoicing, recovered the whole Venetum region, as though it had never been fragmented [*postliminium*].[6] The region went back of its own accord to its old inhabitants, having driven away the foreign tyrants who, emerging from the remnants of the barbarians, had settled in the region and held the people in harsh servitude. This way, Venice extended its dominion over the mainland, endeavoured to give the people new to our league the advantage of good laws and the benefits of peace, and thereby allowed them to defend and preserve the freedom they had regained.

Venice's location in the midst of a lagoon does not allow our citizens to dedicate their energies to land wars and be detained by that occupation without great danger of civil disturbance and tumult. It would require

---

3 This is a reference to "*thumos*" or passion. In the *Republic*, book 4, Plato divided the constituent parts of the human psyche into *nous*, "intellect," *thumos*, "passion," and *epithumia*, "appetite."

4 A veiled criticism of some of his fellow patricians, and possibly of Machiavelli, who was sharply critical (and arguably jealous) of Venice. See also Bowd 2000b, esp. 406 and note 3, and 420–6.

5 Contarini here repeats the common explanation in his time for the extension of Venetian rule over *terraferma*. See also notes 3 and 5 in book 4.

6 See book 4, note 5.

patricians who devoted themselves to conducting land wars to spend a great part of the year on the mainland, breeding horses and training in land fighting. Moreover, free of warfare at home, they would need to venture abroad to gain experience in the art of war, so as to accustom their spirits as well as their bodies to perform that task with merit and in the service to the fatherland. If they did not do that, they would certainly be incompetent, not only as military leaders but also as soldiers. At the same time, their frequent interaction with the mainland and absence from the city would easily give rise to a faction of citizens who were disconnected from the rest. Venice itself would doubtless fall into dissension and civil strife.

In saying this, I have not even mentioned the arrogant thoughts and mischiefs that would have arisen in the minds of the patricians if they had become powerful in arms and commanded a large number of attendants – since it is human nature to incline to the worse. This, as can be easily evinced from ancient accounts, always troubled the Roman Republic: it caused several Roman citizens to defy the laws and the decrees of the Senate, and, in the end, made Julius Caesar a tyrant of the empire. To prevent a plague of this sort from creeping into our city, our ancestors decided that it would be more appropriate to defend the dominion on the mainland with foreign and mercenary soldiers, rather than with Venetians. Provincial taxes are set aside for the cost, since it is fair that troops who are summoned to defend the region should be maintained at its expense. Many allies of our league were assigned to this army, a good number of whom reached the highest rank, and, as a result of their splendid deeds, were rewarded with Venetian citizenship and noble ranks. In our time, the fame of Bartolomeo Colleoni of Bergamo lives on, a most distinguished man and captain-general, who fought in many famous wars and enlarged the empire of Venice. For this reason he was honoured by the Republic with an equestrian statute in a renowned part of the city.[7]

The patricians of Venice were thus deprived of gaining the glory of land wars, consigning that honour to foreigners. The law forbids a Venetian gentleman to command more than twenty-five soldiers. Yet, because of the frequency of wars we face, this law has in practice been abrogated in our own time. When war is imminent, many patricians of higher rank

---

7 The mounted statue of Colleoni (d. 1475) by Andrea del Verrocchio is in the piazza
   next to the Scuola di San Marco and *not* in the piazza before Saint Mark's basilica,
   as Colleoni had willed. A description of Colleoni as a *condottiere* and his equestrian
   statue as a work of art may be found in Wills 2001, 62–5. On the role of *condottieri* in a
   comparative perspective, see Lane 1973, 231–4. Lane recalls that "Florence was a more
   than once . . . tricked by her condottieri; Machiavelli's wounded patriotism added
   vitriol to his denunciation of these mercenaries" (232).

are sent to the army to perform a temporary duty according to the duration and urgency of the war. They serve as treasurers and legates [*provveditori*],[8] and always accompany the captain-general of the army, who is a foreigner and has no authority to do or decide anything without the advice of the legates. Once war ends, each magistrate returns home and surrenders his rank and authority. This is the way that war is conducted and the land army is organized in Venice.

Our city is by nature best suited to sea warfare and naval combat, activities to which the Venetians have always applied themselves. For a city that sits on the sea does not have much to fear from land troops that would come to bring it trouble. It would have been not only unjust but also very inconvenient to muster an army of citizens, transport it to the continent, and wage war against neighbouring nations. Since the most likely attacks to fear would come from the sea and would not be difficult to repel, the whole city devoted its energies to sea affairs, and designed the education of young people for that purpose, strengthening it with practical experience [or the experience of life].

The education of gentlemen has always been, from a very tender age until puberty, to spend time under the tutorship of school masters, learning Latin according to one's capacity. After that age (with the exception of the few who, driven by talent or natural disposition, devoted themselves to the study of letters), all of them apply themselves to the affairs of the sea and their family. Some sail to distant shores, where they work in commercial activities to increase their family wealth, while gaining knowledge of the customs, habits, and laws of men. Many would embark on war galleys, and, from a young age, strengthen their bodies through physical toil and cultivate their minds in sea matters and expertise in naval combat. Venetians have always excelled in these arts. Moreover, a law that has survived until this day prescribes that two youths of noble rank would serve in every armed galley, and in doing so would earn a decent wage at public expenses. Their duty is none other than to acquire the skills and experience in matters pertaining to the sea.[9] To achieve this easily, certain tasks would ordinarily be assigned to them so that they would gain experience and make progress towards undertaking greater tasks. Eight young patricians are sometimes assigned to the greater galleys, where they are trained for the fleet and the challenge of war, or assigned to private citizens engaged in in commercial activities. These

---

8 A reliable and learned discussion of the role and work of *provveditori* who accompanied the armies in the field is in Mallett and Hale 1984.

9 Though this law survived, by Contarini's time it was no longer applied with force and rigour.

young men earn quite a good salary (either from public revenue, or, in the case of ships allocated for commerce, from private funding) while they gain experience in naval and war studies. The law also imposes this duty on the ships of private patricians that are used for public utility, so that the individual ship owner must, from his own funds, pay a salary to one or two young patricians (two if the ship is of considerable size) whose only duty is to acquire experience in naval tasks. These young men are also allowed to carry a certain amount of merchandise on the transport-galleys and private ships to which they have been assigned, without having to pay passage-money. And if they do not have anything to carry, they may sell and transfer this right to other people.

This law provides not only for the training of young people, but also allows patricians of little means, distressed by the scarcity of family wealth, to do the same. It is therefore obvious that our ancestors did not neglect the education of the young, as some people believe, for the salutary effect of this law is that more than two hundred patricians are trained in war-like exercises at the expense of others. In addition, all young noble men, according to the customs of Venice and the practice of the Republic, apply themselves to learning or to the seafaring and maritime discipline. In this way, they greatly benefit themselves, and, to no small extent, the family business as well. These ancient laws and practices still continue in our own time, although many young men, corrupted by ambition or luxury since the expansion of the empire, have neglected their country's institutions. In addition, the number of patricians has increased so much, and so many have become poor due to war and expenses at home, that there are more who need assistance than the law provided for.

Nature has disposed things in such a way that nothing can be permanent among men. No matter how perfectly things seem to have been originally constituted, after some years go by, everything experiences the crumbling deterioration of nature and stands in need of repair. Just as a body that has been sated with its midday meal cannot remain sound unless dinner follows some hours later, it is necessary to bring sustenance and renewal to a declining nature.[10] With the help of God, we too imitate

---

10 In a discussion of Venice's forest bureaucracy, Appuhn (2009, chap. 6, esp. 247, 251–66) draws attention to how forest as well as water shaped Venetians' ideas about the proper relationship between humans and the natural world, setting them apart from northern European views about nature and humans. Whereas Venetians had "an organic understanding of the natural world as a living entity possessing active agency" (simultaneously fragile but manageable), northern Europeans, including Locke, tended to have "a mechanistic view of nature as inert matter subject to the managerial whims of its human masters" (247, 252; see also Appuhn 2000). For a more general discussion, Crouzet-Pavan's (2002, 2000, 2013) research remains fundamental.

this process, and will devise some remedy. In this respect, nothing is lacking in our Republic – but enough has been said about this matter. Now we go through the officers [magistrates] who are in charge of our ships and navies at sea.

II.

Every galley prepared for war has a senior patrician [*virum patritium*] as its captain who has absolute power in that galley, except for the power to punish with death. Just like in a land force where a centurion or the captain of a squadron is responsible for his men, so the galley captain takes care of the sailors and all the things in his galley, which make up its equipment. Every year, even if there is no need, the Venetians arm galleys to protect the sea for seafarers and secure it from pirates. This practice offers safe navigation to honest men who transport their goods without doing harm to anyone. Besides the captains of the galleys, there is a legate over the whole navy, who has power over the entire fleet, including the galley captains. He is like a *provveditore* of the army, and, unless the captain-general of the sea is present, he has both the authority to impose the death penalty and to direct the navy wherever he prefers.

This magistrate in charge of the armed galley is almost always appointed in a time of peace. If circumstances require that the Republic should prepare a grand fleet, then they appoint a captain-general who has high and pre-eminent authority in the fleet. He is also put in charge of the maritime provinces with as great an authority as that possessed by the dictator in the Roman Republic, apart from the fact that in every matter he obeys the authority of the Senate and the decrees of the Republic. However, he is invested with the highest authority over the fleet, the captains, the legates of the fleet, and also over the *podestà* and all the officers who have authority and who exercise a public function in the islands and the maritime regions. So great is his power that, when the captain-general of the fleet arrives in a city, the clergy must immediately approach him and offer him the keys to the gates and the fortress, while the authority of the *podestà* ceases during that time, and it becomes possible to appeal all sentences of magistrates to the captain-general. If he so wishes, he can administer justice and dispense public monies on his own – in short, he alone has authority over all. There is in Venice no other magistrate with higher authority, and therefore it is very rare for a captain-general to be appointed unless the situation absolutely requires it. A power so tremendous that everything depends on the will of a single citizen is not bestowed without very good reason.

At this point we cannot fail to mention a law according to which the captain-general, the *provveditore*, or fleet captain cannot enter the city of Venice with armed galleys – not even when he returns home. As soon as he approaches Istria, a province about one hundred miles from the city, he is required by law to pay and dismiss the sailors. In the past, it was customary at that point for a few people to bring the galleys to Venice, and leave them in the shipyard [the Arsenal] under the canopies built for that purpose, where they would be protected from the winds and rains. Nowadays, this law is not observed the way it was at the time of our ancestors.

We have now examined almost all of the Republic's offices. Our ancestors, however, added to them, like a crown or a top, magistrates we usually call syndics [*sindici*], a vernacular word derived from a Greek noun. We refer to them as "recognitors,"[11] a name that is perhaps new, but appropriate to clarify the function of that office. These are usually appointed for four or five years, and are sent to the mainland as well as the islands and maritime regions of our empire [*terraferma* and *Stato da mar*]. They review the acts of all the *podestà* and other magistrates who have held public positions outside the city. And they can open proceedings against these with almost the same authority as that bestowed on the officers of the Avogaria. For, as Aristotle[12] wisely says, such is our human disposition that those who are in power do not conduct themselves well unless they are checked by another authority. We have now reviewed all the offices held by patricians, which administer the Republic of Venice both inside and outside of the city. It remains to show the way in which our ancestors, the wisest of men, retained the support and confidence of the common people and the multitude.

III.

It is certainly something hard to believe, indeed scarcely credible, that for so many years the multitude, though deprived of a place in government, has never yet refused or been unwilling to support the government of the patrician citizens. Nor has it ever plotted to change the constitution

---

11 Modern historians of Venice refer to them as syndics. Monique O'Connell (2009) shows the structures, processes, practices, and laws that Venice employed to maintain its vast overseas holdings. Chapter 6 of her work focuses on syndics, prosecutions, and scandals, pointing out that in spite of corruption and a gap between ideology and practice, "the Venetian state as a whole governed effectively and with a great deal of stability" (119).

12 *Politics*, books 3 and 4.

of the Republic and thereby gain access to public power. The multitude has always shown itself to be most fond of, and obedient to, the nobility.

Truly, if anyone pays attention not just to the aptness of the site for the defence of the city, but also to our moderation and temperance in governing, he will realize that the multitude has not been completely excluded, for it has shared in the offices and charges that could be entrusted to it without detriment to the common good. He will thus easily discern that in this Republic there has been an equilibrium [or moderation] missing in other communities, both ancient and modern. He will realize that popular riots have always broken out in the others, which eventually overturned every other republic.[13] By contrast, in this city of ours there have never been, for the aforementioned reason, popular riots or sedition by the people – even though, as I said in the beginning, it was necessary to exclude the people from the governance, if the Republic were to be rightly constituted.

In this respect, our ancestors not only followed the authority and reasoning of the greatest philosophers, but also imitated Sesostris, that most ancient legislator of the Egyptians. Sesostris – as shown by Aristotles in *Politics*[14] – instituted that there should be a rank distinction between, on the one hand, soldiers defending the country and citizens deliberating over the public good and exercising justice, and, on the other hand, peasants, craftsmen, and labourers. Still, such a statute could easily lead to the overthrow of a republic, unless one introduced that temperance [balance] in governing that our ancestors wisely instituted.

Thus, in Venice it was constantly ensured that justice was equal for all, and that no one could perpetrate an offence against anyone with impunity, not even to someone from the lowest plebs;[15] for a noble man to offend

---

13 No doubt Contarini was familiar with the history of Florence and how it was portrayed with varying degrees of like (Guicciardini) and dislike (Machiavelli). For that history in a comparative perspective with Venice see, e.g., Giannotti [1540] 1840; Gilbert 1968; Rubinstein 1968. Stephen D. Bowd (2000b) traces the politics and political ideas from 1525 to 1530 of both Venice and Florence, in the wider concern for the defence of liberty. In his renowned history of the Renaissance, Jacob Burkhardt contrasted Florence, "the city of incessant movement," with Venice as a city of "apparent stagnation." There is something to Burkhardt's claim, but it is not the whole story, as Martin and Romano (2000, 15) observe, for Venice, "despite its appearance of stability, was a city of constant change in both its internal social arrangements and its relation with the outside world." For an analysis of Machiavelli's Florence as "a great and wretched city," see Jurdjevic 2014.

14 Book 7, chap. 10, 1329.

15 For a view that argues the opposite, that is, that the judicial system was skewed against the commoners and in favour of patricians, see Ruggiero 1980. For an assessment of Ruggiero's analysis, see Cohn 1981.

a man of the people has always been considered a sacrilege and a terrible crime. And if some reckless patrician ever dared to perpetrate anything of this sort, he knew that he could not get away with it with impunity. In fact, the greater was his reputation or dignity, the greater was the penalty.

Moreover, the Senate attends with great diligence both to the annual provision of grain, and to the plenitude of everything that contributes to the well-being of the patrician citizens and the common people, to that extent that it sometimes disburses a great quantity of public revenue to keep the city from suffering famine. Everyone can evince this from what we said above, when we were dealing with the matter of grain and public health inspectors [*provveditori*]. And these are surely the two main demands that peoples make of the governors of cities: that is, to live comfortably with an abundance of possessions, and to not be at the mercy of powerful citizens who could offend them. If these conditions are granted, people carry on with their business without troubling others.

Our ancestors did not neglect anything related to these two demands. Rather, in many splendid ways they took pains to attend to the people's welfare, and to the indigence of those men who nonetheless busy themselves in honourable activities useful to the Republic, or who once did so but can no longer fulfil their duty because of age or frailty of health. For countless houses have been built in Venice, quite suitable and appropriate for living, which are given for free to these kinds of men; they can live there with their families until the end of their lives without expending their family wealth. Consider also that in the enormous shipyard [Arsenal],[16] which holds the status of a separate town, there are more than a few men who, though they do nothing either because of old age or some injury, still receive stipends and yearly allowances in recognition of the fact that, when they were in their prime of life, they fulfilled their duty in the construction of galleys or in some similar work useful to the Republic. According to an ancient statute, in the [contracts of] purchase and sale of precious goods, both the buyer and the vendor pay a fixed tax on the value of the goods in question, which is assigned to the poor sailors who have become too old for their work. All these excellent statutes give the common people a hand in the administration of the Republic. In addition, there are now several other laws, which – in my opinion – were wisely established by our ancestors to benefit these men, in proportion to their condition, while satisfying the ambition and desire for honour that is implanted in the minds of all, without thereby detracting from the government of the nobility.

---

16 We met the Arsenal in book 4.

The entire people are divided into two social orders:[17] some are of higher rank, while others belong to the lowest plebs, such as artisans and those kinds of men whom Aristotle in *Politics* considers similar to civic servants. In my opinion, both groupings have been attended to, neither unsuitably nor unjustly. Plebians, who by nature do not concern themselves with honour, but rather devote themselves to the pursuit of family wealth, have been granted their own rights and their own honours. They are divided into as many groups as the number of crafts [arts] they spend their lives practising;[18] each group has its own laws, under which they practise their trade. Several men, elected by votes from the whole group, lead them, and it is appropriate to call them leaders of their craft. On their orders, many things are prescribed, and many small disputes resolved. As a result, master artisans who have been granted such authority are gratified by that function and are convinced that they have attained no small dignity, being considered worthy of a position of leadership by men of their class. In addition, there are in each group several other lesser positions that are, nevertheless, held in high esteem. In this way the desire for honour, which seems to be implanted even in the minds of plebeians and the lowest populace, is satisfied and provided for. The upper order, people of higher rank, is more honourable in Venice and also has a more honourable status. Particular offices – honourable and respectable – are assigned to them; the men of noble rank are debarred from them and do not have access to them in any way.[19] There are many offices of such kind, which all the same could not give reason for complaints even to a noble man, given their salary and title of honour.

The order of the secretaries, who assist all magistrates, is the most honourable. This office is only given to men of the people, never to a noble man. Although this office is not illustrious, it is nevertheless honourable. Public records and ledgers recording every matter, private and

---

17 Brian Pullan (1999, 152) observes that Contarini "wrote of a binary division of the residents of Venice": noblemen who were free and people who were servile, enslaved by the need to earn a living. After recalling that others before and after Contarini preferred to recognize a three-tiered ranking (patricians, citizens, and the common people), Pullan notes that Contarini eventually admitted that there were people and people: some were the best respected sort of common people who could be distinguished from the very base common folk engaged in manual work.

18 There were roughly one hundred trade guilds in Venice. For analyses of the role of these guilds in a comparative context, see Mackenney 1987 and Iordanou 2016.

19 A reference to the legally defined status group in Venetian society known as the *cittadini originari*, who composed about 5 per cent of the Venetian population (Romano 1987, 29). See also Introduction, and Pullan 1971.

public, are entrusted to the reliability and diligence of these secretaries.[20] Anyone considered worthy of this task deserves to hold a reputation for being an excellent, honest, and industrious man, and he receives great praise among men. To many of these clerks, an emolument has been assigned that is sufficient not only to preserve their patrimony, but also to augment it.

Those who serve as secretaries of the Senate are from the class of *cittadini originari*, and never from the nobility. This order of administration is more prestigious than the general one, and therefore the office is usually held by *cittadini originari* who are of more honourable birth. They receive good salaries from the treasury, and they are privy to all proceedings of the Senate. They are always present at the deliberations of the Great Council and the Senate, and for this reason they are held in great esteem by the people. From this group, a good number are selected who assist the Ten; they record their acts in the books and are privy to the knowledge of everything done by that council. They hold this office for life, and there is no alternation – as there is in the case of noble men who hold offices, none of which are permanent apart from those of the doge and procurators.

The secretaries to the Senate are also all plebians [i.e., *cittadini* below the patricians]. One secretary, above the rest and held in the greatest of honour, is called the Chancellor of Venice.[21] Every patrician citizen gives way to him, with the exception of the procurators. The chancellor knows all the secrets of the Republic. A great emolument is assigned to him from the revenue of the Republic, and when he dies, he is honoured with a funeral oration. No one in the city of Venice is usually granted this honour apart from the doge or some other extraordinarily worthy citizen (who is "out of the game" – as people say). Apart from these, the honour of a funeral oration is not conferred on anyone else; it is as if the grand chancellor is the doge of the people. This is the only chancellor created in the sessions of the Great Council. All the secretaries are elected by the Ten, and are subject to their censure if they do wrong in the offices they hold.

All the other popular assemblies, such as the guilds of artisans, the leaders of each trade, and several others that I will mention below, depend on the judgment of the Council of Ten and are subject to its authority. They were instituted from the beginning by the authority of that

---

20 Translated in the modern social science idiom of trust and reciprocity, they were fiduciaries of the trust of state officials, that is, patrician rulers.
21 We met the office of grand chancellor in book 3.

council and are under its control. And it was wisely established that the Council of Ten takes precautions so that these associations, instituted for the public good, do not plot against the Republic under the pretence of their office. Indeed, the Ten was originally established as a precaution against this disease, that is, to prevent a conspiracy of evil citizens from perpetrating something against the Republic.

Furthermore, five societies[22] have been created in Venice under the spiritual protection of certain saints, which include countless men from both the plebeian and noble ranks. Each of these has its own livery and emblems, which they do not always wear everywhere, but only when they parade together to honour a member's death or for some similarly solemn function. They usually gather every holiday: first they attend to the sacred mysteries, then they go and visit the churches of their saints to venerate God the Almighty with supplications and solemn pomp. Each of these societies has its own particular house, with a spacious hall where members gather on appointed days to pay homage to their faith. At times they celebrate the sacred rites, and at other times they visit the church of a saint; often they honour the obsequy and funeral of a deceased brother, when one of them has ended his days. They make atonement for his sins with repeated mass prayers. Besides these spacious halls, each of the houses has an appointed chamber in which the leaders of the confraternities assemble. This is an annual meeting, and of no small dignity among the plebeians. The leaders gather together and take counsel about the things to do; they do not fail to attend to the good of the society. Likewise, a large sum of money to distribute to the poor is also entrusted to their responsibility. In times past, these societies were held in great esteem, so that many people, who made testamentary dispositions to distribute their wealth to the poor, appointed fraternal officers as executors, under whose pronouncement the money would be disbursed. As a result of this, some of these confraternities, thanks to the copiousness of resources they must disburse every year for those purposes, are equal in every respect to the procurators of Saint Mark, a most eminent and noble office. Noble men do not have access to this position, that is, the leadership of these societies, even though they are counted among the brothers. This dignity can be conferred only on men of the people, so that in this respect the people imitates the nobility.

---

22 The first of these, the *Scuola di Santa Maria della Caritá*, was founded in the second half of the thirteenth century. By Contarini's time, there were five so-called *scuole grandi* and hundreds of smaller ones known as *scuole minori*. There is a growing literature on these confraternities as mutual aid societies; the works of Brian Pullan (1971) and Richard Mackenney (1987, 1997) remain basic references on the topic.

In order to prevent these confraternities and their leaders from bringing any harm to the Republic, they are supervised by the Ten: they cannot introduce any change, or gather beyond the appointed times, without that council's permission and authority. These honours have been established in our Republic for the men of the people who belong to both orders,[23] so that they were not completely deprived of a share in public administration and civil functions. This system aimed to make the provision of responsibility adequate to their own desire and ambition for honour, ensuring that they did not resent or trouble the order of the nobles.

IV.

With this balance of government, our Republic has been able to achieve what none of the ancient ones did, however illustrious they were. Indeed, for two hundred years, from its very beginnings until our time, the Republic has remained secure not only from the domination of foreign men, but also from significant civil sedition. And this has not been achieved by force, armed garrisons, or a well-fortified citadel, but rather by a just and balanced system of government, such that the people obey the nobility of their own accord and do not wish for any revolution, while retaining a strong affection towards the nobility. And this became apparent in our age. Indeed, all the Christian princes conspired for the utter destruction of Venice's very name. Our army had been routed in a great defeat by King Louis of the French at Cassano, a village in the countryside of Cremona. On one side the Germans were threatening, and on the other side the pope, Julius Romanus, and almost all the mainland regions had defected from the Venetian empire. In that critical situation, the Venetian people, although distressed, did not plot against the nobility, to the point that everyone tearfully offered themselves and their properties for the defence of the Republic – and actually did so in practice.[24]

---

23 Contarini here is not very clear, but by "both orders" he refers to the two orders of plebians and *cittadini* below the patriciate.

24 The events alluded to here occurred in the early stages of the War of the League of Cambrai (see also book 4, note 10). On 14 May 1509, the forces of Louis XII annihilated the main Venetian army in what historians call the Battle of Agnadello, then also known as Vailà, named after the village or place near Cassano. The league's forces subsequently overran most of Venice's territory in northern Italy. In July, however, the Venetians regained control of Padua and successfully resisted an attempt to retake the city by siege (15–30 September). In *The Prince*, Machiavelli noted that in this battle in one day Venice "lost what it had acquired with so much trouble over eight hundred years" (2016, 77). Machiavelli spoke too soon. See also Gleason 2000 and Muir 2000.

The city of Padua was recovered without any trouble because of the extremely good disposition of the inhabitants towards us, even though the Emperor Maximilian had besieged that city with a huge army, gathering supporting forces from everywhere. A vast number of citizens, not only nobles but also of the plebeian order, went of their own accord to defend that city, together with soldiers hired at their own private expense. They accomplished a splendid result in that campaign, so much so that the emperor was forced to withdraw the army without attempting to conquer the city. The greatest challenge having been met, the other cities were also recovered amid the enthusiasm of the peoples seeking refuge from a foreign emperor in the safe harbour of Venice. Surely, this is proof of a just dominion, when one rules over willing subjects.

And if one reflects carefully, he will easily reckon that there is a reason why this has occurred. For every city that has come into the allegiance of the Venetian empire maintains its own laws,[25] and the citizens in each city obtain many honours. Furthermore, several villages situated in the countryside around those cities are governed by the citizens of those cities who hold offices there. Add to this the fact that the *podestà* of the prominent cities, when they administer justice, are assisted by legal experts, whom they consult before taking decisions. This is not a small honour, for which they receive a sizeable recompense. These types of offices may not be filled by noblemen of Venice, but are selected either by the population of the Venetum or, usually, from the allied cities. From this, it can be understood easily that in this Republic the balance that seems to best imitate the nature of things has been introduced. For in the body of a living being, the function of seeing and looking is assigned only to the eyes. The other, less noble functions are left to the other members, which are deprived of the faculty of seeing, but must obey and not dissent from what their eyes communicate to them, nor direct themselves anywhere other than where their eyes direct them. The whole body is structured and maintained in such a way. In a similar manner, in the Republic of Venice the totality of the government is entrusted to the noble order, as though they were the eyes of the city, while the less noble offices are entrusted to the rest of the population. The Venetians live most felicitously as a well-organized body, since the eyes of the Republic do not look after themselves only, but after all the members. And the other parts of the city not only take care of themselves, but also obey these eyes most willingly, as if they were more powerful members of the Republic.

---

25 For the local and interprovincial dynamics this autonomy generated among locals within the republic, see the cases of Friuli discussed in Muir 1993.

And if some republic reaches that level of insanity – as happens in the majority of them – that the people wish to take on the task of seeing and so usurp the office of the eyes, it is inevitable that the whole republic will be immediately overthrown. Or, on the other hand, if the noble citizens only look after themselves, and neglect the other members of the city, then the people will become enraged to the ruin of the nobility and the Republic's situation will undoubtedly worsen and degenerate.

By imitating nature, our ancestors made provisions against both harms. They applied such moderation that no one, other than someone with bad intentions, could find reasons to criticize such a rightful and lawful institution. We pray for God the Almighty to preserve it safely for a long time. For, if one can believe that anything good for men derives from God the Immortal, it must be considered most certain that this has happened to the city of Venice by divine intervention.

References

Primary Sources

Contarini, Gasparo. 1525. *Relazione di Gasparo Contarini ritornato ambasciatore da Carlo V. Letta in Senato a di 16 November 1525*. Rome: Biblioteca Italiana, 2005.
– 1543. *La Republica e i magistrati di Vinegia*. Edited by Vittorio Conti. Florence: Centro Editoriale Toscano, 2003.
– [1543] 1571. *De magistratibus et republica Venetorum*. In *Gasparis Contareni Cardinalis Opera*. Paris: apud Sebastianum Niuellium.
– [1571]. *The Office of a Bishop* [*De officio viri boni et probi episcopi*]. Edited by John P. Donnelly. Milwaukee: Marquette Universit Press, 2002.
– 1599. *The Commonwealth and the Government of Venice*. Edited by Lewes Lewkenor. London: John Windset.

Secondary Sources

Acemoglu, Daron, and James A. Robinson. 2012. *Why Nations Fail: The Origins of Power, Prosperity and Poverty*. New York: Crown.
Achen, Christopher H., and Larry M. Bartels. 2017. *Democracy for Realists: Why Elections Do Not Produce Responsive Government*. Princeton: Princeton University Press.
Appuhn, Karl. 2000. "Inventing Nature: Forests, Forestry, and State Power in Renaissance Venice." *Journal of Modern History* 72: 861–89.
– 2009. *A Forest on the Sea: Environmental Expertise in Renaissance Venice*. Baltimore: Johns Hopkins University Press.
Aristotle. 1962. *Politics*. Edited and translated by Ernest Barker. New York: Oxford University Press.
Bagehot, Walter. (1867) 1968. *The English Constitution*. Oxford: Oxford University Press.

Bellavitis, Anna. 1983. "Serenissima a numero chiuso: Il diritto di cittadinanza a Venezia tra XIV e XV secolo." *Storia e cultura* 12: 62–7.

– 2004. "Ars mechanica e gerarchie sociali a Venezia tra XVI e XVII secolo." In *Le technicien dans la cité en Europe occidentale 1250–1650,* edited by M. Armoux and P. Monnet, 161–79. Rome: Ecole Française de Rome.

Bellavitis, Giorgio. 2009. *L'Arsenale di Venezia: Storia di una grande struttura urbana.* Venice: Marsilio.

Bevilacqua, Piero. 2009. *Venice and the Water: A Model for Our Planet.* Solon: Polar Bear.

Bizzarri, Dina. 1916. "Ricerche sul diritto di cittadinanza nella costituzione comunale." *Studi Senesi* 32: 19–136. http://www.rmoa.unina.it/4615/1/Bizzarri-Ricerche_diritto_cittadinanza.pdf.

Bouwsma, William J. 1968. *Venice and the Defense of Republican Liberty.* Cambridge: Cambridge University Press.

– 1973. "Venice and the Political Education of Europe." In *Renaissance Venice,* edited by J.R. Hale, 45–66. London: Faber and Faber.

Bowd, Stephen D. 1998. "The Contemplative in Action: Vincenzo Querini, Gasparo Contarini and the Shaping of Politics in Renaissance Italy." Doctoral diss., University of Edinburgh, Edinburgh.

– 2000a. "The Republic of Ideas: Venice, Florence and the Defense of Liberty, 1525–1530." *History* 85, no. 279 (July): 404–26. https://doi.org/10.1111/1468-229x.00154.

– 2000b. "'The Tune Is Marred': Citizens and People in Gasparo Contarini's Venice." *European Review of History* 7, no. 1: 83–97. https://doi.org/10.1080/713666729.

– 2010. *Venice's Most Loyal City: Civic Identity in Renaissance Brescia.* Cambridge: Harvard University Press.

Branca, Vittore. 1998. *La Sapienza civile: Studi sull'Umanesimo a Venezia.* Florence: Olschki.

Brennan, Jason. 2017. *Against Democracy.* Princeton: Princeton University Press.

Buchan, Bruce, and Lisa Hill. 2014. *An Intellectual History of Political Corruption.* London: Palgrave Macmillan.

Burke, Peter. 1980. "How Venice Worked." Review of *Politics in Renaissance Venice* by Robert Finlay. *London Review of Books* 2, no. 21 (6 November): 22.

– 1994. *Venice and Amsterdam: A Study of Seventeenth Century Elites.* Cambridge: Polity.

Calabi, Donatella. 1999. "Gli stranieri nella capitale della republica Veneta nella prima età moderna." *Melanges de l'école française de Rome* 111, no. 2: 721–32. https://doi.org/10.3406/mefr.1999.4665.

Casini, Matteo. 1991. "Realtà e simboli del cancelliere grande veneziano in etá moderna (Secc. XVI–XVIII)." *Studi Veneziani* 22: 195–251.

– 2002. "Fra Città-stato e Stato regionale: Riflessioni politiche sulla Repubblica di Venezia in età moderna." *Studi Veneziani* 44: 15–36.

Chambers, David, and Brian Pullan, eds. 2004. *Venice: A Documentary History 1450–1630.* Toronto: University of Toronto Press.

Chittolini, Giorgio. 1991. "Statuti e autonomie urbane: Introduzione." In *Statuti città territory in Italia e Germania tra medioevo ed età moderna,* edited by Giorgio Chittolini and Dietmar Willoweit, 7–45. Bologna: Il Mulino.

Chojnacki, Stanley. 1972. "Crime, Punishment and the Trecento Venetian State." In *Violence and Civil Disorder in Italian Cities 1200–1500,* edited by Lauro Martines, 184–228. Berkeley: University of California Press.

– 1988. Review of *The Venetian Patriciate: Reality versus Myth* by Donald E. Queller. *Journal of Modern History* 60 (September): 599–602. https://doi. org/10.1086/600422.

– 2000. "Identity and Ideology in Renaissance Venice: The Third *Serrata.*" In *Venice Reconsidered. The History and Civilization of an Italian City State, 1297– 1797,* edited by John Martin and Dennis Romano, 263–95. Baltimore: Johns Hopkins University Press.

Ciriacono, Salvatore. 2006. *Building on Water: Venice, Holland and the Construction of the European Landscape in Early Modern Times.* New York: Berghahn.

Cohen, Thomas V. 2008. "Obey and Applaud." Review of *Information and Communication in Venice: Rethinking Early Modern Politics* by Filippo de Vivo. *London Review of Books* 30, no. 11 (5 June): 19–20.

Cohn, Thomas. 1981. Review of *Violence in Early Renaissance Venice* by Guido Ruggiero. *Journal of Social History* 15, no. 2 (Winter): 298–301. http://www. jstor.org/stable/3787117.

Concina, Ennio. 1984. *L'arsenale della Republica di Venezia: Tecniche e istituzioni dal medioevo all'età moderna.* Milan: Mondadori.

Connell, William J. 2000. "The Republican Idea." In *Renaissance Civic Humanism: Reappraisals and Reflections,* edited by James Hankins, 14–29. New York: Cambridge University Press.

Conti, Vittorio. 2002. "The Mechanization of Virtue: Republican Rituals in Italian Political Thought in the Sixteenth and Seventeenth Centuries." In *Republicanism: A Shared European Heritage,* vol. 2: *The Values of Republicanism in Early Modern Europe,* edited by Martin van Gelderen and Quentin Skinner, 73–83. Cambridge: Cambridge University Press.

Coryat, Thomas. 1905. *Coryat's Crudities.* Vol. 1. Glasgow: James MacLehose and Sons.

Cozzi, Gaetano. 1963–4. "Cultura politica e religione nella 'pubblica storiografia' veneziana del '500." *Bollettino dell'Istituto di Storia della Società e dello Stato Veneziano* 5–6: 215–96.

– 1970. "Domenico Morosini e il '*De bene instituta re publica.*'" *Studi Veneziani* 12: 405–58.

- 1973. "Authority and the Law in Renaissance Venice." In *Renaissance Venice*, edited by J.R. Hale, 293–345. London: Faber and Faber.
- 1982. *Repubblica di Venezia e gli Stati italiani: Politica e giustizia dal secolo XVII al secolo XVIII*. Turin: Einaudi.

Crawshaw, Jane L. Stevens. 2012. *Plague Hospitals: Public Health for the City in Early Modern Venice*. London: Routledge.

Crouzet-Pavan, Elisabeth. 2000. "Toward an Ecological Understanding of the Myth of Venice." In *Venice Reconsidered: The History and Civilization of an Italian City State, 1297–1797*, edited by John Martin and Dennis Romano, 39–66. Baltimore: Johns Hopkins University Press.

- 2002. *Venice Triumphant: The Horizons of a Myth*. Baltimore: Johns Hopkins University Press.
- 2013. "Venice and Its Surroundings." In *A Companion to Venetian History, 1400–1797*, edited by E.R. Dursteler, 25–46. Boston: Brill.

Crowley, Roger. 2011. *City of Fortune: How Venice Won and Lost a Naval Empire*. London: Faber and Faber.

Darnton, Robert. 1990. *The Kiss of Lamourette: Reflections in Cultural History*. New York: W.W. Norton.

Davis, Robert. 1991. *Shipbuilders of the Venetian Arsenal: Workers and Workplace in the Preindustrial City*. Baltimore: Johns Hopkins University Press.

de Vivo, Filippo. 2007. *Information & Communication in Venice*. Oxford: Oxford University Press.

- 2011. "How to Read Venetian *Relazioni*." *Renaissance and Reformation* 34: 25–59.

Donnelly, John P. 2002. Introduction to Gasparo Contarini, *The Office of a Bishop*. Milwaukee: Marquette University Press.

Dursteler, Eric R. 2013. "Introduction: A Brief Survey of Histories of Venice." In *A Companion to Venetian History, 1400–1797*, edited by Eric R. Dursteler, 1–24. Boston: Brill.

Epstein, S.R., and Maarten Prak. 2008. "Introduction: Guilds, Innovation and the European Economy, 1400–1800." In *Guilds, Innovation and the European Economy*, edited by S.R. Epstein and Maarten Prak, 1–24. Cambridge: Cambridge University Press.

Fasoli, Gina. 1958. "Nascita di un mito." In AA.VV., *Studi Storici in onore di Gioacchino Volpe per il suo 80°*, vol. 1, 447–79. Florence: Sansoni.

Faugeron, Fabien. 2014. *Nourrir la ville: Ravitaillement, marches et metiers de l'alimentation a Venize dans les derniers siecles du moyen age*. Rome: Ecole Française de Rome.

Febvre, Lucien, and Henri-Jean Martin. 2010. *The Coming of the Book: The Impact of Printing, 1450–1800*. London: Verso.

Ferraro, Joanne M. 2012. *Venice: History of the Floating City*. New York: Cambridge University Press.

Finer, S.E. 1997. "The Republican Alternative: Florence and Venice." In *The History of Government from the Earliest Times*, vol. 2: *The Intermediate Ages*, 950–1023. Oxford: Oxford University Press.

Fink, Zera S. 1940. "Venice and English Political Thought in the Seventeenth Century." *Modern Philology* 38: 155–72. https://doi.org/10.1086/388471.

– 1945. *The Classical Republicans: An Essay in the Recovery of a Pattern of Thought in Seventeenth Century England.* Evanston: Northwestern University Press.

Finlay, Robert. 1980. *Politics in Renaissance Venice.* New Brunswick: Rutgers University Press.

– 2000. "Fabius Maximus in Venice: Doge Andrea Gritti, the War of Cambrai and the Rise of the Habsburg Hegemony, 1509–1530." *Renaissance Quarterly* 53 (Winter): 988–1031.

Finzi, Claudio, ed. 1969. *De bene instituta re publica.* By Domenico Morosini. Collectanea Caralitana. Milan: Giuffrè.

Florio, Maria Stella. 2009. "'So Flourishing a Commonwealth': Some Aspects of Lewkenor's Translation (1599) of Contarini's *La Republica e i magistrati di Vinegia* (1544)." Doctoral dissertation, Università Ca' Foscari, Venice. http://hdl.handle.net/10579/976.

– 2010. "Gasparo Contarini e la traduzione inglese del suo trattato sulla repubblica di Venezia (1543)." *Ateneo veneto* 197, 3rd series, 9 (2): 83–122.

Fortini Brown, Patricia. 1987. "Honor and Necessity: The Dynamics of Patronage in the Confraternities of Renaissance Venice." *Studi Veneziani* 14: 179–212.

– 1991. "The Self-Definition of the Venetian Republic." In *City States in Classical Antiquity and Medieval Italy*, edited by Anthony Molho, K. Raaflaub, and Julia Emlen, 511–27. Ann Arbor: University of Michigan Press.

Fotos, Michael A. 2017. "Public Goods and the Diagnosis of Counter-Intentional Policy Outcomes." In *Institutional Diversity in Self-Governing Societies: The Bloomington School and Beyond*, edited by F. Sabetti and D. Castiglione, 213–38. Lanham: Lexington.

Fragnito, Gigliola. 1969. "Cultura umanistica e riforma religiosa: Il 'De officio boni viri ac probi episcopi' di Gasparo Contarini." *Studi veneziani* 11: 75–189.

– 1983. "Contarini, Gasparo." In *Dizionario Biografico degli Italiani*, vol. 28, edited by Alberto M. Ghisalberti, 172–92. Rome: Istituto della Enciclopedia Italiana.

– 1985. "Aspetti della censura ecclesiastica nell'Europa della Controriforma: L'edizione parigina delle opera di Gasparo Contarini." *Rivista di storia e letteratura religiosa* 21: 3–48.

– 1988. *Gasparo Contarini: Un magistrato veneziano al servizio della cristianità.* Florence: Olschki.

Freeland, Chrystia. 2012. "The Self-Destruction of the 1 Percent." *New York Times Sunday Review*, 14 October. https://www.nytimes.com/2012/10/14/opinion/sunday/the-self-destruction-of-the-1-percent.html.

Fusaro, Maria. 2014. "Politics of Justice/Politics of Trade: Foreign Merchants
    and the Administration of Justice from the Records of Venice's *Giudici
    del Forestier.*" *Melanges de l'Ecole Française de Rome* 126, no. 1. https://doi.
    org/10.4000/mefrim.1665.
Gaeta, Franco. 1961. "Alcune considerazioni sul mito di Venezia." *Bibliotheque
    d'Humanisme et Renaissance* 23, no. 1: 58–75. http://www.jstor.org/
    stable/20674246.
–   1981. "L'Idea di Venezia." In *Storia della cultura veneta: Dal primo Quattrocento
    al Concilio di Trento,* vol. 3, edited by G. Arnaldi and M. Pastore Stocchi, 565–
    641. Vicenza: Neri Pozza.
Gaille, Marie. 2005. "L'ideale della costituzioni mista tra Venezia e Firenze: Un
    aristotelismo politico ambiguo." *Filosofia politica* (April): 63–76.
Giannotti, Donato. (1540) 1840. *Libro della Repubblica de' Viniziani.* Venice: Col
    Tipo del Gondoliere.
Gianturco, Elio. 1938. "Bodin's Conception of the Venetian Constitution and
    His Critical Rift with Fabio Albergati." *Revue de littérature comparée* 18: 684–95.
Gilbert, Felix. 1967. "The Date of the Composition of Contarini's and
    Giannotti's Books on Venice." *Studies in the Renaissance* 14: 172–84. https://
    doi.org/10.2307/2857166.
–   1968. "The Venetian Constitution in Florentine Political Thought." In
    Florentine Studies, edited by Nicolai Rubenstein, 463–500. London: Faber and
    Faber.
–   1969. "Religion and Politics in the Thought of Gasparo Contarini." In *Action
    and Conviction in Early Modern Europe: Essays in Memory of E.H. Harbison,*
    edited by T.K. Rabb and J.E. Siegel, 90–116. Princeton: Princeton
    University Press.
–   1973. "Venice in the Crisis of the League of Cambrai." In *Renaissance Venice,*
    edited by J.R. Hale, 274–92. London: Faber and Faber.
Gilmore, Myron. 1973. "Myth and Reality in Venetian Political Theory." In
    Renaissance Venice, edited by J.R. Hale, 431–44. London: Faber and Faber.
Gleason, Elisabeth G. 1988. "Reading between the Lines of Contarini's Treatise
    on the Venetian State." *Historical Reflections* 15: 251–70.
–   1993. *Gasparo Contarini: Venice, Rome and Reform.* Berkeley: University of
    California Press.
–   2000. "Confronting New Realities: Venice and the Peace of Bologna, 1530."
    In *Venice Reconsidered: The History and Civilization of an Italian City-State, 1297–
    1797,* edited by John Martin and Dennis Romano, 168–84. Baltimore: Johns
    Hopkins University Press.
Gleeson-White, Jane. 2011. *Double Entry: How the Merchants of Venice Created
    Modern Finance.* New York: Norton.
Gordon, Scott. 1999. *Controlling the State: Constitutionalism from Ancient Athens to
    Today.* Cambridge: Harvard University Press.

Greif, Avner, and Joel Mokyr. 2017. "Cognitive Rules, Institutions and Economic Growth: Douglass North and Beyond." *Journal of Institutional Economics* 13, no. 1: 25–52. https://doi.org/10.1017/s1744137416000370.

Griffith, Elizabeth. 2004. "Venice: The Model Turned Upside Down." Paper presented at the European Business History Association 2004 Conference, Barcelona, 16–18 September.

Grubb, James S. 1986. "When Myths Lose Power: Four Decades of Venetian Historiography." *Journal of Modern History* 58, no. 1: 43–94. https://doi.org/10.1086/242943.

Grygiel, Jakub J. 2006. *Great Powers and Geopolitical Change.* Baltimore: Johns Hopkins University Press.

Hale, J.R. 1971. *Renaissance Europe 1480–1520.* London: Fontana.

Halikowski Smith, Stefan. 2017. "Gasparo Contarini's Relazione of November 1525 to the Venetian Senate on the Divergent Dynamics of the Spanish and Portguese World Empires." *Mediterranean Historical Review* 32 (2): 189–235. DOI: 10. 1080/09518967.2017.1396764

Hankins, James. 2010. "Exclusivist Republicanism and the Non-Monarchical Republic." *Political Theory* 38, no. 4: 452–82. https://doi.org/10.1177/0090591710366369.

Harrington, James. (1656) 1992. The Commonwealth of Oceana *and* A System of Politics. Edited by J.G.A. Pocock. New York: Cambridge University Press.

Humphrey, Peter, and Richard Mackenney. 1986. "The Venetian Trade Guilds as Patrons of Art in the Renaissance." *Burlington Magazine* 128: 317–30.

Iordanou, Ionna. 2016a. "What News on the Rialto? The Trade of Information and Early Modern Venice's Centralized Intelligence Organization." *Intelligence and National Security* 31, no. 3: 305–26. https://doi.org/10.1080/02684527.2015.1041712.

– 2016b. "Pestilence, Poverty and Provision: Re-evaluating the Role of the *Popolani* in Early Modern Venice." *Economic History Review* 69, no. 3: 801–22. https://doi.org/10.1111/ehr.12131.

Jacobs, Jane. 1970. *The Economy of Cities.* New York: Vintage.

Jedin, Hubert. 1958. "Gasparo Contarini e il contributo veneziano alla riforma cattolica." In *La civiltà veneziana del Rinascimento,* edited by Diego Valeri et al., 103–24. Florence: Sansoni.

Jensen, K. 1996. "The Humanist Reform of Latin and Latin Teaching." In *The Cambridge Companion to Renaissance Humanism,* edited by J. Kraye, 63–81. Cambridge: Cambridge University Press.

Jones, Eric L. 1997. *The European Miracle: Environments, Economies and Geopolitics in the History of Europe and Asia.* Cambridge: Cambridge University Press.

Jurdjevic, Mark. 2014. *A Great and Wretched City: Promise and Failure in Machiavelli's Florentine Political Thought.* Cambridge: Harvard University Press.

King, Margaret L. 2014. *Venetian Humanism in the Age of Patrician Dominance.* Princeton: Princeton University Press.

Kirshner, Julius. 1973. *"Civitas sibi faciat civem:* Bartolus of Sassoferrato's Doctrine on the Making of a Citizen." *Speculum* 48, no. 4 (October): 694–713. https://doi.org/10.2307/2856224.

Koenigsberger, H.G. 1997. "Republicanism, Monarchism and Liberty." In *Royal and Republican Sovereignty in Early Modern Europe*, edited by Robert Oresko, G.C. Gibbs, and H.M. Scott, 43–74. Cambridge: Cambridge University Press.

Koh, T. 1998. "The Sixth SGH Lecture – Singapore: A New Venice of the 21st Century." Paper delivered at the 9th Annual Scientific Meeting of the Singapore General Hospital, Singapore, 26 April. http://annals.edu.sg/pdf/tkoh.pdf.

Labalme, Patricia H. 1984. "Sodomy and Venetian Justice in the Renaissance." *Tijdscrift voor Rechtsgeschiedenis/Legal History Review* 52, no. 3: 217–54. https://doi.org/10.1163/157181984x00114.

Labalme, Patricia H., and Laura Sanguineti White, eds. 2008. *Venice,* Città Excelentissima*: Selections from the Renaissance Diaries of Marin Sanudo.* Baltimore: Johns Hopkins University Press.

Lane, Frederic C. 1966a. "At the Roots of Republicanism." *American Historical Review* 71 (January): 403–20. https://doi.org/10.2307/1846339.

– 1966b. "Medieval Political Ideas and the Venetian Constitution." In *Venice and History,* 285–308. Baltimore: Johns Hopkins University Press.

– 1973. *Venice: A Maritime Republic.* Baltimore: Johns Hopkins University Press.

Leonhardt, Jurgen. 2013. *Latin: Story of a World Language.* Cambridge: Harvard University Press.

Libby, Lester J. 1973. "Venetian History and Political Thought after 1509." *Studies in the Renaissance* 20: 7–45. https://doi.org/10.2307/2857012.

L'Osservatore Romano. 2017. "[Gasparo Contarini:] Il cardinale che sapeva leggere." 30 December. www.osservatoreromano.va/it/news/ilcardinale-che-sapeva-leggere.

Machiavelli, Niccolo. 2003. *The Discourses.* Edited by Bernard Crick. New York: Penguin.

– 2016. *The Prince.* Edited by William J. Connell. New York: Bedford/St Martin's.

Mackenney, Richard. 1987. *Tradesmen and Traders: The World of the Guilds in Venice and Europe c. 1250–c. 1650.* London: Croom Helm.

– 1997. "The Guilds of Venice: State and Society in the Longue Duree." *Studi Veneziani* 34: 15–43.

Maguire, Henry, and Robert S. Nelson. 2010. *San Marco, Byzantium and the Myths of Venice.* Washington, DC: Dumbarton Oaks Research Library and Collection.

Mallett, Michael. 1973. "Venice and Its Condottieri, 1404–54." In *Renaissance Venice,* edited by J.R. Hale, 121–45. London: Faber and Faber.

Mallett, M.E., and J.R. Hale. 1984. *The Military Organization of a Renaissance State: Venice c. 1400–1617.* New York: Cambridge University Press.

Manzoni, Alessandro. [1827] 1909. *I Promessi Sposi*. (The betrothed). New York: P.F. Collier & Son.

Maranini, Giuseppe. [1927] 1974. *La Costituzione di Venezia. Dalle origini alla serrata del Maggior Consiglio*. Milan: Feltrinelli.

Martin, John, and Dennis Romano. 2000. "Reconsidering Venice." In *Venice Reconsidered: The History and Civilization of an Italian City-State, 1297–1797*, edited by J. Martin and D. Romano, 1–38. Baltimore: Johns Hopkins University Press.

Matheson, Peter. 1972. *Cardinal Contarino at Regensburg*. Oxford: Clarendon.

McNeill, William H. 1974. *Venice: The Hinge of Europe 1081–1797*. Chicago: University of Chicago Press.

McPherson, David. 1988. "Lewkenor's Venice and Its Sources." *Renaissance Quarterly* 41, no. 3 (Autumn): 459–66. https://doi.org/10.2307/2861757.

Mosca, Gaetano. [1896] 1939. *The Ruling Class*. New York: McGraw-Hill.

Mueller, Reinhold C. 1971. "The Procurators of San Marco in the Thirteenth and Fourteenth Centuries: A Study of the Office as a Financial and Trust Institution." *Studi Veneziani* 13: 105–220.

Muir, Edward. 1981. *Civic Rituals in Renaissance Venice*. Princeton: Princeton University Press.

– 1988. Review of *The Venetian Patriciate: Reality versus Myth* by Donald E. Queller. *Renaissance Quarterly* 41 (Summer): 288–91. https://doi:. org/10.2307/2862207.

– 1993. *Mad Blood Stirring: Vendetta and Factions in Friuli during the Renaissance*. Baltimore: Johns Hopkins University Press.

– 1999. "The Sources of Civil Society in Italy." *Journal of Interdisciplinary History* 29 (Winter): 379–406. https://doi.org/10.1017/cbo9780511572777.003.

– 2000. "Was There Republicanism in the Renaissance Republics? Venice after Agnadello." In *Venice Reconsidered: The History and Civilization of an Italian City-State 1297–1797*, edited by J. Martin and D. Romano, 137–67. Baltimore: Johns Hopkins University Press.

Najemy, John. 2006. *A History of Florence 1200–1575*. London: Wiley-Blackwell.

Nederman, Cary J. 2002. "Mechanics and Citizens: The Reception of the Aristotelian Idea of Citizenship in Late Medieval Europe." *Vivarium* 40 (1): 75–102.

Neff, Mary. 1981. "A Citizen in the Service of the Patrician State: The Career of Zaccaria de' Freschi." *Studi Veneziani* 5: 33–66.

Negrato, Claudio. 2012. "Lingua e linguaggio nei dispacci di Gasparo Contarini." Doctoral dissertation, Università Ca' Foscari, Venice. http://hdl. handle.net/10579/1213.

North, Douglass C., John J. Wallis, and Barry R. Weingast. 2013. *Violence and Social Orders: A Conceptual Framework for Interpreting Recorded Human History*. New York: Cambridge University Press.

Norwich, John Julius. 1989. *A History of Venice.* New York: Vintage.

O'Connell, Monique. 2009. *Men of Empire: Power and Negotiation in Venice's Maritime State.* Baltimore: Johns Hopkins University Press.

Ostrom, Elinor. 1990. *Governing the Commons: The Evolution of Institutions for Collective Action.* New York: Cambridge University Press.

– 2005. *Understanding Institutional Diversity.* Princeton: Princeton University Press.

– 2014. "A Behavioral Approach to the Rational Choice Theory of Collective Action." In *Choice, Rules and Collective Action: The Ostroms on the Study of Institutions and Governance,* edited by F. Sabetti and Paul D. Aligica, 121–66. Colchester, UK: ECPR.

Ostrom, Vincent. 1997. *The Meaning of Democracy and the Vulnerability of Democracies: A Response to Tocqueville's Challenge.* Ann Arbor: University of Michigan Press.

Pocock, J.G.A. 1975. *The Machiavellian Moment: Florentine Political Thought and the Atlantic Republic Tradition.* Princeton: Princeton University Press.

– 1992. Introduction to *The Commonwealth of Oceana and A System of Politics,* by James Harrington, vii–xxv. New York: Cambridge University Press.

Psarra, Sophia. 2018. *The Venice Variations: The Architectural Imagination.* London: UCL. https://goo.gl/P552uD.

Pullan, Brian. 1960. "Poverty, Charity and the Reason of State: Some Venetian Examples." *Bollettino dell'Istituto di Storia della Societàe dello Stato Veneziano II:* 17–60.

– 1963–4. "The Famine in Venice and the New Poor Law, 1527–9." *Bollettino dell'Istituto di Storia della Società e dello Stato Veneziano V–VI,* 141–202.

– 1964. "Service to the Venetian State: Aspects of Myth and Reality in the Early Seventeenth Century." *Studi Secenteschi* 5: 95–148.

– 1971. *Rich and Poor in Renaissance Venice: The Social Institutions of a Catholic State.* Oxford: Oxford University Press.

– 1974. "The Significance of Venice." *Bulletin of the John Rylands University Library* (Manchester) 56: 443–62.

– 1999. "Three Orders of Inhabitants: Social Hierarchies in the Republic of Venice." In *Orders and Hierarchies in Late Medieval and Renaissance Europe,* edited by Jeffrey Denton, 147–95. Toronto: University of Toronto Press.

Queller, Donald E. 1986. *The Venetian Patriciate: Reality versus Myth.* Urbana: University of Illinois Press.

Raines, Dorit. 1991. "Office Seeking, Broglio and the Pocket Political Guidebooks in Cinquecento and Seicento Venice." *Studi Veneziani* 22: 137–94.

– 2003. "Cooptazione, aggregazione e presenza al Maggior Consiglio: Le casate del patriziato veneziano, 1297–1797." *Storia di Venezia Rivista* 1: 1–64.

Rakove, Jack. 2002. "The Political Presidency: Discovery and Invention." In *The Revolution of 1800: Democracy, Race and the New Republic,* edited by James P.P. Horn, J. Lewis, and Peter S. Nuf, 30–58. Charlottesville: University of Virginia Press.

Riesenberg, Peter. 1992. *Citizenship in the Western Tradition: Plato to Rousseau.* Chapel Hill: University of North Carolina Press.

Robey, David, and John Law. 1975. "The Venetian Myth and the 'De Republica Veneta' of Pier Paolo Vergerio." *Rinascimento* 15: 3–59.

Rodrik, Dani. 2002. "Institutions, Integration and Geography: In Search of the Deep Determinants of Economic Growth." http://ksghome.harvard/edu/~.drodrik.academic.ksg/papers.html (last accessed 2004).

Romano, Dennis. 1987. *Patricians and Popolani: The Social Foundations of the Venetian Renaissance State.* Baltimore: Johns Hopkins University Press.

– 1996. *Housecraft and Statecraft: Domestic Service in Renaissance Venice, 1400–1600.* Baltimore: Johns Hopkins University Press.

– 2007. *The Likeness of Venice: A Life of Doge Francesco Foscari 1373–1457.* New Haven: Yale University Press.

Rösch, Gerhard. 2000. "The *Serrata* of the Great Council and Venetian Society, 1286–1323." In *Venice Reconsidered: The History and Civilization of an Italian City-State 1297–1797*, edited by John Martin and Dennis Romano, 67–88. Baltimore: Johns Hopkins University Press.

Rose, Charles J. 1974. "Marc Antonio Venier, Renier Zeno and 'the Myth of Venice.'" *The Historian* 36, no. 3: 479–97. https://doi.org/10.1111/j.1540-6563.1974.tb01536.x.

Ross, James Bruce. 1970. "Gasparo Contarini and His Friends." *Studies in the Renaissance* 17: 192–232. https://doi.org/10.2307/2857063.

– 1972. "The Emergence of Gasparo Contarini: A Bibliographical Essay." *Church History* 41, no. 1 (March): 22–45. https://doi.org/10.2307/3164684.

Rubenstein, Nicolai, ed. 1968. *Florentine Studies.* London: Faber and Faber.

Ruggiero, Guido. 1980. *Violence in Early Renaissance Venice.* New Brunswick: Rutgers University Press.

Sabetti, Filippo. 2000. *The Search for Good Government: Understanding the Paradox of Italian Democracy.* Montreal: McGill-Queen's University Press.

– 2010. *Civilization and Self-Government: The Political Thought of Carlo Cattaneo.* Lanham: Lexington.

Sabetti, Filippo, and Paul Dragos Aligica, eds. 2014. *Choice, Rules and Collective Action: The Ostroms on the Study of Institutions and Governance.* Colchester, UK: ECPR.

Savorana, Alberto. 2018. *The Life of Luigi Giussani.* Montreal: McGill-Queen's University Press.

Setti, Cristina. 2014. "La terza part a Venezia: L'Avogaria di Comun tra Politica e Prassi Quotidiana (secoli XVI–XVII)." *Acta Historie* 22, no. 1: 127–44.

Shaw, James E. 2006. *The Justice of Venice: Authorities and Liberties in the Urban Economy.* Oxford: British Academy.

Siedentop, Larry. 2000. *Democracy in Europe.* London: Allen Lane.

Skinner, Quentin. 2002. *Visions of Politics.* New York: Cambridge University Press.

Tenenti, Alberto. 1973. "The Sense of Space and Time in the Venetian World of the Fifteenth and Sixteenth Centuries." In *Renaissance Venice*, edited by J.R. Hale, 17–46. London: Faber and Faber.

Terpstra, Nicholas. 2006. "'Republics by Contract': Civil Society, Social Capital and the 'Putnam Thesis' in the Papal State." *Storicamente* 2, no. 29: 12–31. https://storicamente.org/terpstra.

Tocqueville, Alexis de. (1835) 1969. *Democracy in America*. Vol 1. New York: Harper.

Trexler, Richard C. 1980. *Public Life in Renaissance Florence*. Ithaca: Cornell University Press.

Trivellato, Francesca. 2008. "Guilds, Technology and Economic Change in Early Modern Venice." In *Guilds, Innovation and the European Economy, 1400–1800*, edited by S.R. Epstein and Maarten Prak, 199–231. Cambridge: Cambridge University Press.

van Gelderen, Martin, and Quentin Skinner, eds. 2002. *Republicanism: A Shared European Heritage*. 2 vols. Cambridge: Cambridge University Press.

Ventura, Angelo. 1981. "Scrittori politici e scritture di governo." In *Storia della cultura veneta: Dal primo Quattrocento al Concilio di Trento*, edited by G. Arnaldi and M. Pastore Stocchi, 513–63.

Ventura, Pietro. 1995. "Le ambiguità di un privilegio: La cittadinanza napoletana tra cinque e seicento." *Quaderni storici* 30, nos. 88–90 (2): 385–416.

Venturi, Franco. 1971. *Utopia and Reform in the Enlightenment*. Cambridge: Cambridge University Press.

– 1979. "Venice et, par occasion, de la liberté." In *The Idea of Freedom: Essays in Honor of Isaiah Berlin*, edited by Alan Ryan, 195–210. Oxford: Oxford University Press.

Viggiano, Alfredo. 2013. "Politics and Constitution." In *A Companion to Venetian History, 1400–1797*, edited by Eric R. Dursteler, 47–84. Boston: Brill.

Voigt, Stefan. 2013. "How (Not) to Measure Institutions." *Journal of Institutional Economics* 9: 1–26.

Waquet, Françoise. 2001. *Latin, or The Empire of a Sign*. London: Verso.

Weiner, Greg. 2012. *Madison's Metronome: The Constitution, Majority Rule and the Tempo of American Politics*. Lawrence: University Press of Kansas.

Wills, Garry. 2001. *Venice – Lion City: The Religion of Empire*. New York: Simon & Schuster.

Wilson, Peter H. 2016. *The Holy Roman Empire: A Thousand Years of European History*. Cambridge: Harvard University Press.

Winch, Donald. 2002. "Commercial Realities, Republican Principles." In *The Value of Republicanism in Early Modern Europe*, edited by Martin van Gelderen and Quentin Skinner, 293–310. Cambridge: Cambridge University Press.

Index

The letter *f* in parentheses following a page number denotes a figure.

THE LORENZO DA PONTE ITALIAN LIBRARY

General Editors: Luigi Ballerini and Massimo Ciavolella

Pellegrino Artusi, *Science in the Kitchen and the Art of Eating Well* (2003). Translated by Murtha Baca and Stephen Sartarelli. Introduction by Luigi Ballerini. Foreword by Michele Scicolone.

Lauro Martines, *An Italian Renaissance Sextet: Six Tales in Historical Context* (2004). Translated by Murtha Baca.

Aretino's Dialogues (2005). Translated by Raymond Rosenthal. Introduction by Margaret Rosenthal.

Aldo Palazzeschi, *A Tournament of Misfits: Tall Tales and Short* (2005). Translated by Nicolas J. Perella.

Carlo Cattaneo, *Civilization and Democracy: The Salvemini Anthology of Cattaneo's Writings* (2006). Edited and introduced by Carlo G. Lacaita and Filippo Sabetti. Translated by David Gibbons.

Benedetto Croce, *Breviary of Aesthetics: Four Lectures* (2007). Translated by Hiroko Fudemoto. Introduction by Remo Bodei.

Antonio Pigafetta, *The First Voyage around the World (1519–1522): An Account of Magellan's Expedition* (2007). Edited and introduced by Theodore J. Cachey Jr.

Raffaello Borghini, *Il Riposo* (2008). Edited and translated by Lloyd H. Ellis Jr.

Paolo Mantegazza, *The Physiology of Love and Other Writings* (2008). Edited with an introduction and notes by Nicoletta Pireddu. Translated by David Jacobson.

Renaissance Comedy: The Italian Masters, Volume 2 (2008). Edited with an introduction by Donald Beecher.

Renaissance Comedy: The Italian Masters, Volume 1 (2008). Edited with an introduction by Donald Beecher.

Cesare Beccaria, *On Crimes and Punishments and Other Writings* (2008). Edited by Aaron Thomas. Translated by Aaron Thomas and Jeremy Parzen. Foreword by Bryan Stevenson. Introduction by Alberto Burgio.

Leone Ebreo, *Dialogues of Love* (2009). Edited by Rossella Pescatori. Translated by Cosmos Damian Bacich and Rossella Pescatori.

Boccaccio's Expositions on Dante's Comedy (2009). Translated by Michael Papio.

My Muse Will Have a Story to Paint: Selected Prose of Ludovico Ariosto (2010). Translated with an introduction by Dennis Looney.

Giacomo da Lentini, *The Complete Poetry* (2018). Translated and annotated by Richard Lansing.

Remo Bodei, *Geometry of the Passions: Fear, Hope, Happiness: Philosophy and Political Use* (2018). Translated by Gianpiero W. Doebler.

Scipio Sighele, *The Criminal Crowd and Other Writings on Mass Society* (2018). Edited with an introduction and notes by Nicoletta Pireddu. Translated by Nicoletta Pireddu and Andrew Robbins. With a foreword by Tom Huhn.

Gasparo Contarini, *The Republic of Venice* (2020). Edited with an introduction by Filippo Sabetti. Translated by Giuseppe Pezzini with Amanda Murphy.

NOW, SAVE MONEY ON ALL YOUR TRAVELS!
Join Frommer's™ Dollarwise® Travel Club

Saving money while traveling is never a simple matter, which is why, over 29 years ago, the **Dollarwise Travel Club** was formed. Actually, the idea came from readers of the Frommer publications who felt that such an organization could bring financial benefits, continuing travel information, and a sense of community to value-conscious travelers all over the world.

In keeping with the money-saving concept, the annual membership fee is low—$18 (U.S. residents) or $20 U.S. (Canadian, Mexican, and other foreign residents)—and is immediately exceeded by the value of your benefits which include:

1. The latest edition of any TWO of the books listed on the following pages.

2. A copy of any one Frommer City Guide.

3. An annual subscription to an 8-page quarterly newspaper, *The Dollarwise Traveler*, which keeps you up-to-date on fast-breaking developments in good-value travel in all parts of the world—bringing you the kind of information you'd have to pay over $35 a year to obtain elsewhere. This consumer-conscious publication also includes the following columns:

Hospitality Exchange—members all over the world who are willing to provide hospitality to other members as they pass through their home cities.

Share-a-Trip—requests from members for travel companions who can share costs and help avoid the burdensome single supplement.

Readers Ask . . . Readers Reply—travel questions from members to which other members reply with authentic firsthand information.

4. Your personal membership card, which entitles you to purchase through the club all Frommer publications for a third to a half off their regular retail prices during the term of your membership.

So why not join this hardy band of international Dollarwise travelers now and participate in its exchange of information and hospitality? Simply send $18 (U.S. residents) or $20 U.S. (Canadian, Mexican, and other foreign residents) along with your name and address to: Frommer's Dollarwise Travel Club, Inc., 15 Columbus Circle, New York, NY 10023. Remember to specify which *two* of the books in section (1) and which *one* in section (2) above you wish to receive in your initial package of member's benefits. Or tear out the next page, check off your choices, and send the page to us with your membership fee.

FROMMER BOOKS
PRENTICE HALL TRAVEL
15 COLUMBUS CIRCLE
NEW YORK, NY 10023

Date_____

Friends:
Please send me the books checked below:

FROMMER™ GUIDES

(Guides to sightseeing and tourist accommodations and facilities from budget to deluxe, with emphasis on the medium-priced.)

☐ Alaska	$14.95	☐ Japan & Hong Kong	$13.95
☐ Australia	$14.95	☐ Mid-Atlantic States	$14.95
☐ Austria & Hungary	$14.95	☐ New England	$14.95
☐ Belgium, Holland & Luxembourg	$14.95	☐ New York State	$14.95
☐ Bermuda & The Bahamas	$14.95	☐ Northwest	$14.95
☐ Brazil	$14.95	☐ Portugal, Madeira & the Azores	$13.95
☐ Canada	$14.95	☐ Skiing Europe	$14.95
☐ Caribbean	$14.95	☐ Skiing USA—East	$13.95
☐ Cruises (incl. Alaska, Carib, Mex, Hawaii, Panama, Canada & US)	$14.95	☐ Skiing USA—West	$13.95
☐ California & Las Vegas	$14.95	☐ South Pacific	$14.95
☐ England & Scotland	$14.95	☐ Southeast Asia	$14.95
☐ Egypt	$13.95	☐ Southern Atlantic States	$14.95
☐ Florida	$14.95	☐ Southwest	$14.95
☐ France	$14.95	☐ Switzerland & Liechtenstein	$14.95
☐ Germany	$14.95	☐ Texas	$13.95
☐ Italy	$14.95	☐ USA	$15.95

FROMMER $-A-DAY® GUIDES

(In-depth guides to sightseeing and low-cost tourist accommodations and facilities.)

☐ Europe on $40 a Day	$15.95	☐ New York on $60 a Day	$13.95
☐ Australia on $30 a Day	$12.95	☐ New Zealand on $40 a Day	$13.95
☐ Eastern Europe on $25 a Day	$13.95	☐ Scandinavia on $60 a Day	$13.95
☐ England on $50 a Day	$13.95	☐ Scotland & Wales on $40 a Day	$13.95
☐ Greece on $30 a Day	$13.95	☐ South America on $35 a Day	$13.95
☐ Hawaii on $60 a Day	$13.95	☐ Spain & Morocco on $40 a Day	$13.95
☐ India on $25 a Day	$12.95	☐ Turkey on $30 a Day	$13.95
☐ Ireland on $35 a Day	$13.95	☐ Washington, D.C. & Historic Va. on $40 a Day	$13.95
☐ Israel on $40 a Day	$13.95		
☐ Mexico on $35 a Day	$13.95		

FROMMER TOURING GUIDES

(Color illustrated guides that include walking tours, cultural & historic sites, and other vital travel information.)

☐ Australia	$9.95	☐ Paris	$8.95
☐ Egypt	$8.95	☐ Scotland	$9.95
☐ Florence	$8.95	☐ Thailand	$9.95
☐ London	$8.95	☐ Venice	$8.95

TURN PAGE FOR ADDITONAL BOOKS AND ORDER FORM.

A

FROMMER CITY GUIDES

(Pocket-size guides to sightseeing and tourist accommodations and facilities in all price ranges.)

☐ Amsterdam/Holland	$5.95	☐ Minneapolis/St. Paul	$5.95
☐ Athens	$5.95	☐ Montréal/Québec City	$5.95
☐ Atlantic City/Cape May	$5.95	☐ New Orleans	$5.95
☐ Belgium	$5.95	☐ New York	$5.95
☐ Boston	$5.95	☐ Orlando/Disney World/EPCOT	$5.95
☐ Cancún/Cozumel/Yucatán	$5.95	☐ Paris	$5.95
☐ Chicago	$5.95	☐ Philadelphia	$5.95
☐ Dublin/Ireland	$5.95	☐ Rio	$5.95
☐ Hawaii	$5.95	☐ Rome	$5.95
☐ Las Vegas	$5.95	☐ San Francisco	$5.95
☐ Lisbon/Madrid/Costa del Sol	$5.95	☐ Santa Fe/Taos/Albuquerque	$5.95
☐ London	$5.95	☐ Sydney	$5.95
☐ Los Angeles	$5.95	☐ Washington, D.C.	$5.95
☐ Mexico City/Acapulco	$5.95		

SPECIAL EDITIONS

☐ A Shopper's Guide to the Caribbean	$12.95	☐ Manhattan's Outdoor Sculpture	$15.95
☐ Beat the High Cost of Travel	$6.95	☐ Motorist's Phrase Book (Fr/Ger/Sp)	$4.95
☐ Bed & Breakfast—N. America	$11.95	☐ Paris Rendez-Vous	$10.95
☐ California with Kids	$14.95	☐ Swap and Go (Home Exchanging)	$10.95
☐ Caribbean Hideaways	$14.95	☐ The Candy Apple (NY with Kids)	$12.95
☐ Guide to Honeymoon Destinations		☐ Travel Diary and Record Book	$5.95
(US, Canada, Mexico & Carib)	$12.95		

☐ Where to Stay USA (Lodging from $3 to $30 a night) $10.95
☐ Marilyn Wood's Wonderful Weekends (NY, Conn, Mass, RI, Vt, NH, NJ, Del,Pa) $11.95
☐ The New World of Travel (Annual sourcebook by Arthur Frommer previewing: new travel trends, new modes of travel, and the latest cost-cutting strategies for savvy travelers.) $14.95

SERIOUS SHOPPER'S GUIDES

(Illustrated guides listing hundreds of stores, conveniently organized alphabetically by category.)

☐ Italy	$15.95	☐ Los Angeles	$14.95
☐ London	$15.95	☐ Paris	$15.95

GAULT MILLAU

(The only guides that distinguish the truly superlative from the merely overrated.)

☐ The Best of Chicago	$15.95	☐ The Best of Los Angeles	$14.95
☐ The Best of France	$16.95	☐ The Best of New England	$15.95
☐ The Best of Hong Kong	$16.95	☐ The Best of New York	$14.95
☐ The Best of Italy	$16.95	☐ The Best of San Francisco	$14.95
	☐ The Best of Washington, D.C.	$14.95	

ORDER NOW!

In U.S. include $2 shipping UPS for 1st book; $1 ea. add'l book. Outside U.S. $3 and $1, respectively.

Allow four to six weeks for delivery in U.S., longer outside U.S.

Enclosed is my check or money order for $_____

NAME_____

ADDRESS_____

CITY_____ STATE_____ ZIP_____

A